CW00548757

BIG DATA IN EDUCATION

The digital future of learning, policy and practice

Sara Miller McCune founded SAGE Publishing in 1965 to support the dissemination of usable knowledge and educate a global community. SAGE publishes more than 1000 journals and over 800 new books each year, spanning a wide range of subject areas. Our growing selection of library products includes archives, data, case studies and video. SAGE remains majority owned by our founder and after her lifetime will become owned by a charitable trust that secures the company's continued independence.

Los Angeles | London | New Delhi | Singapore | Washington DC | Melbourne

BIG DATA *IN* EDUCATION

The digital future of learning, policy and practice

Ben Williamson

Los Angeles | London | New Delhi
Singapore | Washington DC | Melbourne

Los Angeles | London | New Delhi
Singapore | Washington DC | Melbourne

SAGE Publications Ltd
1 Oliver's Yard
55 City Road
London EC1Y 1SP

SAGE Publications Inc.
2455 Teller Road
Thousand Oaks, California 91320

SAGE Publications India Pvt Ltd
B 1/I 1 Mohan Cooperative Industrial Area
Mathura Road
New Delhi 110 044

SAGE Publications Asia-Pacific Pte Ltd
3 Church Street
#10-04 Samsung Hub
Singapore 049483

Editor: James Clark
Assistant editor: Robert Patterson
Production editor: Nicola Carrier
Copyeditor: Solveig Gardner Servian
Proofreader: Kate Campbell
Marketing manager: Dilhara Attygalle
Cover design: Sheila Tong
Typeset by: C&M Digitals (P) Ltd, Chennai, India
Printed in the UK

© 2017 Ben Williamson

First published 2017

Apart from any fair dealing for the purposes of research or private study, or criticism or review, as permitted under the Copyright, Designs and Patents Act, 1988, this publication may be reproduced, stored or transmitted in any form, or by any means, only with the prior permission in writing of the publishers, or in the case of reprographic reproduction, in accordance with the terms of licences issued by the Copyright Licensing Agency. Enquiries concerning reproduction outside those terms should be sent to the publishers.

Library of Congress Control Number: 2017931037

British Library Cataloguing in Publication data

A catalogue record for this book is available from the British Library

ISBN 978-1-47394-799-3
ISBN 978-1-47394-800-6 (pbk)

At SAGE we take sustainability seriously. Most of our products are printed in the UK using FSC papers and boards. When we print overseas we ensure sustainable papers are used as measured by the PREPS grading system. We undertake an annual audit to monitor our sustainability.

CONTENTS

ABOUT THE AUTHOR

Ben Williamson is a Lecturer in the Faculty of Social Sciences at the University of Stirling, UK. His research focuses on educational policy and digital technology, with a particular emphasis on the involvement of networks of technical, commercial, philanthropic and scientific experts in data-driven educational governance. He has previously published his research in a range of education, sociology and policy studies journals, maintains a research blog at https://codeactsineducation.wordpress.com/, and on Twitter he is @BenPatrickWill.

PREFACE

Big data, algorithms, data mining, analytics, machine learning and AI have become some of the most significant technical developments and concepts of recent years. Today's most successful companies are those that can provide an engaging digital service while also compelling users to provide data that can then be mined using sophisticated analytics technologies. Google's search algorithms provide access to information while tracking the online habits of users. Facebook collects data about its users to monitor and enhance their engagement with their timelines and newsfeeds. Amazon, Netflix and Spotify analyse user information to make automated recommendations of media that users might like. Meanwhile, wearable health devices gather information about physical health and fitness and prompt their users to make healthy lifestyle choices, and business intelligence software helps organizations make better strategic decisions.

In our everyday lives spent living with digital hardware and software, we are constantly generating information that can be used to identify where we go, what we like, who we know, how we feel, what we do, what we consume and so on. A consequence is that we can be watched by organizations that can access our data. Government agencies have sought to access social media networks to identify and track people's online activities. Police forces have been experimenting with predictive analytics technologies that can calculate where and when crime is most likely to take place, and who is most likely to commit it. Facebook has been experimenting on its users by manipulating their news feeds in order to change their moods. Even elections are now fought through computational propaganda that spreads through social media networks thanks to trending algorithms and detailed profiles of users' behaviours, preferences and tastes.

Whether you like it or not, a data-based version of yourself exists out there, scattered among different databases as data points in massive torrents of big data. Data mining, algorithms and analytics processes are increasingly being put to work to know and understand you, and also to know and understand the wider populations, communities and societies to which you belong. And as technical innovation in machine learning and artificial intelligence makes technologies smarter, new kinds of machines are emerging that are designed to interact with you by collecting and analysing your activities in real-time in order to learn about you, and adjust to serve your needs and interests.

Public awareness of these activities is emerging as media coverage about social media, government online snooping and computational propaganda has grown.

Some of these issues have become the stuff of popular culture. The UK television show *Humans*, for example, dramatizes current concerns about robotics, automation and artificial intelligence, with its cast of 'synthetic humans' undergoing 'machine learning' as they seek survival in the human world. The satirical novel *The Circle* by Dave Eggers, about a social media company that seeks perfect knowledge through seamless surveillance, has been turned into a major Hollywood film. The Australian TV series *The Code* depicts a shady world of governmental big data agencies and private sector surveillance contractors. Finally, the movie *Margin Call* dramatizes what happened in the financial crash when risky computer models and algorithms developed to process huge financial data began to operate beyond the control of their designers. Far from being merely technical, code, data, algorithms, artificial intelligence and machine learning are now firmly embedded in society and culture, as well as in economics and politics.

Big data is now becoming a key part of the educational landscape too. The same kind of learning machines that share our lives with us on social media, on our smartphones and on the Web take on a special importance as they begin to occupy the educational field. According to many of the enthusiasts we will encounter in this book, big data can help people learn more, learn faster, and learn better. Applications and services that process big data can help students in schools, colleges and universities by providing feedback on their measured progress, and recommendations on what to do to improve. They can help policymakers learn about institutional and system performance, and generate insights for future policy intervention. They can help teachers review and evaluate courses as they can track students' engagement and achievement, and enable school and university leaders to review and evaluate institutional and staff performance at the same time. As machines are designed to get ever smarter and more responsive and adaptable as they learn from data, it is claimed, they will become embedded in education all the way from policymaking to practice.

'Big data' has become a contested term that is used diversely by different groups. The simple technical definition is that big data consists of information collected in huge volume, of highly diverse variety, which is collected at extreme velocity. Rather than working with a strict technical definition of big data, big data can be better understood as an emerging social phenomenon and as a powerful concept that has attained critical importance in recent years. Big data is also inseparable from the software programs, algorithms and analytics required to collect and manage it, all of which requires diverse forms of specialist expert practice to be performed. A whole industry of textbooks, manuals, conferences and training courses is available for those wishing to specialize in data mining, analytics and machine learning. There are people behind big data – not just data scientists, but software developers and algorithm designers, as well as the political, scientific and economic actors who seek to develop and utilize big data systems for their diverse purposes. And big data is also about the people who constitute it, whose lives are recorded both individually and at massive population scale. Big data, in other words, is simultaneously technical and social. Technical in that it is the product of software programs and processes; social because it is produced and used by human operatives working in specific organizational settings, and is generated from the everyday lives of people around the globe. As a source of knowledge, big data also has the power to change how and what we know about society and the people and institutions that occupy it.

Big data has prompted much future-gazing. With access to huge quantities of information, it seems, comes the potential of better knowledge of behaviours, institutions, even whole societies. Better data-driven knowledge might then be used to catalyse new innovations or interventions in everything from business and entertainment to government and public services. The field of education has emerged as a key site for the production of visions of the data-driven future. This book illustrates how future visions of education have been animated by key ideas related to big data.

As a concept and as a set of technical possibilities, big data has captured the imagination of businesses, think tanks, non-profit philanthropic foundations, politicians and policymakers alike, which have seen big data as a potentially limitless new reserve of insights into how education systems and institutions function, how teachers perform, and how learners achieve. For its supporters, the potential insights available from big data might be used as intelligence to be used in the design of new courses, new resources, new policies and new practices. Smart learning machines based on artificial intelligence might even become available that can act as digital assistants to teachers and students alike, intelligently spotting patterns in any educational activity and then providing real-time feedback to improve it, or perhaps even to automate it.

Big data in education is as much an imaginative resource to be mined for future possibilities as it is an emerging technical reality. As this book demonstrates, however, imagining the future of education with big data is catalysing real developments that are set to impact on educational processes worldwide.

ACKNOWLEDGEMENTS

This book first emerged from a seminar series funded by the Economic and Social Research Council (grant reference ES/L001160/1) that I led and organized from 2013–2015. 'Code Acts in Education: Learning through code, learning to code' was intended to generate a critical interdisciplinary conversation about the role of software, code, algorithms and digital data between educational researchers, educators, social scientists and various organizations with an interest in technologies in education. The series proved to be the catalyst for a programme of research and writing that has finally culminated in this book. I would like to acknowledge and thank several colleagues for their collaboration on Code Acts in Education: Richard Edwards, Tara Fenwick, Sian Bayne, Jeremy Knox, Sarah Doyle, Lyndsay Grant and Alison Oldfield. Many of the brilliant speakers we invited to present their work at Code Acts helped to set the stage for the material developed in the book – thanks to all who took part. Some of the material in the book has also benefited from direct collaboration with Carlo Perrotta, Deborah Lupton, Jessica Pykett, Selena Nemorin, Jen Ross, John Morgan and Bethan Mitchell.

In the three years that this work has been ongoing, my children, Cormac and Carys, have both started primary school. Though schools have of course been capturing children in numerical form for a very long time, it has been fascinating as a parent to witness the extent of data work that goes on in schools today. Much of it remains in pencil and paper format, but Cormac and Carys have entered school as data collection, analysis and presentation is becoming increasingly digitized. As parents we can now monitor from home how they're getting on at school – academically, socially, emotionally, behaviourally – through new glossy web-based tools. Data are even becoming the source of pride for young children, but they are also becoming parts of big databases distantly hosted on powerful cloud servers. Young people are being inserted into sprawling networks of hardware and software that are managed by commercial technology companies and promoted by the latest political priorities. Cormac and Carys, this book is for you, and it is animated by my disquiet about the digital shadow versions of you that are being produced through data as you set off on your educational journeys. That's why mummy and daddy love taking you away to the woods, lochs and mountains of Scotland so much. Thanks, as ever, to Vanessa for getting us everywhere – you drive, I'll read the map.

ABOUT THE BOOK

In the introductory first chapter, I describe how education is becoming increasingly 'digitized' and 'datafied'. Through digitization, more and more aspects of education – from the early years through school, higher education and on into lifelong learning – are being conducted through software programs that have been written in code, and that rely on algorithms for their functioning. The process of datafication has involved diverse forms of information about education being rendered in machine-readable digital data, which can then be subjected to sophisticated forms of processing, calculation, analysis, interpretation, visualization and circulation. The chapter details how digitization and datafication reinforce each other, and how they have begun to animate the imaginations and visions of powerful social actors. Adopting the concept of 'sociotechnical imaginaries', in the chapter I explore how 'desirable' future visions for education based on digital data are now being projected and enacted.

Chapter 2 provides a historical and conceptual map for an understanding of big data. It demonstrates how a concern with data has become central to the activities of businesses, cities, governments, think tanks, and social scientific practice itself. The central contention of the chapter is that big data needs to be understood critically. It is not just an accurate statistical reflection of the social world as some data scientists contend, but a key source of social power that, through the technical experts that collect, clean and calculate it, is actively intervening in how social worlds are known, seen and then acted upon. But big data cannot exist on its own; it requires a massive complex of software, code, algorithms and infrastructures for its collection and analysis. Chapter 3 will detail the work that software does in the organization of big data to illuminate how code and algorithms are implicated in the organization of data-driven institutions, spaces and everyday life.

Subsequent chapters provide detailed examinations of how sociotechnical imaginaries of digital data in education are being developed and diffused into real-world contexts. Chapter 4 focuses on the ways that education policy is increasingly accomplished through digital policy instruments that enable policy data to flow across the system in real-time and continuously. Learning analytics and educational data mining tools, the focus of Chapter 5, enable the tracking, monitoring and real-time prediction of student activities, behaviours and sentiments within the pedagogic apparatus of the classroom. Focusing on the emerging field of 'educational data science', the chapter will detail the different forms that educational data mining and analytics now take – from administrative and academic analytics at the institutional level to granular, individualized learning analytics that offer feedback within the physical classroom itself.

Chapter 6 then focuses on educational technologies that have been designed to collect data about learners' bodies, emotions and behaviours. It highlights how new kinds of 'affective computing' devices have been produced to generate a constant stream of information about students' movements and feelings, and how new behaviour management devices are being used to collect and visualize information about individuals' conduct. Current developments in 'cognitive-based systems', 'artificial intelligence', 'machine learning' and 'neural networks' promise to produce increasingly 'intelligent' educational technologies, able to adapt and respond to the learner – the subject of Chapter 7. The specific contribution of this chapter will be to understand the interdependencies of big data technologies and neuroscience in plans for the future design of cognitive classrooms where humans and machines act together as symbiotic systems.

In Chapter 8 the focus shifts on to the idea that young people themselves can learn to write computer code and conduct digital data analyses. This chapter documents how 'learning to code' and 'digital making' initiatives are part of a concerted effort shared across government, the commercial technology sector, and civil society to mould citizens as productive participants for a digitized and data-driven future. The conclusion highlights an important context for further work in this area: the increasing phenomenon that people learn about the world through social media, and the consequences this is exerting for collective and political life as social media filter, curate and personalize access to information based on users' data profiles.

I

INTRODUCTION

Learning machines, digital data and
the future of education

In October 2015, over 1,000 young software developers and hackers attended HackingEDU, a three-day educational hackathon held at the San Mateo Event Center in San Francisco. Originally launched at the 2014 Google Summit, the annual HackingEDU event – the 'world's largest educational hackathon' – is intended to help software developers and programmers, most of them college students, 'revolutionize the education industry' while competing for over US$100,000 in prizes (Hunckler, 2015). Featuring expert workshops, panel discussions and guest speakers, HackingEDU 2015 was supported by major technology companies including IBM, Google, Uber, PayPal and Automattic, as well as by successful educational technology businesses such as Chegg and EdModo. It emphasized the ways in which technologies might be used to 'disrupt' and 'revolutionize' education, much as 'Uber revolutionized the transportation industry based on a simple concept: press a button, get a ride', as the event's partnership director phrased it (Uber 2015). The technology projects produced during HackingEDU 2015 included titles such as Learnization, CereBro, PocketHelp, QuizPrep, BrainWars and StudyTracker, almost all of them relying on a combination of digital data and database technologies and constructed by their young designers using a variety of programming languages, software programs and hardware devices.

Elsewhere in San Francisco, many other fledgling edtech projects are annually developed through the support of edtech 'incubator' or 'accelerator' programs. Incubators typically help entrepreneurs and new startups to test and validate ideas, while accelerators turn products into scalable businesses, often through direct equity investment, and help provide entrepreneurs with legal, IT and financial services along with mentorship, working space and access to educators, entrepreneurs, business partners and potential investors (Gomes 2015). For example, Imagine K12 is 'a startup accelerator focused on education technology':

> Our goal is to improve your company's chances of success. We do this through a combination of strategic advice and mentorship, a series of speakers and seminars designed to help founders make better decisions, value-added networks of entrepreneurs and educators, and $100,000 of initial funding. ... Companies begin receiving support from Imagine K12 immediately upon their acceptance, including $20k of funding. ... [A]ll accepted startups are required to move to Silicon Valley for an intensive four-month program. (Imagine K12 2015)

Edtech incubator and accelerator programs like Imagine K12 provide the space, support and investment required for programmers to write educational technologies, and ultimately act as mechanisms that might realize the 'revolutionary' ambitions of entrants to competitions like HackingEDU. Notably, Imagine K12 has since merged with another accelerator program, Y Combinator, an organization established by billionaire PayPal founder Peter Thiel, a major donor and spokesperson during Donald Trump's US presidential campaign in 2016.

A key educational technology advocate, Thiel has supported and funded many companies and startups that focus on 'revolutionizing' education through data-driven software applications (Levy 2016). For new startups that successfully graduate from the incubation and acceleration stage, entrepreneurial investors from Silicon Valley have been funding educational technology projects with unprecedented financial enthusiasm since about 2010 (EdSurge 2016). With webs of political support and entrepreneurial investment for educational technology growing, a new digital future for education is being imagined and pursued in governmental and private sector settings alike, with significant consequences for learning, policy and practice.

HackingEDU is an important event with which to start this book for a number of reasons. It locates education as it currently exists as a problematically broken system which is in need of revolutionizing. It proposes that the solution is in the hands of software developers and hackers who can write code. It suggests that the availability of masses of educational data can be used to gain insights into the problems of education, and to find solutions at the same time. And it also demonstrates how private sector technology companies have begun to fixate on education and their own role in fixing it. Incubators and accelerators such as Imagine K12 and Y Combinator can then step in with entrepreneurial experience to grow new products into successful startup businesses, to enable programmers to fine-tune the code and algorithms required to make their product run, and to gain financial investment required to push it out into practice. The promise appears simple. Take a model like Uber, the mobile app that has transformed taxi services by harvesting locational data from its millions of users, and then translate that model into a template for educational reform. Fund, incubate and accelerate it until it performs optimally. All it takes to revolutionize education for the future is a few million lines of software code and big piles of digital data.

Digitizing and Datafying Education

The goal of this book is to understand and detail how digital data and the code and algorithms that constitute software are mixing with particular political agendas, commercial interests, entrepreneurial ambitions, philanthropic goals, forms of scientific expertise, and professional knowledge to create new ways of understanding, imagining and intervening in education. Education is now a key site in which big data and algorithmic techniques of data mining and analysis performed with software are proliferating and gaining credibility.

Yet the quantitative increase in data brought about by recent developments and the qualitative effects they are beginning to exert in education have gone largely unnoticed amid much more high-profile concerns about the data mining conducted by social media companies on their users, targeted online advertising that is driven by consumer data, or the data-based forms of surveillance being practised by governments (van Dijck 2013). A 'new apparatus of measurement has drastically expanded' with the availability of digital data in diverse areas of public and private life, 'allied with a set of cultural changes in which the pursuit of measurement is seen to be highly desirable' (Beer 2016a: 3). Education, by contrast, appears more 'ordinary':

> Given that so much attention has already been paid to social media corporations and governmental and security agencies, what we now need to attend to is other, more ordinary actors, as social media data mining becomes ordinary. (Kennedy 2016: 7)

This book takes up the challenge of investigating the digital data technologies, organizations and practices that are increasingly becoming integrated into many aspects of education. A vast apparatus of measurement is being developed to underpin national educational systems, institutions and the actions of the individuals who occupy them.

While the pursuit of educational measurement has a long history stretching back to the nineteenth century (Lawn 2013), it is being extended in scope, enhanced in its fidelity, and accelerated in pace at the present time as new technologies of big data collection, analysis and feedback are developed and diffused throughout the system (Beneito-Montagut 2017; Selwyn 2015). Similarly, schools, colleges and universities have employed e-learning programs for many years in their pedagogic and instructional processes (Selwyn 2011), but with big data and analytics processes now increasingly augmenting them, these resources can now adapt to their users and 'talk back' to educators (Mayer-Schönberger and Cukier 2014). Software and digital data are becoming integral to the ways in which educational institutions are managed, how educators' practices are performed, how educational policies are made, how teaching and learning are experienced, and how educational research is conducted.

The presence of digital data and software in education is being amplified through massive financial and political investment in educational technologies, as well as huge growth in data collection and analysis in policymaking practices, extension of performance measurement technologies in the management of educational institutions, and rapid expansion of digital methodologies in educational research. To a significant extent, many of the ways in which classrooms function, educational policy departments and leaders make decisions, and researchers make sense of data, simply would not happen as currently intended without the presence of software code and the digital data processing programs it enacts.

To fully appreciate how digital data are being generated and exerting material effects in education, then, it is essential to view data and the software code and algorithms that process it in relation to a range of other factors that frame their use.

Political agendas relating to education policy and governance, commercial interests in the educational technology market, philanthropic and charitable goals around supporting alternative pedagogic approaches, emerging forms of scientific expertise such as that of psychology, biology and neuroscience, as well as the practical knowledge of educator professionals, all combine with new kinds of data practices and digital technologies. That is, the mobilization of digital data in education happens in relation to diverse practices, ways of thinking, ambitions, objectives and aspirations that all shape how data is put to use, define the tasks and projects through which data is deployed, and co-determine the results of any form of educational data analysis. The role and consequences of digital data in education cannot be understood without appreciating their relations with the other ordinary features of education – policies, accountability mechanisms, commercial imperatives, charitable intentions, scientific knowledge and professional practice.

In this sense, the subject of this book is the combined process of 'datafying' and 'digitizing' education. Putting it simply, 'datafication' refers to the transformation of different aspects of education (such as test scores, school inspection reports, or clickstream data from an online course) into digital data. Making information about education into digital data allows it to be inserted into databases, where it can be measured, calculations can be performed on it, and through which it can be turned into charts, tables and other forms of graphical presentation. 'Digitization' refers to the translation of diverse educational practices into software code, and is most obvious in the ways that aspects of teaching and learning are digitized as e-learning software products. If you want to build some digital e-learning software, you have to figure out how to do that in lines of code: to encode educational processes into software products. Diverse aspects of education from policy, leadership, management and administration to classroom practice, pedagogy and assessment are now increasingly subjected to processes of digitization, as software is coded and algorithms are designed to augment and rework everyday tasks and processes across the education sector.

Datafication and digitization support and complement one another in myriad ways. For example, when a piece of e-learning software is coded in digital form, it is often designed in such a way that it can generate information about the ways that it is used (visible in, for example, the log files that demonstrate how a user has interacted with the software). That information can then be used, as analysable digital data, to help the producers of the software learn more about the use of their product, data which can then be used to help inform the writing of better code (a software patch, upgrade or update) or the programming of new software products altogether. To take another example: when millions of learners around the world all take a standard global test, the activities they undertake ultimately contribute to the production of a massive database of test results. Making sense of the vast reserves of data in such a database can only be accomplished using software that has been coded to enable particular kinds of analyses and interpretations. The software does not have to be especially appealing – the datafication of education depends to a significant degree on the digital coding undertaken to produce very mundane software products like spreadsheets and statistical analysis packages – but it is certainly becoming more seductive with the ready availability of highly graphical forms of data visualization software, as well as more accessible and easier to use. With both educational technologies and educational data, processes of digitization and datafication support and reinforce each other.

In short, much of education today is being influenced and shaped by the production of lines of code that make digital software function, and by the generation of digital data that allows information about education to be collected, calculated and communicated with software products. Does this matter? Yes, it matters urgently, because the coding of software products for use in education, or the application of coded devices that can process educational digital data, are beginning to transform educational policies, pedagogies and other practices in ways which have so far been the subject of very little critical attention.

As new kinds of software are developed for use in educational contexts that rely on both software code and digital data, we are beginning to see new ways in which schools, universities, educational leaders, teachers, students, policymakers and parents are influenced. Schools are being turned into data-production centres, responsible for constantly recording and auditing every aspect of their performance (Finn 2016). Leaders are being called on to act on their data to improve the institutions they manage (Lewis and Hardy 2016), often using 'learning management systems' to assist in administrative tasks (Selwyn et al. 2017). Students are becoming the subjects of increasingly pervasive data mining and data analytics packages that, embedded in educational technologies and e-learning software, can trace their every digital move, calculate their educational progress and even predict their probable outcomes (Suoto-Otero and Beneito-Montagut 2016). Students in universities are experiencing ever-greater use of online tools to measure their progress (Losh 2014), with their assignments being entered into massive global plagiarism detection databases (Introna 2016). At the same time, university managers are required to make use of complex performance indicator metrics and institutional data dashboards to facilitate decision-making and planning (Wolf et al. 2016). Even early years settings such as nurseries are increasingly required to collect data on young children's development so that it can be tracked against national and international benchmarks (Roberts-Holmes 2015; Moss et al. 2016), which is mirrored by the growing use of analytics technologies in adult education and professional learning (Fenwick and Edwards 2016).

Beyond the spaces of learning, policymakers are increasingly exhorted to develop data-driven or 'evidence-based' policies that are crafted in response to insights derived from digital data (Sellar 2015a), including school inspection data presented on institutions' 'data dashboards' (Ozga 2016). Parents, too, are encouraged to become educational data analysts who use digital 'school comparison' websites to inform their choices about which schools to enrol their children in (Piattoeva 2015). For teachers, a new industry in educational 'talent analytics', or 'labour market analytics', has even appeared (Beneito-Montagut 2017), with fully-automated software products like TeacherMatch acting as 'advanced education talent management' platforms for the recruitment, assessment, professional development and 'talent investment' of teachers, using matching algorithms to match schools with staff just like a social media dating service (TeacherMatch 2015).

Many commercial organizations are changing their business models and practices to engage in education, such as Google with its Google Apps for Education suite of free-to-use cloud services for schools (Lindh and Nolin 2016). Meanwhile, existing commercial 'edu-businesses' such as Pearson – a global education textbook publisher – have moved to become prominent educational software providers and key collectors of educational data (Hogan et al. 2015). Commercial tools for data collection, processing and analysis are finding their way into the discipline of educational research, knowledge production and theory generation too, in ways that are reshaping how education is known and understood (Cope and Kalantzis 2016). And finally, an increasing number of private sector 'data brokers' are starting to collect education-related data, curate and aggregate it using analytics tools, and sell it back to education stakeholders (Beneito-Montagut 2017).

It's not just the people and organizations of education that are affected by the recent acceleration of data-processing software, but curriculum, pedagogy and assessment too. The notion of a curriculum containing the content-knowledge to be taught in schools is itself being challenged, as new kinds of 'adaptive' learning software are developed that can semi-automate the allocation and 'personalization' of content according to each learners' individual data profile (Bulger 2016). Pedagogy is being distributed to automated machines such as 'teacher bots' and 'cognitive tutors': computerized software agents designed to interact with learners, conduct constant real-time analysis of their learning, and adapt with them (Bayne 2015). And the notion of assessment as a fixed event is being supplanted by real-time assessment analytics and computer-adaptive testing, which automatically assess each learner on-the-go and adapt to their responses in real-time (Thompson 2016). What is even meant by 'learning' is being questioned with the collection of datasets so large that enthusiasts believe they can reveal new truths about learning processes that educational researchers working within disciplinary frameworks such as psychology, sociology and philosophy have been unable to detect before (Behrens 2013).

Many of these developments and innovations with digital software and data in education exist technically, but they are also the product of extensive claims, promotional activity and imaginative marketing which centres on the idea that technical solutions have the capacity to transform education for the future. Businesses with products to sell, venture capital firms with return on investment to secure, think tanks with new ideas to promote, and policymakers with problems to solve and politicians with agendas to set have all become key advocates for data-driven education. Of course, we need to be at the very least cautious about many of the claims made about the transformative and revolutionary potential of many new developments, if not downright sceptical – and, indeed, a little resistant.

But the point I pursue throughout is that what we are currently witnessing are signs of a new way of thinking about education as a datafied and digitized social institution. Seriously powerful organizations are at work in this space, organizations with a forceful and influential shared imagination concerning the future of education. It is easy to be dismissive of the claims-making, hype and hubris that surround emerging developments like learning analytics and computer-based cognitive tutors. But it's less easy to dismiss these developments and the claims that support them when you can see that some of the world's richest and most powerful companies are dedicating extraordinary research and development resources to them; when you can read reports advocating and sponsoring them by influential think tanks; when you hear that politicians are backing them; when you discover that enormous sums of venture capital and philanthropic funding are being invested to make them a reality.

A shared vision of the digitization and datafication of education is emerging. Diverse ideas and actors have combined to produce collective imaginative resources that can be used to animate research and development (R&D) practices, to persuade politicians, to generate investment, and to galvanize new practices (Jasanoff 2015). Of course, education has long been a site of future imagination. A 'dominant myth of the future of education' in recent years has been one that 'emerges out of an instrumental conception of education as primarily concerned with serving the formal economy' (Facer 2011: 8). Visions of data-driven education complicate this dominant myth of the future. While economic fantasies of human capital development persist, they are being supplemented and extended by dreams of new forms of governance and citizenship, new scientific aspirations of psychological optimization and cognitive enhancement, and new commercial objectives to insert private sector technologies and practices into public education.

Myths and imaginative visions, moreover, can become material realities when given technical form and inserted into social contexts. The developments traced out in the following chapters are all parts of a new emerging imaginary of the digital future of data-driven education that appears to be considered desirable, and that many organizations and individuals seem to agree could and should be attained through putting new technical developments into practice in the present. The twin processes of digitization and datafication form the basis for the book, but the practices of coding educational technologies of various kinds and of datafying education through diverse techniques are all also situated contextually and are animated by a particularly powerful imaginative resource which envisions education as a massively data-driven and software-supported social institution. The difference that digital data make in education is the result of the highly diverse efforts of programmers, project managers, businesses, startup accelerator programs, policymakers and politicians, think tanks and innovation labs, school managers, leaders, and educators themselves – the material practices of all of them shaped by an imagined vision of a digitized and datafied future which has become increasingly pervasive, persuasive and seemingly desirable.

Datafying Education

'Datafication' refers to the transformation of many aspects of education into quantifiable information that can be inserted into databases for the purposes of enacting different techniques of measurement and calculation. Datafication itself has a long history, detailed more fully in Chapter 2. Recent developments such as the establishment of data labs and data centres for educational data mining and analysis, and the proliferation of specific products such as learning analytics, adaptive learning software and computerized tutors, all rely on the constant collection of masses of digital data. Large-scale educational data has been available from the aggregation of test results or school census information for decades. The key shift with big data is that it is now collected in or near real-time directly as learners interact with software systems. That is to say, large-scale datasets have been historically gathered primarily through assessments and data collection events that have to be separated off from the normal rhythms of the classroom; big data are captured from within the pedagogic machinery of the teaching and learning process itself by being pieced together from the millions of data points that are generated as learners click on content and links, engage with digital educational materials, interact with others online, and post responses to challenges. Digital course content, online courses, e-textbooks, digital simulations, and more, provide the front-end interface for the production of educational big data, behind which lies a sophisticated back-end infrastructure of data collection, information storage, algorithmic processing, and analytics and data visualization capacities.

Underlying these developments is a set of powerful animating visions or imaginaries of datafication. The authors of *Learning with Big Data: The Future of Education* (Mayer-Schönberger and Cukier 2014) imagine that big data will 'reshape learning' through 'datafying the learning process' in three significant ways: (1) through real-time feedback on online courses and e-textbooks that can 'learn' from how they are used and 'talk back' to the teacher; (2) individualization and personalization of the educational experience through adaptive learning systems that enable materials to be tailored to each student's individual needs through automated real-time analysis; and (3) probabilistic predictions generated through data analytics that are able to harvest data from students' actions, learn from them, and generate predictions of individual students' probable future performances. The authors imagine school as a 'data platform' where the real-time datafication of the individual is becoming the 'cornerstone of a big-data ecosystem', and in which 'educational materials will be algorithmically customized' and 'constantly improved' (Mayer-Schönberger and Cukier 2014).

A significant amount of data-driven activity has been undertaken in the higher education sector, through widespread use of learning management systems and online programs such as MOOCs (Massive Open Online Courses) (Knox 2016). But schools are also being targeted for datafication. The US think tank the Center for Data Innovation has produced a report advocating a vision of a 'data-driven education system' for schooling. 'U.S. schools are largely failing to use data to transform and improve education, even though better use of data has the potential to significantly improve how educators teach children and how administrators manage schools', its author claims (New 2016: 1). Instead, the think tank argues that a data-driven education system should achieve four main goals:

> *Personalization*: Educators dynamically adjust instruction to accommodate students' individual strengths and weaknesses rather than continue to utilize a mass production-style approach.
>
> *Evidence-Based Learning*: Teachers and administrators make decisions about how to operate classrooms and schools informed by a wealth of data about individual and aggregate student needs, from both their own students as well as those in comparable schools across the nation … rather than by intuition, tradition, and bias.
>
> *School Efficiency*: Educators and administrators use rich insight from data to explore the relationships between student achievement, teacher performance, and administrative decisions to more effectively allocate resources.
>
> *Continuous Innovation*: Researchers, educators, parents, policymakers, tech developers, and others can build valuable and widely available new education products and services to uncover new insights, make more informed decisions, and continuously improve the education system. (New 2016: 2)

These goals for data-driven education systems accurately capture the dominant imaginary related to the collection and use of data in schools. 'Personalization' has become perhaps the main keyword of data-driven education, emphasizing systems and processes that can be intelligently tailored to the individual students. The use of evidence to perform comparisons across institutions and systems has a long lineage in education policy, but with digitization is becoming much easier and quicker to conduct. Achieving efficiency is paramount for schools, with performance management tools now available to ensure that students, teachers and administrators are all producing measurable outputs. And as larger and larger quantities of data become available – as masses of educational big data – new patterns and insights are being sought to address the goals of various stakeholders, such as the improvement agendas of policymakers and the new product development plans of businesses. The imagined datafication of schools is to be attained through pursing these goals of personalization, evidence-based learning, efficiency and continuous innovation.

How do such goals and imaginative visions look in practice? Compelling examples of how the datafication of schools might look in the imagined near future of education are provided by Silicon Valley 'startup schools'. Startup schools are new educational institutions designed as alternatives to the mainstream state schooling model, and they originate in the technology entrepreneurship culture of Silicon Valley, the technofinancial heart of the global tech industry. A prominent example is AltSchool, set up in 2013 by Max Ventilla, a technology entrepreneur and former Google executive. It 'prepares students for the future through personalized learning experiences within micro-school communities', and its stated aim is to 'help reinvent education from the ground up' (AltSchool 2015a). A recent profile of its founder claimed that 'when Ventilla quit Google to start AltSchool, in the spring of 2013, he had no experience as a teacher or an educational administrator. But he did have extensive knowledge of networks, and he understood the kinds of insights that can be gleaned from big data' (Mead 2016). After establishing in four sites in San Francisco as a 'collaborative community of micro-schools', AltSchool later expanded to Brooklyn and Palo Alto, with further long-term plans for new schools and partnerships across the US. It has since hired executives from Google, Uber and other successful Silicon Valley startups, many with experience of big data projects. The AltSchool chief technology officer, formerly the engineer in charge of the Google.com homepage and search results experience, has stated that 'I am highly motivated to use my decade of Google experience to enable the AltSchool platform to grow and scale' (AltSchool 2015a). The AltSchool 'platform' is described as a new 'central operating system for education', one designed according to 'technology-enabled models' that are transforming other industries and institutions, such as Uber and Airbnb (AltSchool 2015b).

The models it refers to are those of the datafication of other sectors. Airbnb represents the datafication of accommodation letting. Uber has thoroughly datafied taxi services. AltSchool has been programmed to run on the same basic model, or operating system, as these datafied sectors. Thus, it depends on a sophisticated data analytics platform. Its suite of digital tools is intended to 'make personalized education a reality', which it seeks to accomplish by supporting teachers to 'develop Personalized Learning Plans and to capture student progress toward them':

We also create platforms for efficient classroom administration so teachers have more quality face-to-face time with their students. ... To ensure we are always learning from what happens outside the classroom, we build digital tools to support collaboration between teachers, parents and students. ... Our project-based education approach truly comes alive when supported by carefully curated learning tools. We mentor each student in the use of technology for learning and help them skilfully navigate today's information terrain. (AltSchool 2016)

The data platform driving AltSchool is not just a technical system: it has been constructed to support a particular cultural vision of education as being 'personalized' around each individual. Personalization is its dominant ideal, and it is personalization that has been achieved successfully within the commercial social media activities of many Silicon Valley companies. For instance, Google search results are automatically personalized to each user based on their web search history. The Facebook timeline is personalized around the friends graph it constructs about each user's social network connections. The logic of personalization drives the ways in which social media platforms make recommendations for people to follow, consumer goods to buy, memes to share and so on. The culture and techniques of personalization from the commercial social media sphere are inserted into schooling through spaces such as AltSchool, and built in to its data platforms as a technical back-end complement to the front-facing cultural vision of education it projects. AltSchool ultimately balances and assembles a range of resources that appear unproblematically to crisscross the traverse between technological ideals and educational concepts.

Beyond technical and cultural similarities with the datafying priorities of the tech industry, the startup school also enjoys the financial benefits of Silicon Valley startup culture. On its establishment, AltSchool originally raised US$33 million in venture capital funding, with another US$100 million investment in 2015, including donations from Facebook's Mark Zuckerberg and the venture capital firm Andreeson Horowitz (AltSchool 2015b). AltSchool is, then, thoroughly governed, managed and financed through the discourses and material practices of Silicon Valley startup culture. Its operating system is modelled on social media data analytics. Its funding is almost exclusively generated through venture capital and tech philanthropy. Its engineering and design team are applying their social media expertise in data dashboards, algorithmic playlisting, adaptive recommender systems and app development to the development of new personalized edtech devices and platforms. The datafication of education prototyped by AltSchool, and other startup school models, is not just a technical accomplishment but the product of a financial investment model for Silicon Valley startups that has been trialled in other sectors, transplanted into education, and appears to be on the cusp of being scaled-up as a competitive market solution to the problem of mainstream schooling. Technology visionaries and imaginative entrepreneurs like Max Ventilla are becoming high-status education reformers, using their technical expertise in software development and data analytics, combined with the entrepreneurial business expertise required to generate investment, as powerful resources to attract others to their educational visions.

As the AltSchool example demonstrates, big data is not just technical. It is, rather, the 'manifestation of a complex sociotechnical phenomenon that rests on an interplay of technological, scientific, and cultural factors':

> While the *technological dimension* alludes to advances not only in hardware, software, but also infrastructure and the *scientific dimension* comprises both mining techniques and analytical skills, the *cultural dimension* refers to (a) the pervasive use of ICTs in contemporary society and (b) the growing significance and authority of quantified information in many areas of everyday life. (Rieder and Simon 2016: 2, italics in original)

Throughout the chapters that follow, the datafication of education is treated as the contingent materialization of future visions, technologies and skilled scientific techniques, as well as of political, commercial and philanthropic ambitions, all of which are combining into hybrid sociotechnical systems for data-driven measurement and management.

Digitizing Education

Datafication of education requires learning environments to be highly instrumented to collect information (Cope and Kalantzis 2015). This means the learning environment needs to be increasingly digitally-mediated, or digitized, as AltSchool's technical 'operating system' demonstrates. The use of the term 'digitization' refers to 'the process of converting information from analog into discrete units of data that can be more easily moved around, grouped together, and analysed' (Gregory et al. 2017: xviii) using computer technologies. With the digitization of education into information that can be processed by a computer, software and the code that enacts it becomes a significant influence in how education is organized. Software code has become a system for regulating many of the practices and processes of education, teaching and learning.

Described in more detail in Chapter 3, it is important from the outset to acknowledge that code is both a product – the end-result of the work of programmers, working in real material conditions, with their own professional cultures and values, and whose coding practices are shaped by business plans and objectives – and as a productive force in the world (Kitchin and Dodge 2011). By describing code as 'productive' registers the ways in which code is programmed to perform tasks that it then enacts (or, to use the specific computational term, 'executes'). Code instructs a software program to 'do something' on a computer, and in that basic sense it can be seen as productive. But it is also productive because writing code to execute a particular kind of task also fundamentally alters the nature of the task it is being instructed to perform (Mackenzie 2006).

In this book I focus on the ways that turning educational things into code then loops back to change education. However, to think of code just in technical terms, as a script for instructing software written in specific programming languages, would be misleading. It is certainly the case that e-learning software, policy databases and school management programs depend on lines of code for their functioning. But that code has itself to be written, or produced, as noted earlier. Programmers have to craft it, using specific kinds of programming languages and code repositories. Those programmers work according to the business plans, project management schedules and objectives of their employers. Those business plans are the operational manifestation of powerful future visions. The code produced to make software programs function is also dependent on financial investment, funding programmes and economic priorities. This goes beyond the straightforward allocation of programmers' salaries and includes the work of entrepreneurs in securing venture capital for software startups, of politicians providing tax incentives for technology companies, and of philanthropists making donations to finance new technical innovations. The software programs that enact much of education today, in other words, are also the product of imaginative business and political programmes.

An illustrative example of how digital imaginaries, software, finance and politics are interwoven in the contemporary transformation of education is provided by Edtech UK. This organization is 'a new strategic body set up to help accelerate the growth of the UK's education technology sector in Britain and globally':

> the new body is a 'front door' for industry, investment and government and a convening voice for all of the education and learning technology sector including educators, startups, scale up and high growth companies, large corporations, investors, regulators and policy makers. The focus of Edtech UK is to help support, showcase and develop the sector, with a focus on creating more jobs, developing new skills, understanding what works and driving economic growth. Its focus will be global from the outset with an ambitious programme of work to take the Best of British edtech companies to the world and be a launchpad for the world's best education and learning organisations to base themselves and grow in the UK. (Edtech UK 2015)

Edtech UK has been established by the Education Foundation, which describes itself as 'the UK's first independent, cross sector, education think tank' and is 'focused on three priorities: education reform, technology and innovation'. Since 2011 it has led an 'edtech incubator' for new educational technology companies; worked with Facebook on a guide for educators; sought to influence policy development at a national level including running Britain's first Education

Reform Summit in partnership with the Department for Education and the Secretary of State for Education; developed a corporate partners network with Facebook, IBM, Pearson, HP, Randstad Education, Cambridge University Press, McKinsey, Skype, Sony, Google and Samsung; and delivered policy roundtables, conferences, summits, and media events around educational technology in both the UK and USA. Itself an 'incubated' project of the Education Foundation, Edtech UK was launched by Boris Johnson, then Mayor of London, with the support of the UK government departments of Business, Innovation and Skills, and of Trade and Industry, as well as by a private sector coalition of organizations from the technology sector.

Political aspirations and financial capacity, as well as technical expertise and a vision of the future of educational technology, are all combined in the activities of Edtech UK. It has powerful political support, it is modelled on financial lobbying and accelerator organizations, and it mobilizes a hybrid discourse of investment, venture capital, startup and scale-up, and economic growth. Its corporate brochure for attracting new edtech startups to London promises extraordinary benefits. It references a 'large and profitable market' for educational technology; the benefits of 'flexible procurement' regulation which allows schools autonomy in their choice of technology suppliers; proximity to global edtech companies like Pearson and Knewton and the presence of 'talent, venture capital, co-working space, government support, seed funding and events' in London; seed enterprise investment, tax breaks and 'entrepreneurial relief' for early-stage companies; plus, it claims, the incentives of 'global education technology sector spending at $67.8bn in 2015 and a global "e-learning" market worth $165bn, which is poised to reach $243.8bn by 2022' (Education Foundation 2015). It is only amid the political, financial and commercial activities of Edtech UK that the work of programmers in producing educational technologies can take place.

Edtech UK is a compelling example of how the digitization of education – through support for new edtech startup companies – relies on the financial flows that make up the lines of information in a bank account, as well as on establishing political lines of linkage, as much as on the lines of code that actually make the software work. As Lynch (2015) conceptualizes it in *The Hidden Role of Software in Education*, a new kind of 'software space' made of code, algorithms and data produced by commercial actors, programmers and analysts is nowadays working alongside both the 'economic space' of investment, funding and finance and the 'political space' of educational policymaking and governance, then exerting its influence on the 'practice space' of teaching and learning. Edtech UK is emblematic of how imaginative future visions, software, economics and politics combine and interrelate with one another to impact on the practice spaces of education. The digitization of education is not simply about the translation of educational practices into software products, but about the manifold ways in which code comes into being, according to particular values, priorities and objectives, and in accordance with specific kinds of aspirations for the future of education.

The Digital Imagination and Materiality of Education

The examples of AltSchool, Edtech UK, Center for Data Innovation and HackingEDU we have encountered so far provide us with some sense of the imagined possibilities of datafication and digitization being associated with education. The aim of this book is neither to uncritically celebrate these developments, nor to debunk them. Instead, my intention is to consider how the twin processes of datafication and digitization are emerging from, and simultaneously reinforcing, a particular kind of reimagining of the future of education. Some sense of this reimagining is apparent from AltSchool's emphasis on personalized learning supported by data analytics platforms, and from Edtech UK's involvement in seeking to grow a future edtech market through both business and political networks. How to make sense of the work of imagination that underpins these diverse and emerging approaches?

In order to do this kind of analysis, I make use of the concept of 'sociotechnical imaginaries' from the field of science and technology studies (STS). By sociotechnical imaginaries, what is meant are 'collectively held, institutionally stabilized, and publicly performed visions of desirable futures, animated by shared understandings of forms of social life and social order attainable through, and supportive of, advances in science and technology' (Jasanoff 2015: 4). Sociotechnical imaginaries are not just science fiction fantasies: they constitute the visions and values that catalyse the design of technological projects. The dreamscapes of the future that are dreamt up in science laboratories, technical R&D departments, software companies and entrepreneurs' offices sometimes, through collective efforts, become stable and shared objectives that are used in the design and production of actual technologies and scientific innovations – developments that then incrementally produce or materialize the desired future. Through sociotechnical imaginaries, transformative scientific ideas, technological objects and social norms become fused in practice and help to sustain social arrangements or create new rearrangements in cultures, institutions and routines. Sociotechnical imaginaries are therefore the product of specifically political acts of imagination, because they act as powerful aspirational and normative visions of preferred forms of social order.

The concept of sociotechnical imaginaries has been taken up to understand the visions and values that underpin digital developments such as social media and search engines. The capacity to imagine the future is becoming a powerful constitutive element in social and political life, particularly as it infuses the technological visions and projects of global media companies (Mager 2016). Organizations such as Google and Facebook, Apple and Amazon can be understood as dominant producers of sociotechnical imaginaries, whose aspirations are therefore becoming part of how collectively and publicly shared visions of the future are accepted, implemented and taken up in daily life. As a variation on the term 'sociotechnical imaginary', Mager (2015: 56) describes 'algorithmic imaginaries' that emerge from 'a very specific economic and innovative culture' associated with Silicon Valley technology companies, and which privilege their originators' 'techno-euphoric interpretations of Internet technologies as driving forces for economic and social progress'.

The production of such desirable imaginary futures is both social and technical, which is why they are referred to as 'sociotechnical'. That is to say, such futures are produced by particular social groups within specific social contexts, and they are also projected through the design of particular kinds of technologies – or express a view of particular futures in which those kinds of technologies are imagined to be integral, embedded parts. Unpacking sociotechnical imaginaries requires research that focuses on 'the means by which imaginaries frame and represent alternative futures, link past and future times, enable or restrict actions in space, and naturalize ways of thinking about possible worlds' (Jasanoff 2015: 24). In slightly different terms, the imagining of a 'digital future' projects a kind of 'mythology' (a set of ideas and ideals) that animates, motivates and drives forward technical development but is always much more contested and messily realized, and never as simple, straightforward or idealized as it is imagined to be (Dourish and Bell 2011).

Imaginaries in this sense act as models or diagrams to which certain actors hope to make reality conform, serving as 'distillations of practices' for the shaping of behaviours and technologies for visualizing and governing particular ways of life and forms of social order (Huxley 2007: 194). Sociotechnical imaginaries animate technical projects and social organization, and provide models for ways in which certain spaces and places might be designed and arranged. The organization of societies in this sense depends on shared imaginative resources, language and practical techniques that combine in the materiality of 'fabricated spaces' – that is, spaces that have been 'realized' in the form in which they have been imagined (Rose 1999a: 33). In other words, sociotechnical imaginaries are often enacted and materialized through linguistic and concrete practices in ways that weave the underlying vision into the fabric of society. Thus, while sociotechnical imaginaries 'can originate in the visions of single individuals or small collectives', they can gather impetus 'through blatant exercises of power or sustained acts of coalition building' to enter into 'the assemblages of materiality, meaning and morality that constitute robust forms of social life' (Jasanoff 2015: 4). Fabricated spaces, then, are the result of imaginaries that have been realized and materialized through particular technical, discursive and practical acts.

We can understand new educational projects and places such as AltSchool as the fabricated material product of a specific sociotechnical imaginary of education. It has been brought into existence as a new fabricated space of education through discursive and material means as ways of realizing a future that is seen by its advocates and sponsors as desirable and possible to attain. In other words, AltSchool itself acts as an imaginary model for the future spaces of schooling that it is seeking to fabricate in reality through operationalizing its technical platforms, and which it is supporting discursively through reference to specific kinds of progressive educational thinking. Moreover, we can think of AltSchool as an extension of Silicon Valley, translating its particular culture and spaces of innovation to the education sector. AltSchool represents the sociotechnical imaginary of Silicon Valley relocated to the materiality of the classroom. Given AltSchool's aspirations to scale its model to other sites, we can appreciate how AltSchool functions as the material product of a sociotechnical imaginary which defines how education in the future might be, could be, or perhaps even *should* be, and that might shape and delimit the everyday practices of all those who inhabit it. In this sense, the current sociotechnical imaginaries and mythologies of education, in which digitization and datafication will play a significant role, are already becoming the lived reality of education – with all of the mess and potential contestation that entails – and need to be critically examined for the material effects they might exert.

Researching Digitization and Datafication In Education

If imaginary spaces become material zones to inhabit, they can therefore exert real consequences on those who experience them. To tease open the material consequences of emerging sociotechnical imaginaries of education, it is important to look closely at the software that will make such spaces operational. Researching the digitization and datafication of education therefore requires some novel methodological and conceptual approaches. Although the science, technology and society (STS) concept of sociotechnical imaginaries can help to understand the future visions that are animating and catalysing recent and ongoing technical development, we also need methods and concepts to grasp their (actual or potential) material consequences and effects. The emerging field of digital sociology has begun to address how digital technologies, software and data are being embedded into all kinds of social and cultural activities, institutions, relations and processes (Orton-Johnson and Prior 2013):

> For some theorists, the very idea of 'culture' or 'society' cannot now be fully understood without the recognition that computer software and hardware devices not only underpin but actively constitute selfhood, embodiment, social life, social relations and social institutions. (Lupton 2015a: 2)

For digital sociologists, digitization has important implications for our ways of knowing, studying and understanding the social world, which demand interdisciplinary approaches drawing from a longer history of internet studies, media and cultural studies, science and technology studies, surveillance studies and computational social science (Daniels et al. 2016; Halford et al. 2013).

Digital sociology, then, confronts the ways in which 'new digital media, the data they produce and the actors involved in the collection, interpretation and analysis of these data' now increasingly structure and shape the social world (Lupton 2015a: 17–18). It seeks to understand, for example, how people's everyday lives are increasingly mediated through routine digital transactions with governments, commercial organizations and public institutions; how space is experienced through mobile devices; how social media has become part of social networks; and how we learn about the world through new digital media forms. Many of the central preoccupations of sociologists, such as identity, power relations and inequalities, social networks, structures and social institutions, now need to be considered from the perspective of the ongoing digitization and datafication of many aspects of society.

'Software studies' has emerged as an interdisciplinary orientation to the study of software, and includes research from the arts, philosophy, humanities, geography, cultural studies and the social sciences. Studies of software tend to share two key emphases. They focus on the software, programs and social cultures that produce effects in social life from a critical social scientific and cultural perspective, and on the social and material work that contributes to its production. Software studies seek to engage with the 'stuff of software' and:

> to see behind the screen, through the many layers of software, logic, visualization, and ordering, right down to the electrons bugging out in the microcircuitry, and on, into the political, cultural and conceptual formations of their software, and out again, down the wires into the world, where software migrates into and modifies everything it touches. (Fuller 2008: 1)

This is clearly a tall methodological order, requiring expertise in the technicalities of software, the political and cultural processes involved in its production, and the social consequences that occur as it then spreads into highly diverse practices of work, leisure, politics, culture, economics, social relations and so on.

In order to establish a set of methodological parameters for such research, Kitchin and Dodge (2011: 246) have usefully defined a 'manifesto for software studies':

> Rather than focus purely on the technical, it fuses the technical with the philosophical to raise questions about what software is, how it comes to be, ... how it does work in the world, how the world does work on it, why it makes a difference to everyday life, the ethics of its work, and its supporting discourses. Software studies then tries to prise open the black boxes of algorithms, executable files, [database] structures, and information protocols to understand software as a new media that augments and automates society.

Their manifesto particularly highlights the need for critical research on the ways in which code emerges, how it performs, and how it seduces and disciplines. In terms of how code emerges, they urge for greater attention to the knowledge, practices, materials and marketplaces that are involved in the production of code, and the political, economic and cultural contexts that frame its production. They suggest performing detailed ethnographic studies of how developers produce code, and the life of software projects, to understand how software is created and how it is put to work in specific contexts.

Kitchin and Dodge then suggest that software studies might attend to the ways in which code performs. By this they mean analysing in detail 'the contextual ways in which code reshapes practices with respect to industry, transportation, consumption, governance, education, entertainment and health', as well as 'knowledge production, creative practice, and processes of innovation', and studying how code 'makes a difference' to those spaces and contexts through imbuing them with the capacity to do new types of work (Kitchin and Dodge 2011: 249). They also argue that code seduces and disciplines, largely because it offers people real benefits in terms of convenience, efficiency, productivity and creativity, whilst also enforcing more pervasive forms of surveillance and management. In particular, Kitchin and Dodge note how software is supported by powerful and consistent discourses, such as those of safety, security, empowerment, productivity, reliability, economic advantage, which persuade people to willingly and voluntarily embrace it. As such, software and code are amenable to forms of documentary and discourse analysis.

'Critical data studies' is another emerging body of interdisciplinary research that engages with the datafication of many aspects of society. A special issue on the topic of critical data studies introduced the field as a 'formal attempt at naming the types of research that interrogate all forms of potentially depoliticized data science and to track the ways in which data are generated, curated, and how they permeate and exert power on all manner of forms of life' (Iliadis and Russo 2016: 2). Iliadis and Russo (2016: 5) further highlight the identification of social data problems and the design of critical frameworks for addressing them. As a set of approaches to the critical examination of various forms of digital data – including big data, open data and data infrastructures – as well as the diverse practices of data science as a social, professional and technical discipline, critical data studies has found purchase with geographers, sociologists, philosophers and researchers of education.

In one of the first publications detailing critical data studies, the geographers Dalton and Thatcher (2014) set out seven defining commitments: (1) situate data regimes in temporal and spatial context; (2) reveal data as inherently political and expose whose interests they serve; (3) unpack the complex, non-deterministic relationship between data and society; (4) illustrate the ways in which data are never raw but always intentionally generated; (5) expose the fallacies that data can speak for themselves and that exhaustive big data will replace smaller-scale sampled data; (6) explore how new data regimes can be used in socially progressive ways; and (7) examine how academia engages with new data regimes and the opportunities of such engagement.

In another article outlining concepts and methods for critical data studies, Kitchin and Lauriault (2014) seek to provoke researchers to unpack the complex 'assemblages' that produce, circulate, share/sell and utilize data in diverse ways. Data assemblages, as they define them, consist of technical systems of data collection, processing and analysis, but also the diverse social, economic, cultural and political apparatuses that frame how they work. In this broad sense, a data assemblage includes: (1) particular modes of thinking, theories and ideologies; (2) forms of knowledge such as manuals and textbooks; (3) financial aspects such as business models, investment and philanthropy; (4) the political economy of government policy; (5) the materiality of computers, networks, databases and analytics software packages; (6) specific skilled practices, techniques and behaviours of data scientists; (7) organizations and institutions that collect, broker or use data; (8) particular sites, locations and spaces; and (9) marketplaces for data, its derivative products, its analysts and its software.

Approaching critical data studies in terms of sociotechnical data assemblages is productive for research into the production and use of educational data. This book provides a series of explorations of big data as it is entering into the complexities of education and reworking teaching, learning, assessment, governance and educational research itself. For the field of education research, big data is a new and emerging phenomenon about which there remains limited knowledge (Beneito-Montagut 2017). In the following chapters, I combine the focus on sociotechnical imaginaries with digital sociology, software studies and critical data studies approaches as a methodological strategy to perform a series of critical analyses of the ways in which assemblages involving software code, algorithms and digital data are making a difference in education.

This is not to suggest that existing approaches to educational research, description and explanation are irrelevant. Rather, part of my aim is to demonstrate that educational research can be productively extended by engaging with software and data from a critical perspective. Studies of educational policy, for example, have already begun to engage with the software packages and data infrastructures that enable policy information to be collected, and that also allow policies to penetrate into institutional practices. In the following chapters I seek to understand how some of the software technologies penetrating education today have come into existence and inquire into the imaginaries that animate them; to explore the forms of expertise and knowledge they work in relation with; to examine how they are being put to work in specific contexts and spaces and how they are shaping particular practices; and to explore how they are promoted and supported by certain discourses emanating from diverse public, private and philanthropic sectors.

Learning Machines

By working with concepts of sociotechnical imaginaries and critical approaches to software and data, I aim to show how powerful future visions are fast being turned into the ordinary artefacts that are enabling digitization and datafication in education. A useful term to capture these artefacts of educational digitization and datafication is 'learning machines'. This is a term I borrow from Michel Foucault. In his highly influential work on regimes of discipline, Foucault (1991) traced some of the ways in which schools function to supervise and discipline pupils, particularly through techniques like timetabling, sitting them in rows in classrooms, and organizing them in ranks according to age, performance, behaviour, knowledge and ability. Together, Foucault (1991: 147) argued, these techniques 'made the educational space function like a learning machine, but also as a machine for supervising, hierarchizing, rewarding … according to the pupils' progress, worth, character, application, cleanliness and parents' fortune.' He detailed how classrooms functioned by placing pupils in categories, classifications and rankings based on constant assessments of their qualities, age, development, performance and behaviour. Through techniques of ordering and ranking pupils according to diverse categories, Foucault argued, 'the classroom would form a single great table, with many different entries', and he noted that classrooms are 'mixed spaces' – 'real' insofar as they consist of buildings, rooms and furniture, but 'also ideal, because they are projected over this arrangement of characterizations, assessments, hierarchies' (1991: 148).

The categorization and tabularization of educational institutions, spaces, processes and individuals is perhaps the ideal aim – or dominant imaginary – of big data in education. In this sense, what Foucault designated learning machines takes on new resonance in the era of big educational data. The learning machines being imagined and built today consist of computational technologies that can capture and process data about learning; that can intervene in learning practices, processes and institutions; that can 'learn' from the data they process; and that can be understood as techniques of power, instruments for the control of activity, behaviours and bodies, and processes of knowledge generation. They are smart learning machines, the material and operational form of the sociotechnical imaginary of big data in education. Through big data, schools, colleges, universities and other informal learning contexts are becoming 'machine[s] for learning, in which each pupil, each level and each moment, if correctly combined', are becoming 'permanently utilized in the general process of teaching' by a 'precise system of command' which operates 'according to a more or less artificial, prearranged code' (Foucault 1991: 165–6). The smart learning machines associated with digitization and datafication in education are the product of lines of code, in the technical sense, that also enforce particular codes of conduct. Digital software allows institutions, practices and people to be constantly observed and recorded as data; those data can then be utilized by learning machines to generate insights, produce 'actionable' intelligence, or even prescribe recommendations for active intervention. The ideal sociotechnical imaginary of big data in education is now being materialized and operationalized through smart learning machines, made of software code and data, which might inhabit real educational spaces.

2

CONCEPTUALIZING DIGITAL DATA

Data mining, analytics and imaginaries

Digital data have become central to the activities of businesses, governments, media companies, think tanks, cities and scientific innovation, as well as to the everyday lives of billions around the globe. Commercial organizations including supermarkets, online retailers, financial institutions, entertainment and social media companies, transport providers and many more, depend on gathering huge quantities of data from their customers and users in order to optimize the running of their operations. In the universe of the big web companies, Amazon, Netflix and Spotify have enough data on customers both individually and en masse to be able to predict media preferences and make individualized, micro-targeted recommendations (Beer 2013). Google and Facebook collect data from each click a user makes, using those data to construct detailed profiles about users' tastes, preferences and interests that can then be used to tailor and personalize the content they receive – as well as to sell to third parties for targeted digital advertizing – and subtly shape their overall social media experience (van Dijck 2013). Even Disney World has become a massively data-based commercial operation: its visitors are all issued with bespoke wristbands (MagicBands) which constantly transmit information about their location in the park, menu choices in the restaurants, waiting times for rides, the shows they watch – everything they do. Disney's engineers can then analyse this data in specialist Disney Research labs to generate insights about better optimizing the park and its attractions. This 'DataLand' has reimagined 'a theme park as an experimental city', where 'data surveillance' is part of 'the world's largest and most diverse experiment in wearable data fashion' (Bogost 2014).

Governments are trying to do the same thing as Disney World but at the scale of national populations. Through personal information contained in the barcode of your passport, plus biometric details scanned from your irises in an eye-scanner at an airport, national governments can keep a decent record of your travels. When you file a tax return online, or when you access another online digital government service, it can track your interactions with the state, since, it has been claimed, 'many or even most government departments and agencies "are" their information systems and digital presence – the only part of them with which many citizens will interact' (Dunleavy and Margetts 2015). Politics itself is experiencing an 'analytics turn' characterized by the increased use of 'experimental data science methods to interrogate large-scale aggregations of behavioral information from public voter records and digital media environments, with the aim of organizing and mobilizing key segments of the electorate to vote and to publicly and privately share their decision with others' (Chadwick and Stromer-Galley 2016: 284).

When Edward Snowden, the whistle blower from the US National Security Agency (NSA) leaked files to the media in 2014, it became clear how some powerful government agencies have built back doors into social media sites, enabling them to harvest information about millions of people as they go about their daily lives online. This has raised significant concerns about surveillance and privacy invasion by both commercial and governmental actors (Lyon 2014). Political think tanks, too, are increasingly turning to digital data as a source for gauging the pulse of the public and then recommending policies and government interventions on that basis (Miller 2014).

Journalism is both undergoing a transformation, in the shape of digital journalism and data journalism, and experiencing a massive crisis as traditional news outlets are threatened by virally populist social media stories and online sources of fake news (Albright 2016a). This is bringing about a situation where a concern for 'facts' and 'truth' is being usurped by concerns for clicks, engagement metrics and revenue-generation via digital advertising. In turn, this is exacerbated by the rise of 'post-truth politics' whereby politicians and their political advisers spin salacious stories that are more likely to circulate in social media networks and resonate emotionally with the population (Viner 2016). Thus, while mining data may be beneficial for gaining either political or journalistic insights into the public mood and key events, social media, fake news and post-truth politics combined are also radically reshaping people's exposure to information. At the same time, the data gained from users' clicks and links is used to further customize their experience around their existing interests and worldviews rather than challenging them with countervailing perspectives.

A similar commitment to mining big data for insights can be found in many techniques of urban governance and city management. This is particularly the case in 'smart cities' – emerging urban spaces that are instrumented with sensor devices, surveillance equipment and the data collection capacities to track and monitor people through their smartphones:

> The old city of concrete, glass and steel now conceals a vast underworld of computers and software. Linked up via the Internet, these devices are being stitched together into a nervous system that supports the lives of billions in a world of huge and growing cities. … This digital upgrade to our built legacy is giving rise to a new kind of city – a 'smart city'. (Townsend 2013: xii)

In such cities where 'machines run the world on our behalf', urban managers can conduct real-time diagnostics of the city – using the results from digital data to allocate resources, manage traffic and transportation, and monitor energy use – and even monitor social media posts from Facebook and Twitter to gather insights into public sentiment expressed about certain urban locations, services and events. The city appears to be becoming smart, even a 'sentient city', as it learns from the data it collects and acts responsively to perform more optimally (Shepard 2011).

In these and other ways, people's everyday lives are being transformed by digital data. This is perhaps most obvious for those individuals who use their mobile phones or wearable fitness and health-tracking devices to monitor their physical exercise. The Quantified Self movement has become a global phenomenon, with people using devices such as Fitbit bands, Apple watches and other sensor-enabled devices to track their movement, record their sleep patterns, monitor their sex lives, report their feelings, calculate their calorific input and output, and far more (Lupton 2016). Even more commonly, through interacting with social media, people are becoming both consumers of data produced by others, as well as producers of data – in the shape of profile updates, posts, images, videos, comments, likes, recommendations and so on (Beer 2013).

With the rise of the Internet of Things (IoT) – objects with internet connections, such as smart fridges, smart thermostats and even smart toothbrushes that are able to monitor their own use – the everyday material environment itself is becoming more alive with data, as buildings, offices, homes and individual devices all interact and communicate with one another without human intervention (Thrift 2014). In this context of intense interaction between people and smart things, data makes a difference to everyday lives as people become parts of vast networks of movements of data: 'Just as we may speak of "sentient cities", we may also refer to the "sentient citizen" – a digital data emitting node in the Internet of Things' (Michael and Lupton 2015: 6). If we use the Web, we are all shadowed by our 'data double', a version of ourselves compiled from digital traces of our activities (Haggerty and Ericson 2001; Raley 2013). With the rise of automated assistants like Google Now, Apple's Siri and Facebook's M, a vast database of every individual user is now being compiled, a database containing enough information about us for systems to become seemingly intelligent and sentient in their subsequent interactions with us.

The role of digital data in education has, perhaps oddly, been rather neglected. While the emergence of new developments like educational data mining may not appear immediately as spectacular as Disney World's data labs, as powerful as government digital services, as responsive as smart cities, or as pervasive as the Internet of Things, they are equally as important. In fact, many organizations are already proposing that educational institutions could be run as digital data-led spaces, modelled on exactly the same kind of imaginings that have galvanized the datafication of Disney, the growth of digital government, the smartening up of cities and the interconnecting of things into powerfully responsive webs that are becoming more knowing, sentient and aware of themselves. Along these lines, there are already programs to rethink education in smart cities; there are adaptive learning technologies that respond to their users in ways that appear sentient; there are wearable devices to track and monitor learners' academic progress as well as their movements and emotions. These developments, and more, will be introduced and discussed in the chapters that follow, but first it is necessary to grasp some of the complexity and diversity of what is meant when we talk about digital data and big data.

Defining Data

Digital data technologies have expanded in reach and influence significantly in recent years. While the concept of data in relation to digital technologies is obviously a product of the twentieth century, the use of the term is much older. In English usage, 'data' dates back to the seventeenth century, with the ideas underlying it later coming to play a significant role in opening up the conceptual space for subsequent innovations in statistics and information technology (Rosenberg 2013). 'Data' itself is derived etymologically from the Latin *dare*, meaning 'to give'. In this etymological sense, 'data' signifies something that is given or taken for granted; data constitute the raw elements that can be abstracted, measured and recorded from various phenomena and turned into evidence or facts. As such, the concept of data was linked to seventeenth- and eighteenth-century attempts to move away from theological knowledge claims based on scriptures, to scientific facts and evidence, and the assumption that data were meaningful regardless of context, medium, format, language or producer (Kitchin 2014a). From the eighteenth-century perspective, 'data are apparently before the fact: they are the starting point for what we know, who we are, and how we communicate', and were often perceived as transparent, self-evident, neutral and objective, 'the fundamental stuff of truth itself' (Gitelman and Jackson 2013: 2–3).

When we use the word 'data', however, we are usually referring to those elements that are 'taken' (*capere*) or selected, not those units that have been given by nature to the scientist. Kitchin (2014a: 3) claims that instead of 'data' we should more accurately refer to 'capta', and although this would obviously confuse matters, he argues that it highlights how:

> data harvested through measurement are always a selection from the sum total of all data available – what we have chosen to take from all that could potentially be given. As such, data are inherently partial, selective and representative, and the distinguishing criteria used in their capture has consequences.

In this sense, data need to be understood as social products – as units of measurement that have been taken from a phenomenon according to the conventions by which they have been generated. In other words, much work has to be put into the generation of data; they are never just 'raw' material that, once 'discovered', underpin the production of evidence or information (Bowker 2008). Rather, 'data require our participation. They need us' (Gitelman and Jackson 2013: 6).

Data are, in other words, not given, but taken or selected according to diverse social factors such as expert knowledge, professional conventions and the practices of those that design and work with the technologies; organizations and institutions within which data are collected, calculated and communicated; political, financial and marketplace contexts that shape the conditions for data use; the material availability of devices to enact the generation of data; and the legal and ethical frameworks, technical standards, laws and regulations that govern all stages of the production and use of data. In other words, data 'do not exist independently of ideas, techniques, technologies, systems, people and contexts' (Kitchin 2014a: 24).

First Wave Big Data

The sociotechnical arrangement of many aspects of the contemporary world now increasingly depends on various database systems, and the processes of ordering, sorting, counting and classification they enact (Mackenzie 2012). Though digital database technologies are clearly a twentieth-century invention, they have long genealogical roots. Large-scale data collection and statistical analysis have a very long history across governmental, commercial and academic sectors, for example in national censuses, consumer loyalty schemes, and the production of massive scientific knowledge databases (Bowker 2008). The even newer concept of big data itself has a fragmented past which is tied up in the complex histories of computerization, military funding, commercialization, academic research agendas and changing forms of government regulation, as well as being built upon historical modes of inquiry such as social physics, spatial analysis and other earlier forms of computational and statistical analysis of social data (Barnes and Wilson 2014; Rieder and Simon 2016).

Current interest in big data can therefore be seen as continuous with the 'avalanche of printed numbers' associated with the rise of statistics and other novel knowledge production and sorting processes of the mid-1800s, such as those of census offices, libraries and museums, and especially those bureaucratic practices of social data collection such as counting rates of sickness, disease, poverty, crime and so on (Hacking 1990). The use of statistics and forms of measurement has been integrally connected to how governments have sought to understand and control populations for several centuries, which pre-dates but also anticipates current enthusiasm around both large-scale data and digital big data:

> Knowledge of the things that comprise the very reality of the state is ... called 'statistics.' Etymologically, statistics is knowledge of the state, of the forces and resources that characterize a state at a given moment. ... [Statistics is] a set of technical knowledges that describes the reality of the state itself. (Foucault 2007: 274)

Thus, the techniques of statistics that first began to appear in the seventeenth century and later proliferated in the nineteenth-century revolution in 'printed numbers' could furnish governments with knowledge of the population, its quantity, its wealth, its natality, health and mortality, its trade and taxes, its military resources and so on, all of which could constitute the content of governmental knowledge. Statistical knowledge of the population could therefore be seen as a key source of governmental power, enabling 'a machinery of government to operate from centres that calculate' (Rose 1999a: 213).

These analogue statistical forms of 'social data' anticipated the rise of political, commercial and academic interest in the concept and practices of big data by well over a century (Beer 2016a). The nineteenth-century avalanche of analogue numbers was the 'first wave of big data', brought about as 'people reached for quantification when chaos from a massive shift in the sociotechnical world ensued' from the industrial revolution (Ambrose 2015: 218). This had significant implications for social organization, control and governance. The nineteenth-century 'collection of social data had a purpose – understanding and controlling the population in a time of significant social change' – which brought about changed understandings of individuals, groups and populations, and influenced how they might be acted upon through new social institutions (Robertson and Travaglia 2015). By this time, it had become common to treat data as the result of an investigation or experiment, rather than a unit of a phenomenon given in advance.

Of course, many of the analogue bureaucratic and statistical practices of the past are continued today. For example, many government departments routinely collect administrative data about individual citizens, such as birth records, social security payment records, educational attainment records, health records, employment records, benefits records, court records, tax records and records of one's death. These data form an administrative timeline of each individual of the population, and can be aggregated and analysed to build up detailed accounts of social trends and behaviours. In the UK, the Administrative Data Research Network administers access to these data, linking them together to offer the opportunity to develop a statistical picture of society that might be used to influence future government policy. The ambition to use large datasets to provide insight into societal and individual behaviours underpins new and emerging efforts to mine the digital deluge of big data.

Digital Big Data

While so-called 'first wave big data' was associated with nineteenth-century statistical practice, the twenty-first century's 'second wave of big data' (Ambrose 2015) is much more dependent upon digital technologies and associated data practices. The data that can be collected and stored are now not just statistical, quantitative or numerical in nature, but can also be qualitative and non-numeric, as with text, pictures, video and sound. Big data is possible because of massive increases in telecommunication bandwidth and information flow, connecting data storage systems that allow for huge information stockpiling, network servers and server farms, and enhanced digital computational capacities to make sense of the data (Hilbert 2016; Kitchin 2014a). Digital data are, in other words, enabled by the material availability of specific devices, without which they could be neither collected and stored nor analysed and interpreted. Like all forms of data, digital big data are in this sense never 'raw' because they have to be first captured, then translated into quantifiable, encodable and machine-readable characteristics which enable them to be identified, classified, ordered or sorted through data processing algorithms which are themselves reliant upon material hardware (Bowker 2008).

Although big data has become a popular term and a hyped concept in recent years, definitional clarity in relation to big data is surprisingly elusive. In technical terms, big data refers to data sets that are huge in volume (at the scale of petabytes, exabytes and zettabytes); highly diverse in type and nature; generated continuously at great velocity in or near real-time; exhaustive in scope (enabling the capture of entire populations – or 'n=all' – rather than sampled selections); fine-grained in resolution at the level of indexing individual units; combinable with other networks of datasets; and flexible and scalable enough for new fields to be added and to expand in size rapidly (Boyd and Crawford 2013; Mayer-Schönberger and Cukier 2013; Kitchin 2014a, 2014b). Kitchin and McArdle (2015) suggest that exhaustivity and velocity are perhaps the two most key traits of big data systems. These qualities of big data are in contrast to earlier methods of data collection and analysis that progressed using data produced in tightly controlled ways using sampling techniques that limited their scope, variety, temporality and size (Kitchin and McArdle 2015).

However, big data is not just a material phenomenon, but a powerful concept with a long history that is tied to earlier forms of social data collection and population management:

> when thinking about Big Data we need to consider its history as being tied-up with particular ways of thinking. We then need to consider how this thinking is enacted in the development of certain infrastructures and in the industry of data analytics. This is to see Big Data as the entwinement of both a phenomenon and a concept. Big Data itself, with its capacity to track lives through archived and classified forms of individuated data, can be placed then within the genealogical lineage of the modern state. (Beer 2016b: 1)

As a result, it is not always clear what constitutes big data in practice. The contested definitional nature of big data is captured in the question 'What makes big data, big data?' by Kitchin and McArdle (2015), who note that many systems described as big data often fail to meet the definitional criteria offered by the literature (e.g. huge in volume, highly varied, collected in real-time, able to be extended in scale and related to other datasets, exhaustive rather than sampled, and fine-grained in resolution). Rather, big data has become 'loose in its ontological framing and definition', often 'treated like an amorphous entity that lacks conceptual clarity', and 'while there has been some rudimentary work to identify the "genus" of big data ... there has been no attempt to separate out its various "species" and their defining attributes' (Ibid. 2015: 4–5). In other words, there may be many kinds of big data with different characteristics and nature.

Data Analytics, Data Mining and Machine Learning

However big data is defined, all digital data need to be processed and analysed to help make sense out of them. Hilbert (2016: 139) even suggests that the 'full name' for big data is 'big data analytics', since 'independent from the specific peta-, exa- or zettabytes scale, the key feature of the paradigmatic change is that analytic treatment of data is systematically placed at the forefront of intelligent decision-making'. Building on established statistical methods and models, new data analytics and data mining technologies have been developed in recent years to detect, classify and extract associations and patterns from large datasets utilizing advances in information management and storage, data handling, modelling algorithms, machine intelligence and expert systems.

The processing and analysis of abundant, varied, exhaustive and messy big data has become possible only due to high-powered computational techniques that are 'rooted in research concerning artificial intelligence and expert systems that have sought to produce machine learning that can computationally and automatically mine and detect patterns and build predictive models and optimize outcomes' (Kitchin 2014b: 2). Data analytics methods:

> promise to help us gain insight into public opinion, mood, networks, behaviour patterns and relationships. Data analytics and machine learning are also ostensibly paving the way for a more intelligent Web 3.0 ... and they envision new strategies for forecasting, targeting and decision-making in a growing range of social realms, such as marketing, employment, education, health care, policing, urban planning and epidemiology. (Andrejevic et al. 2015: 1)

Techniques of data mining, though, are not altogether new: they have been developing in scientific settings and industry research for at least the last half-century, and now include a vast array of techniques including pattern recognition, statistical modelling, decision trees, neural networks, perceptrons, logistic and linear regression models, machine learning and many others (Mackenzie 2015).

Of all data analytics methods, machine learning is perhaps the most prominent. Machine learning is the term to describe 'intelligent' software systems featuring adaptive algorithms, designed in statistical programming languages such as R, that can be taught to anticipate and predict how people act. As a particular predictive practice of data mining, machine learning is now embedded in many of the platforms that mediate everyday life. Machine learning relies on adaptive algorithms and statistical models that can be 'fed training data'; these are, crudely speaking, 'taught algorithms' that can learn from being taught with example data (Gillespie 2014b). Customized search engine results, social media suggestions and online consumer recommendations are all examples of machine learning at work.

The significance of machine learning systems is that they exhibit some tendencies of emergence, adaptivity, anticipation and prediction. By being trained with past data, machine learning produces taught algorithms that can interact with both people and other machines, and adapt in response. Taught algorithms enable the digital environment to 'learn' from and about users, and to 'talk back' in the shape of feedback and recommendations for future actions. This is not to say that machine learning can proceed entirely without human oversight. Machine learning systems have to be constantly re-trained in an iterative process of monitoring, adjusting, revising and optimizing as the accuracy and generalizability of the predictive models they generate are themselves checked and analysed (Mackenzie 2015).

With recent technical advances, however, it is increasingly possible for machine learning systems to learn more autonomously. Whereas conventional machine learning algorithms depend on being trained and re-trained with example data (sometimes termed 'supervised learning'), newer machine learning systems based on techniques such as neural networks and deep learning are designed with the capacity to process and learn from natural language, interactions with users, and other unstructured data ('unsupervised learning') in ways that emulate the neural networks of the human brain. Machine learning and predictive analytics software are part of a world, therefore, in which 'probabilistic outcomes' and predictions about the future now prevail, with significant implications for how individuals think about and anticipate their own futures (Mackenzie 2013). The capture and processing of big data through the taught algorithms of machine learning systems can be found in consumer businesses, financial industries, governmental database services, and in the media, as well as in new forms of surveillance.

However, serious questions need to be raised about the process that Mackenzie (2015: 431) describes as 'the production of prediction'; that is, the sociotechnical work that goes into making the predictive practices of machine learning possible. Notably, he highlights that machine learning can only learn from:

a data sample that has already been classified or labelled by someone. The existence of the classifications is crucial to the work of the techniques. The classification becomes what the data mining techniques seek to learn or model so that future instances can be classified in a similar way. (2015a: 433)

Likewise, Gillespie (2014b) has argued that the values and assumptions that go into the selection and preparation of the training data are central to the way in which the machine learning algorithm can learn from the data. The human act of training the algorithm to identify and learn from things that have been classified or labelled clearly indicates how machine learning is a form of work or production performed by people working in specific labour conditions, within institutional frameworks, according to professional commitments, worldviews and disciplinary theories about the ways in which the world works. These contextual factors are consequential to the ways in which machine learning is trained, re-trained and checked to ensure the accuracy and generalizability of its models, and have significant implications for how data may be communicated and visualized.

Data Visualization

Given the complexity and vastness of big data, it has become essential to find ways of communicating it effectively to make sense to various audiences. The graphical display of big data through data visualization is increasingly employed to make visible and comprehensible complex datasets and models that would otherwise be difficult to conceptualize, and to reveal patterns, structures and interconnections that might otherwise remain hidden. Although the visual register has long been used 'to summarise and describe datasets through statistical graphs and charts, diagrams, spatialisations, maps, and animations' (Kitchin 2014a: 106), recently, social science and humanities researchers have developed a strong interest in data visualization in specific relation to big digital datasets. The abundance of data visualizations, through 'many kinds of visual forms such as scatter plots, line graphs, histograms, boxplots, heatmaps and various other kinds of specialized data graphic' all play roles in the practices of data mining, analytics and machine learning as 'part of the toolkit of data miners and "data scientists" employed to navigate, transform or otherwise explore data' and thus 'persuade people to do things or help them to decide what to do' (Mackenzie 2015: 437).

Through the application of 'visual analytics', data visualizations can reveal patterns and build visual models and explanations. Visualization acts as a way of simplifying and reducing the complexity of the interaction of variables to graphical and diagrammatic form; it is an advanced semiotic technique whereby diverse quantities and qualities of data are transformed and standardized into a common visual metric. But the 'database aesthetics' of data visualization can also be used as a form of visual argumentation or rhetoric:

> Not only are data abstract and aggregative, but also data are mobilized graphically. That is, in order to be used as part of an explanation or as a basis for argument, data typically require graphical representation and often involve a cascade of representations. ... Data visualization amplifies the rhetorical function of data, since different visualizations are differently effective, well or poorly designed, and all data sets can be multiply visualized and thereby differently persuasive. (Gitelman and Jackson 2013: 12)

Consequently, visual methods give the data meaning; they translate measurements into curves and trends; and they make the data amenable to being inserted into presentations and arguments that might be used to produce conviction in others. In other words, data visualization gives numbers some pliability to be shaped and configured as powerful and persuasive presentations. The visualization of data is no neutral accomplishment but amplifies the rhetorical or persuasive function of data, allowing it to be employed to create arguments and generate explanations about the world, and to produce conviction in others that such representations, explanations and arguments depict the world as it really appears – as 'visualized facts' (Kitchin et al. 2015).

In terms of the production or generation of data visualization, researchers therefore need to examine the actors involved in producing visualizations, ask what data they are using, how those data have been formed, as well as 'what software is used in the analysis, what code or algorithms shape the data and the visualization', in order to 'treat these visuals seriously as they come to envision the social world' (Beer 2013: 118–19). Visual analytics methods imply a combination of humans and algorithms working symbiotically, with the algorithmic ordering of the visual data subtly working alongside the user in the construction of meaningful images, diagrams, graphs and tables (Kitchin 2014a). As Rose et al. (2014) have identified, any visualization produced using software and digital data is ultimately 'made' as it circulates around a network of offices and computer screens; as it is worked on by a variety of designers, visualizers, project managers, programmers and data analysts; and as it encounters various software programmes and hardware devices. As such a visualization might be understood as an 'interfacial site' created through networks of human bodies at work with various kinds of software and hardware, facilitated by vast repositories of code and databases of fine-grained information, thus highlighting:

> the changes wrought to meaning-making by the emergence of digital networks through which data are constantly mobile, shifting and proliferating, moving between different actors and media, ported and patched, altered and designed, collaged and commented on. (Rose et al. 2014: 401)

The visualization of the world described here is a complex sociotechnical act involving a variety of actors and technologies with the persuasive power to shape people's engagement and interaction with the world itself.

Big Data Infrastructures and Practices

As the discussion of big data generation and visualization has already begun to indicate, any attempt to define big data cannot be confined to technical classifications such as the 3Vs (volume, variety and velocity) alone. Rather than reducing big data simply to a list of characteristics, it is more useful to think of it in terms of a sociotechnical system. This means being alert to the social conditions of its production, as well as to its productive effects in the world. Kitchin and Lauriault (2014: 6) have described a highly relational 'data infrastructure' as:

> a complex socio-technical system, composed of many apparatuses and elements that are thoroughly entwined, whose central concern is the production of data. A data assemblage consists of more than the data system/infrastructure itself, such as a big data system, an open data repository, or a data archive, to include all of the technological, political, social and economic apparatuses that frames their nature, operation and work.

The concept of a data infrastructure is particularly important as, in simple terms, an infrastructure is the physical, material and organizational structure that underlies and orchestrates social, political and economic life. Infrastructures consist of massive technical systems such as the telecommunication and informational networks of electronic communication, energy and power networks, water and waste networks, the networks of transport and travel, each of them underpinned by dense thickets of standards, protocols and classification systems, and which are increasingly coordinated by computer programs, software, algorithms and code that define how they should function.

As Bowker and Star (1999: 35) have defined it, 'infrastructure is sunk into, inside of, other structures, social arrangements, and technologies'; it is a historically worked-out set of technologies, routines, conventions of practice and organizational structures. An infrastructure is not merely a technical system, then, but constituted through the relations between many interlocking technical, social and discursive elements to form the 'material instantiation or embodiment of some wider social and political movements' (Beer 2013: 23). As such, infrastructures are both technical, built on data technologies and associated software packages, but also social and human accomplishments, requiring new kinds of knowledge workers, designers, engineers and so on. They also consist of built-in political and social assumptions or aspirations, so that 'seemingly purely technical issues, like how to name things and how to store data, in fact constitute much of human interaction and much of what we come to know as natural' (Bowker and Star 1999: 326).

While data infrastructures underpin the organization of many aspects of contemporary societies, it is important to consider the 'data practices' that generate digital data within such infrastructures. An 'algorithmically driven social infrastructure' requires significant human labour and resource extraction, and should not simply be regarded as a technical system (Orton-Johnson et al. 2015). Taking this further, Ruppert et al. (2015) have detailed that big data come into being through social and technical practices in specific expert settings, practices which do not just generate those data but also 'order, manage, interpret, circulate, reuse, analyse, link and delete them' according to 'the normative, political and technical imperatives and choices … [of] the actors and institutions that shape big data'. They also then point out that the social and technical generation of data, and the ways these data are interpreted and made meaningful, are also *generative* of particular effects and social implications, since data and the algorithms that process them are consequential to 'what is known', and can influence decision-making and other activities (Ruppert et al. 2015). A data infrastructure, then, is not just technical but also practical in the sense that it needs to be enacted through the work of various actors and institutions, and practical in the additional sense that the data produced might also then become *practicable* and consequential to the actions of those who encounter those data and make decisions on the basis of the meaning extracted from them.

The data practices associated with big data are largely those undertaken by data scientists, software engineers and programmers – the originators of big data systems – but could also be extended to include the users of big data, those who make meaning out of datasets and visualizations and employ those meanings and interpretations in their decision-making practices and other activities. Referring to the former, Gehl (2015: 414) has characterized 'the rare subject capable of mining these messes':

> the Data Scientist, armed with … a large pile of data, algorithms and not a little genius. As with past generations of knowledge workers, the data scientist is called forth to tame the excesses of our constant sharing and mine it for new knowledge and produce valuable new techniques of social management.

As the ideal-type knowledge worker of the big data era, the figure of the data scientist, Gehl (2015: 420) argues, is a 'sexy and rare' hybrid product of various threads, including the long history of statistical analysis, computational power, advances in algorithms within the field of computer science, new forms of information storage and retrieval, new programming languages, and entrepreneurialism.

These new data scientific experts of the social world have been termed 'algorithmists' – experts in computer science, mathematics and statistics, as well as policy, law, economics and social research – who can undertake big data analyses across commercial, political and scholarly sites (Mayer-Schönberger and Cukier 2013). Big data require data science algorithmists as a kind of super-class of scientific expertise. They are the knowledge workers whose code, algorithms and analytics will extract meaning from masses of data, who will be able to perform analyses on it, visualize it for the consumption of others, and who will produce the insights, facts and evidence on the basis of which others might be persuaded what to do.

At the other end of the data practice spectrum are those actors who encounter data and work with it in the enactment of their everyday lives. For example, school teachers, leaders and schoolchildren themselves are both producers of data and also subjects of data (Finn 2016). More broadly, big data might be approached in terms of the practices of data users, such as those social media users who are engaged in 'playing' with data when they participate in Facebook, Snapchat, Instagram, Twitter and so on (Beer 2013). Many of the major commercial companies responsible for the generation and analysis of big data from social media have dedicated extensive research and development to human–computer interaction (HCI) to 'optimize' the interaction of users with data:

> information providers conduct a great deal of research trying to understand, and then operationalize, how humans habitually seek, engage with, and digest information. … Most notably in the study of human-computer interaction (HCI), the understanding of human psychology and perception is brought to bear on the design of algorithms and the ways in which their results should be represented. (Gillespie 2014a: 174)

Big data itself has become a valuable resource for HCI researchers and developers, who are able to utilize masses of data about users' information processing practices to inform the design of new software interfaces and functionality. As a result, the practices of the data user are significantly 'configured' (Woolgar 1991) and constrained by the design choices made during the development of the user interface that mediates the users' interaction with the data.

Social Consequences of Big Data

Though big data may not be a settled and uncontested term, the consequences of big data in the wider social world are now the subject of serious academic debate, particularly in relation to the tracking and monitoring of individual and social behaviours and activities. In the contemporary 'dataverse':

> Data about me are stored in thousands of virtual locations… . As that data is reworked, processed through an online algorithm or spat out to somewhere and somewhen to the computer screen of a vigilant operator, my possibilities for action are being shaped. … As people, we are … becoming our own data. (Bowker 2013: 168)

This is a context in which datafication – the transformation of social action into online quantified data to enable real-time tracking, monitoring and predictive analysis of people's behaviour – has become a new paradigm in science and society, and in which there is an increasingly 'dataist' trust in the objective quantification of all kinds of human behaviour and sociality (van Dijck 2014: 198). As Gehl (2015: 414) notes, 'data mining, analysis and resulting practices are aimed at "ordinary" people to manage and exploit their desires, movements and sociality.' He adds that:

> The informationalization of knowledge, coupled with advances in digital storage and the concretization of so many utterances – from the corporate world to antiterrorist agencies to the world of digitized online interaction – leads to our current *epistemé*, that of big data, the dream of N = all, wherein every social problem can be solved. (2015: 418)

Big data are socially consequential because they are seen as the source of 'actionable intelligence', or insights so robust that they can be used to recast 'all complex social situations either as neatly defined problems with definite computable solutions or as transparent and self-evident processes that can be easily optimized – if only the right algorithms are in place!' (Morozov 2013a: 5). The technical solutionist approach is animated by the belief that specific details can be 'effortlessly recovered' from synthetic data, and 'the idea that everything can be settled and anticipated if only we can find the right system or set of algorithms' (Thrift 2014: 1263).

The promise of objective datafication and algorithmic solutionism is premised on the epistemology that data analytics and pattern recognition methods and techniques applied to big data can reveal meaningful connections, associations, relationships, effects and correlations about human behaviours without the need for prior hypotheses, theoretical frameworks or further experimentation. This assumes that 'through the application of agnostic data analytics the data can speak for themselves free of human bias or framing, and that any patterns and relationships within big data are inherently meaningful and truthful' (Kitchin 2014a: 132).

Yet, as already noted, data do not exist naturally as a raw or truthful representation of an underlying reality; they have to be brought into being through social, methodological and technical practices, and are constantly shaped as they move between human actors, software platforms, and institutional structures and settings, all framed by social, political and economic contexts (Bowker 2008). In other words, big data do not present an impartial 'view from nowhere':

> The rationalist fantasy that enough data can be collected with the 'right' methodology to provide an objective and disinterested picture of reality is an old and familiar one: positivism. This is the understanding that the social world can be known and

explained from a value-neutral, transcendent view from nowhere in particular. …
But the advent of Big Data has resurrected the fantasy of a social physics, promising
a new data-driven technique for ratifying social facts with sheer algorithmic processing power. (Jurgenson 2014)

The notion that big data can provide universal insight into human behaviour
and sociality returns us to the idea that data comes before the fact, that data are
given from nature as units of a phenomenon or the fundamental elements of
truth itself. Jurgenson (2014) deeply questions the 'myths of objectivity and
political disinterestedness' associated with big data, not least because it 'cannot
be understood outside the powerful nexus of data science and social-media
companies. It's where the commanding view-from-nowhere ideology of Big
Data is most transparent; it's where the algorithms, databases, and venture
capital all meet'.

The notion of big data as a value-free window on to fundamental universal
truths about individual behaviours and social activities is itself politically and
ideologically motivated (it's a view from *somewhere*, not from nowhere), as well
as technically embedded in the design of the material instruments that enable
big data to be collected and analysed. It downplays how the design of a big data
system to capture and calculate data is governed by the political choices, social
standpoints, specific cultural understandings, and even outright biases and
prejudices of its programmers, while presuming the data 'passively collected by
computers to be objective. But computers don't remember anything on their
own. … This replicates their existing bias and simultaneously hides that bias to
the degree their findings are regarded as objectively truthful' (Jurgenson 2014).

If big data systems are designed with in-built biases, then the social consequences of such systems as they make social worlds and individual behaviours
known as 'facts' and 'evidence' are serious. In the field of surveillance, for example, techniques such as 'predictive policing' and data analytic 'pre-crime'
methods depend on the use of data to produce objective predictions about individuals' likelihood to commit a crime, which:

then acts back on those with whom the data are associated, informing us who we
are, what we should desire or hope for, including who we should become. The algorithms grip us even as they follow us. … [T]he price of our freedom in both political
and consumer contexts is our shaping or conditioning by algorithms. (Lyon 2014: 7)

The kind of 'pre-emptive' and 'future-tense' anticipation enabled by practices
such as predictive policing are based on 'human–algorithm relations' where there
is 'a deliberate intention to reduce someone's range of options' through 'future-
oriented preventative measures' (Lyon 2014: 5). Significant claims have been
made that predictive policing systems exhibit racial bias, disproportionately
directing police attention on to particular ethnic groups.

Predictive profiling also extends into other areas of everyday life. In the domain of popular culture, familiar online services such as Amazon, Google, Netflix, Spotify and Facebook all rely on database systems that are able to collect data from people's everyday activities, then sort and classify individuals on the basis of their tastes, judgments and choices in order to generate results and recommendations – and therefore to shape cultural preferences and 'make taste' (Beer 2013). New forms of data analytics and data mining 'also have the potential to usher in new, unaccountable and opaque forms of discrimination and social sorting based not on human-scale narratives but on incomprehensibly large, and continually growing, networks of interconnections' (Andrejevic et al. 2015: 1).

The ways in which individuals are profiled, and their tastes predicted, depend on machine-learning algorithms that have been trained to match individuals to larger patterns of media consumption. These techniques serve to reinforce particular pre-existing cultural preferences, so that everyday life becomes lived in a kind of 'echo chamber' or 'filter bubble' (Pariser 2015) where alternative cultural and political perspectives are filtered out of the individual's social media experience in favour of material that is popular or self-validating. In effect, the algorithm chooses how to stage the individual's encounter with culture, based on choices made by its designers. Pariser (2015) notes that the way an algorithm narrows what content one consumes is almost as strong as individual choices, and concludes that 'each algorithm contains a point of view on the world. Arguably, that's what an algorithm is: a theory of how part of the world should work, expressed in math or code'.

The methods of data mining and analytics are significant, then, because they turn digital data about people into profiles and evaluations that can be compared with and matched to categories and classifications in databases. Such techniques then enable individuals to be allocated services, targeted for advertising, and offered a range of personalized recommendations and 'push' notifications.

The Big Data Imaginary

In the previous chapter, I detailed how 'sociotechnical imaginaries' are future visions of society that are reflected in the design of technical projects. As Jasanoff (2015: 4) elaborates:

> It often falls to … institutions of power to elevate some imagined futures above others, according them a dominant position …. Imaginaries, moreover, encode not only visions of what is attainable through science and technology, but also of how life ought, or ought not, to be lived.

Other authors have developed this idea to account for the specific imaginaries emerging around the design of data analysis techniques and software. For Housley (2015) a latent goal of the 'Big Data Imaginary' (his capitalization) is to configure 'social organization and relations according to mathematical principles' derived from 'the empirical focus of data science'. Rieder and Simon (2016: 4) have detailed four specific characteristics of the sociotechnical big data imaginary: (1) extending the reach of automation, from data collection to storage, curation and analysis, and covering increasingly large parts of the analytical and decision-making process; (2) by capturing massive amounts of data and focusing on correlations rather than causes, big data claims to reduce the need for theory, models and human expertise; (3) expanding the realm of what can be measured, in order to trace and gauge movements, actions and behaviours in ways that were previously unimaginable; and (4) aspiring to calculate what is yet to come, using smart, fast and cheap predictive techniques to support decision making and optimize resource allocation across many sectors. Through this big data imaginary of 'mechanical objectivity', they suggest, advocates of big data are 'applying a mechanical mindset to the colonization of the future' (Rieder and Simon 2016: 4).

As an automated means for tracking people and things at massive scale and scope in order to predict the future, big data has great utility in the imaginations of governments and businesses, and has brought data science methods directly into the realm of political and commercial calculations and interventions. The big data imaginary of an institution of power such as data science, then, motivates excursions into the material world, and seeks to make it amenable to its underlying goals and aspirations of mechanical objectivity, empiricism, prediction and optimization. As noted in the previous chapter, imaginaries also infuse the design and organization of specific projects, which act as models of the future to which their advocates hope to make reality conform.

With the current proliferation of a big data imaginary across different sectors of society, it is possible to see society as increasingly constituted by different 'data spaces' or 'datascapes' (Lippert 2015). For example, hospitals depend on a constant flow of data, without which they might become unmanageable. Digital data are integral to many workplaces and working practices. Cities are becoming reimaged as significant datascapes, where many urban functions and processes are monitored through digital flows of data. In everyday life, we constantly move between different data spaces as we carry mobile devices around with us that change our experience of the material spaces we inhabit. But these data spaces should not be thought of as natural – they are made up in thought and action by the designers of the data systems that enact them, according to particular ways of thinking about the functioning of the spaces for which they are intended. Schools are perhaps typical data spaces, or 'data centres' (Finn 2016), which are increasingly designed to function according to a shared imaginary in which the collection, calculation and communication of digitized educational data are seen as desirable and attainable.

The concepts of a big data imaginary, and of fabricated datascapes, are useful because they alert us to the ways in which particular ideas, imaginings, ambitions and desires are manifested in the materiality of particular spaces, and of the ways in which such spaces might then function to shape the actions and behaviours of those individuals and groups that move in and through them (Rose 1999a; Huxley 2007). As a material phenomenon, big data is framed by 'the discourse, terminology and rhetoric that surrounds it and which ushers and affords its incorporation into the social world':

> This is not to say that the specific material properties of Big Data are somehow unimportant, but rather that the way that these data are framed in particular rationalising discourses also needs to be treated carefully if we are to form a more detailed appreciation of the social implications of those data. It could be argued that in many ways the power dynamics of Big Data are to be found just as much in the way that those data are labelled and described as it is in the actual data themselves. (Beer 2016b: 2)

The datascapes produced by a big data imaginary are generated through the imaginative work of specific social actors, through which big data become enmeshed in performing and producing their visions of the social order. As Jasanoff (2015: 22) articulates it, 'space and social order are co-produced in part through the spread of ideas and practices – and indeed ideologies – across times and territories'. The notion of a big data imaginary and its associated datascapes, then, captures the ways in which associated ideas spread into specific spaces and, once located there through particular practices and technologies, act to shape social and individual behaviours and actions to conform to the same shared vision.

Actors with authority to shape the public imagination construct stories of progress in their statements about big data, but these actors are of course not just governmental authorities:

> Imaginaries, moreover, are not exclusively the property of state actors. National sociotechnical imaginaries may permeate into popular culture, finding expression in the mass media and in non-official genres ... or the popular writings of prominent individuals. Multinational corporations increasingly act upon imagined understandings of how the world is and ought to be, playing upon the perceived hopes and fears of their customers and clients, and thereby propagating notions of technological progress and benefit. (Jasanoff 2015: 27)

In particular, 'coalitions between corporate interests and the media, through advertising and outright control, are increasingly likely to play a pivotal role in making and unmaking global sociotechnical imaginaries' (Jasanoff 2015: 27).

In relation to big data, it is clear that the making of imaginaries is being performed by such coalitions, as big data companies and data scientists broker relationships with one another (e.g. the partnership between Twitter and MIT's Social Machines laboratory) to form powerful alliances generating ideas and visions that might percolate into popular culture as well as into governmental thought and thus animate new technological projects and innovations.

The big data imaginary projects a particular view of how diverse activities (in education, entertainment, healthcare, policing, business, government and elsewhere) ought to be conducted. Van Dijck and Poell (2013) have argued that all kinds of actors are increasingly required to act within what they define as 'social media logic', a logic constituted by the norms, strategies, mechanisms and economies that underpin the incorporation of social media activities into an ever-broader range of fields. Social media logic refers to the strategies, mechanisms and economies that underpin the dynamics of social media platforms, and includes *programmability, popularity, connectivity and datafication*. In contemporary society most institutions – including business, government, education, arts, entertainment, law – have become part of this logic. *Programmability* can be defined as 'the ability of a social media platform to trigger and steer users' creative or communicative contributions, while users, through their interaction with these coded environments, may in turn influence the flow of communication and information activated by such a platform' (2013: 5). *Popularity* includes techniques for filtering and prioritizing popular items, boosting the popularity of certain people, things, issues, topics or ideas, and therefore influencing people by directing attention. The term *connectivity* highlights how social media platforms mediate users' experiences and define how connections take shape, 'a strategic tactic that effectively enables human connectedness while pursuing automated connectivity' through 'algorithmically connecting users to content, users to users, platforms to users, users to advertisers, and platforms to platforms' (2013: 8–9). Finally, *datafication* involves the quantification of content into data that allows companies to develop techniques of predictive and real-time analytics. Through datafication, social media software appears to empower users while at the same time empowering platforms to steer and exploit users' activities. Social media platforms therefore have a built-in architecture for mining online traffic for indicators of trending topics, keywords, sentiments, public viewpoints and so on:

> Much of social media data's value lies in their real-time 'live' appearance: platforms claim they can track instantaneous movements of individual user behavior, aggregate these data, analyze them, and subsequently translate the results into valuable information about individuals, groups, or society at large. (van Dijck and Poell 2013: 10)

Like social media logic, the notion of a big data imaginary likewise captures the ways in which various norms, values, strategies and so on that are associated with big data are now being projected into diverse spaces of activity, but also acknowledges that these mechanisms are instantiations of a future vision that is increasingly shared and seen as desirable and attainable.

Conclusion

Education is a key sector of society in which a big data imaginary is now beginning to animate practices. Following a long historical rise in the use of data in education systems, education is currently being subjected to increasingly intensive software-mediated processes of datafication, and is being treated as a 'computational' project, that is:

> the 'modelling' of education through digital data ... [and] algorithmically driven 'systems thinking' – where complex (and unsolvable) social problems associated with education can be seen as complex (but solvable) statistical problems. Thus, digital data are accompanied by a heightened sense of 'solutionism'. This leads to a recursive state where data analysis begins to produce educational settings, as much as educational settings producing data. (Selwyn 2015: 72)

The interdependence of digital data and educational settings mean that concerns of digital data collection and analysis, enacted through the statistical models and processes programmed into database technologies, take precedence over more individual, historical, moral and humanist concerns. In this sense, 'what counts' as education when it comes to digital data is what can be *counted*.

In this chapter I have sought to clarify the concept of big data, and particularly developed a conceptual account of how a 'big data imaginary' of the future of education is now being made attainable through certain kinds of big data practices and projects. Education is one significant sector of society where the big data imaginary is becoming shared and stabilized sufficiently for it to be seen as a desirable and attainable future reality, one that might be materialized through the deployment for new and emerging software for the collection, calculation and communication of educational data. As the big data imaginary is animating the data practices that produce material developments and technical projects, new educational datascapes are emerging – spaces designed to capture data, or that function through data analytics processes to be responsive and adaptable to feedback.

Throughout this book I treat data practices as social and technical instantiations of particular future visions – as practices that operationalize imaginaries in the present, often in ways that are more messy in practice than anticipated or desired. By mobilizing the idea of a big data imaginary along with the emphasis on data infrastructures and practices, what I am seeking to register is the formation and circulation of a 'desirable' educational future associated with (and made attainable through) data practices and the infrastructure of technologies, conceptual framings, discourses, knowledges, institutions and cultures in which they take place. The result of such an imaginary is the proposed production of smarter learning software systems – or learning machines – that might transform educational practices, processes, policies and institutions, although the materialization of such an imaginary of education in practice is likely to be more contested and messy than its advocates might imagine.

Together, I mobilize the concept of a big data imaginary, an attention to data infrastructures and practices, and an alertness to the emergence of new aspirations around the management of educational practices, institutions and individuals as a framework for the analyses offered in subsequent chapters. In short, education is being reimagined as a sector that might be governed through specific data practices located in wider sociotechnical infrastructures. However, in order for data to be collected, calculated and communicated, it is also necessary for it to be processed through software. The next chapter details how software, and the code and algorithms that enact it, are also implicated in the emerging data practices that might make the big data imaginary of education into an attainable material reality.

3
SOFTWARE, CODE AND ALGORITHMS

Programming, automating and governing everyday life

S oftware, the code that it is programmed in, and the algorithms that enact it, have become incredibly powerful influences in everyday life. Such is its reach and penetration that some commentators have described the emerging conditions of a 'software society', one where all contemporary media have been transformed by being remediated through software; where human social communication and relations are filtered through software platforms and interfaces; and where many of the social, cultural, political and economic institutions of society – schools, universities, hospitals, airports, cities, military bases, science laboratories, businesses, retailers – depend on software for their functioning and existence (Manovich 2013).

By contrast, many educational critics have lamented the lack of technological transformation of institutions such as schools and universities (Selwyn 2016). Technology has been viewed as a way of changing, improving or even revolutionizing institutions that have remained, it is claimed, anachronistically wedded to the same kinds of practices, processes and pedagogies for well over a century. But such claims miss the point that schools and universities are already dependent on software for their everyday operations.

Many of the ways in which software penetrates education is highly mundane. Increasingly, school registers are kept via software (Boden 2016). Key institutional data is recorded in spreadsheets and stored on software servers (Selwyn 2016). Classrooms contain computers and whiteboards that require software to run presentations, multimedia and interactive packages, and there is even seating plan software to allocate students to specific sitting positions according to criteria held in school databases (Selwyn et al. 2017). Curriculum materials and guidance – often produced by large 'edu-businesses' – can be accessed online, sometimes for a fee and sometimes as freely available 'open' educational resources (Edwards 2015). Students' work is also routinely entered into plagiarism detection software, where it can be compared with massive databases of text (Introna 2016). Internal communications between staff take place via email or intranet platforms, while external communication and institutional marketing is increasingly mediated via the Web rather than paper-based channels. Classroom management software that can be used to monitor students' use of computer software and internet use, as well as access their internet history, are becoming commonly used in classrooms (Big Brother Watch 2016).

More than that, schools and universities are all part of vast and complex informational networks, obliged to upload and share information that can then be collated and displayed (often publicly, in the form of data visualizations constructed through software packages) as a measurable record of institutional performance (Anagnostopoulos et al. 2013). Software technologies may not have transformed the teaching and learning aspects of education as some enthusiasts would wish, but clearly constitute an active (if often mundane) presence in many pedagogic, administrative and governance tasks.

The dependence of any single educational institution on software was vividly illustrated to me recently by a student on a teaching placement in a local high school. During her placement, extensive school rebuilding works were taking place. One morning, the builders accidentally cut through the main wiring that connected the school to the Internet. The student described to me a chaotic three-day period during which staff could not access lesson resources, administrators could not communicate with senior management or parents, and school leaders could not keep in touch with various external authorities and agencies. Of course, easy workarounds were found, but the episode illustrates how, in often very mundane everyday ways, we have come to rely on software as a kind of invisible presence in our lives – not least in educational institutions – which often only reveals the depth of its penetration when it breaks down (Mackenzie 2006).

With the emergence of big data in education, software is taking on an even more pronounced role. As Ford (2015) has commented in relation to big data more generally, 'data management is the problem that programming is supposed to solve. But of course now that we have computers everywhere, we keep generating more data, which requires more programming, and so forth'. In other words, the problems arising from the contemporary deluge of data is demanding new kinds of programming solutions, with the result that the datafication of everything is speeding up demand for the production of new software in a recursive cycle. This is especially the case in education where new products are constantly being produced that generate new data; data that often requires new software to be programmed for its adequate collection, storage and analysis. Before detailing the new educational software of big data collection and analysis, however, it is important to provide an overview of what software is and how it is influencing society. This requires an engagement with code and algorithms, including their origins in the history of computer science and software development.

Computer Science and Software

To understand software, it is important to acknowledge its disciplinary origins in the field of computer science. Born out of a combination of mathematical logic, the mechanization of calculation, storage and control, and the development of electronic circuits in electrical engineering in the mid-twentieth century – as well as philosophical questions about how humans should interact with complex control machinery – computer science began to coalesce as a discipline in its own right only in the 1950s. It wasn't until the late 1960s that the first disciplinary university curriculum in computer science became available in the shape of Donald Knuth's canonical *The Art of Computer Programming: Fundamental Algorithms* (Cerruzzi 2012). It was the publication of this text that established the programming of computer code and the study of algorithms as the dominant focus for the discipline. It also signalled that while practical training in programming was an 'important by-product' of an education in computer science, the development of programming skills was not as significant as mathematical analysis and theory development (Ensmenger 2010).

The emphasis on abstract theory over technical skill represented a historical cleavage in the fledgling discipline of computer science. When computing first emerged as a professional practice, a 'coder' was seen merely as a 'glorified clerical worker' and the task of coding was almost exclusively performed by women, who were expected to 'code into machine language the higher-level mathematics developed by male scientists and engineers. Coding implied manual labor, and mechanical translation or rote transcription; coders were obviously low on the intellectual and professional hierarchy' (Ensmenger 2010: 35). The actual art of 'programming', as it came to be known in the late 1940s, consisted of a number of distinct steps (including mathematical conceptualization, algorithm selection and numerical analysis) only the last of which was the 'coding' done by female coders. Computer science and programming, or software development, have been running on parallel but separate trajectories ever since.

While the core agenda for computer scientists is to understand the nature of computation, often working on abstract problems of analysis and theory, the agenda for software developers is to write useful programs by applying abstract concepts on to concrete program structures (Hayes 2015). The cultures of computer science and software development are very different: computer scientists and software developers work in different settings, attend different conferences, belong to different professional associations, and have very different ways of working, with different worldviews, systems of thinking, and professional practices. They are distinctly different 'cultures of code' (Hayes 2015). Even by the end of the 1960s, in fact, programmers were already calling themselves 'software engineers' in order to imply that their tasks were equivalent with the established branches of engineering, such as civil, mechanical, aerospace, chemical, electrical and environmental engineering (Bogost 2015).

However, it was with the invention and manufacturing of the silicon chip and the microprocessor, and the fast growth of Silicon Valley in California in the latter decades of the twentieth century that software development fully escaped the disciplinary enclosures of computer science (Castells 1996; Cerruzzi 2012). It is the history of computer software rather than computing that forms the basis of the computer revolution of the mid- to late-twentieth century:

> What makes the modern electronic computer so unique in all the history of technology – so powerful, flexible, and capable of being applied to such an extraordinarily diverse range of purposes – is its ability to be reconfigured, via software, into a seemingly infinite number of devices. In fact, it is this ability to be programmed via software that has come to encapsulate the essence of modern

computing ... . What matters is that it is programmable. ... Software transforms the latent power of a theoretically general-purpose machine into a specific tool for solving real-world problems. (Ensmenger 2010: 5)

Although computers clearly do consist of hardware, it is software that has come to define what a computer is and what it can be used for. As computing historian Ensmenger (2010: 6–7) notes, 'software is the interface between the computer and society', one that deeply informs how we think of ourselves and our environment, and which acts as an enabler of diverse cultural, economic and political aspirations. These historical notes make it clear that the production of code is inseparable from social context: that the digital materialities of software and hardware with which we live cannot just be reduced to lines of code and sequences of algorithms.

Producing Code

In technical terms, software is simply a set of instructions, written in computer code, which instructs a computer. Whenever we speak of software, we are talking of something that is utterly constituted by code and that is structured and operationalized through algorithms – sets of steps or processes which specify how to transform a given set of inputs into an output. Code is the instructional script that makes software work, and is constructed by programmers using specific programming languages, while programming is the art and science of putting together algorithms and instructions that can be automatically read and translated by a machine in order to process data and *do* something. As such, software 'cannot be understood apart from its constitution through and through as code. Code, even defined in the minimalist technical sense ..., cuts across every aspect of what software is and what software does' (Mackenzie 2006: 2–3).

At the same time, however, it is hard to pinpoint what code is and what code does without acknowledging that it is inextricably interwoven with larger social and technical systems that include machines, people and processes:

software is an ideal illustration of what the historians and sociologists of science call a sociotechnical system ... in which machines, people and processes are inextricably interconnected and interdependent. ... Software is where the technology of computing meets social relationships, organizational politics, and personal agendas. All technologies are to a certain extent social constructions, but in the case of software, the social dimensions of technology are particularly apparent. (Ensmenger 2010: 8)

Understood as a social creation, it is clear that software is the product of code that has to be written by programmers. The sheer diversity of software products, however, means that myriad different programming practices exist. According to Ford (2015), there are approximately 18 million professional software developers worldwide, programming software for everything from the Web and smart phones to security systems and scientific software packages, all using programming languages including Java, JavaScript, C, C++, Objective-C, and C#, PHP and Python. Each of these languages itself has its own long history of development, with vast libraries and repositories of pre-existing code often made available for free for others to copy, paste and use. International standards defined by expert technical committees under the International Organization for Standardization (IOS) regulate each of these programming languages, ensuring they are used consistently worldwide.

Much of what is taken for granted about software therefore depends on the 'mundane acquisition and exercise of technical skills in programming and configuring code' (Mackenzie 2006: 3). Programmers inhabit a contemporary 'codescape' where they learn and develop coding practices and programming languages through a sheer abundance of educational and pedagogical activities related to code and code-related events such as trade shows, conferences, competitions, publications such as books, training manuals and journals, and websites, video tutorials, blogs, discussion forums and news groups (Mackenzie 2006).

In this sense, code needs to be understood as the product of technical R&D, commodity production, business development, professional associations, pedagogical activities and programming practices combined, plus all the political, economic, material and cultural contingencies that contribute to its production. As Kitchin and Dodge (2011: 24) have shown, as a product, code is inseparable from a range of other materials and discourses:

- *Material objects and spaces*: computer hardware, display screens, disk drives and disks, network interfaces, network telecomms infrastructures, hardware peripherals, desks, offices.

- *Discursive and material assemblages of knowledge*: flow charts, manuals, magazines, mailing lists, blogs.

- *Standards and classifications*: data standards, file formats, interfaces, communication protocols, intellectual property regimes such as copyrights, trademarks and patents.

- *Practices and experiences*: ways of doing, coding cultures, hacker ethos, norms of sharing or stealing code.

- *Subjectivities and identities*: coders, programmers, hackers, sellers, marketers, business managers, product managers, entrepreneurs.

- *Organizations*: corporations, consultants, start-ups, government agencies, manufacturers, retailers, universities, conferences, clubs, professional associations and societies.

- *Marketplaces*: coder recruitment agencies, commercial investment, venture capitalism.

Many social scientific researchers of software and code have therefore approached it from a 'sociotechnical' perspective as something that is thoroughly interwoven with and inseparable from its social processes of production (Fuller 2008).

In this vein, to understand what code is and what it does, Mackenzie (2006) argues, it is essential to understand it not merely as a technical artefact – lines of code – but (1) as the product of an *originator* (whether a programmer, a software engineer, a corporation, a hacker or so on); (2) as things or people that act as its *recipients* and are solicited by code to do something (whether a user, another programmer or a software program executing commands); and (3) as something else that is represented or prototyped (such as a desktop user interface representing a set of office activities, a graphic image manipulation program representing a photography studio, a visualization program representing the practices of a scientific laboratory and so on). This recognition is important because it registers how code emerges from particular human decisions made during its production. These decisions, once materialized and mobilized in software, can then exert material effects in the world. The writing of code is accomplished by 'practised hands' which include software developers and programmers who, through programming languages, are producing new kinds of 'coded writings' that, through their commodification and global distribution 'via the medium of the screen' as websites, software packages and so on, mediate the spaces in which they appear (Thrift 2005: 153–4). 'If coders don't run the world, they run the things that run the world', Ford (2015) argues.

Productive Code

In addition to being a *product* of programming practice, code needs also to be understood as a *producer* of social consequences. In other words, it has productive effects in the world. Code can 'make things happen' by virtue of its 'execute-ability' or its ability to perform tasks according to encoded instructions (Mackenzie and Vurdubakis 2011: 6). Code is not inert but an 'increasingly capable actor performing in the world' (Kitchin and Dodge 2011: 248). It is fundamentally performative, and perpetually produces dynamic outputs by changing an input from one state to another through sequences of commands and processing operations in an autonomous fashion. As a consequence, code is always located within diversely produced social, cultural, economic and political contexts, and has become 'a vital source of social power' that increasingly 'augments and automates society' (Kitchin and Dodge 2011: 246). As Mackenzie (2006: 48) argues, 'code textures worlds': it increasingly affects our notions of agency (who does what), materiality (what we can touch, see and hear), and sociality (how we form attachments and collective belonging). From these perspectives, code is woven into the substrate of contemporary society, as a layer of our personal perceptions, sensations and transactions, and it crystallizes new social formations, publics and groups.

However, coded technologies are never just innocent technical devices. Because code is produced in specific technical settings, through the work of technical experts working within complex social, political and economic contexts, it represents particular ways of approaching the world that derive from the world-views of its originators and that are projected on to its recipients. Thus software is produced by programmers (originators) with particular sensibilities, epistemological assumptions and worldviews, in collaboration with institutions and corporations with their own particular philosophies of the world, ambitions and resources. These systems of thought and their manifestation into sequences of code and algorithmic processes make a difference to their recipients, to how people do work in the world, how problems are solved, how people relate to one another, and to a variety of contexts in which code reshapes practices, such as in consumption, government, entertainment, health and education. As such, computer code is:

> the manifestation of a system of thought – an expression of how the world can be captured, represented, processed, and modelled computationally with the outcome subsequently doing work in the world. Programming then fundamentally seeks to capture and enact knowledge about the world … in order to augment, mediate, and regulate people's lives. (Kitchin and Dodge 2011: 26)

These sociotechnical approaches to code view it both as a product of social relations and decisions made by programmers, and code as a process which produces certain forms of action (Fuller 2003). In this sense, contemporary society is becoming a thoroughly 'hybrid progeny of computer code and of social codes of conduct' (Mackenzie and Vurdubakis 2011: 16). And this means that code makes a difference to everyday life, agency and sociality; it mediates, augments and ultimately *produces* collective political, cultural and economic life (Kitchin and Dodge 2011).

However, the code that programmers produce is not always as productive as hoped. As the professional programmer Ceglowski (2016) puts it:

> Our intentions are simple and clear. First we will instrument, then we will analyze, then we will optimize. … But the real world is a stubborn place. It is complex in ways that resist abstraction and modelling. It notices and reacts to our attempts to affect it. Nor can we hope to examine it objectively from the outside, any more than we can step out of our own skin. … Approaching the world as a software problem is a category error that has led us into some terrible habits of mind.

He notes in particular that programmers have created powerful tools of social control by building 'the greatest surveillance apparatus the world has ever seen' in the form of 'vast amounts of permanently stored personal data about entire populations', an example of how an 'enthusiastic group of nerds has decided to treat the rest of the world as a science experiment' (Ceglowski 2016). Others have noted that programmers are often oblivious to the social effects of the code they write and the software they produce (Thrift 2005). As highly-skilled engineers and computational problem-solvers, they often possess little knowledge of the wider social contexts in which their products will work:

An engineer is a professional who designs, builds, and maintains systems. But to engineer means skillfully, artfully, or even deviously contriving an outcome. To engineer is to jury-rig, to get something working more or less, for a time. Sufficiently enough that it serves an immediately obvious purpose, but without concern or perhaps even awareness of its longevity. (Bogost 2015)

Cast as software engineers, programmers are responsible not only for engineering technical systems, but for unconsciously engineering social outcomes.

Additionally, much of the influence of code in society has been made possible because of a steady proliferation of discourses and collective imaginings around software. A consistent set of discourses has promoted and supported the deployment of code, algorithms and software across many domains of contemporary social, political, economic and cultural life (Beer 2017). These discourses are persuasive and powerful: software seduces and disciplines people to willingly and voluntarily 'submit to the agency of software' (Kitchin and Dodge 2011: 249). These discourses legitimate, justify and work to persuade people to believe and act in relation to the logic of software and code, to imagine the world according to the representations that are possible with code.

The Social Power of Algorithms

As already highlighted, a significant dimension of the power of software and code is that of the algorithm. Although algorithms have become the focus of extensive media attention in the last few years – particularly as social media companies such as Facebook and Google have come under scrutiny – algorithms are, in fact, deceptively complex to define. Kitchin (2017) demonstrates how algorithms need to be understood as: (1) 'black boxes' that are hidden inside intellectual property and impenetrable code; (2) 'heterogeneous systems' in which hundreds of algorithms are woven together in relation with datasets, companies, programmers, standards and laws; (3) 'emergent' and evolving systems that are constantly being refined, reworked, and tweaked; and (4) complex, unpredictable, and fragile systems that are sometimes miscoded, buggy, and 'out of control'. As a consequence, it may make little sense to interrogate any algorithm singularly, but rather to unpack complex 'algorithmic systems'. In addition, although 'algorithm' may be a 'digital keyword' for our times, technical communities such as computer scientists and programmers may be using it in very different ways to social scientists, journalists or the wider public (Gillespie 2014b).

In computer science terms, an algorithm is simply a precise, mechanical set of step-by-step instructions designed to complete a particular computing process in such a way that requires 'no human intuition or guesswork' (MacCormick 2012: 3). All computer algorithms are more or less meaningless without sources of data. Algorithms require some form of input, such as an unsorted list of data, to transform into an output. A search algorithm, for example, works upon a vast database of information that must be indexed, parsed and stored in advance to facilitate fast and accurate information retrieval. This involves companies such as Google crawling the Web collecting and indexing information, logging search queries and links clicked, in order to generate the data required to allow the search algorithms to function autonomously. However, algorithms are more than simply computer science abstractions and routines for sorting and structuring data. They also exert profound effects as they come into contact with the world.

Although computer scientists and social scientists are not always thinking of the same thing when they talk about an algorithm, social science has now begun to acknowledge their profound social effects and power. The development of new forms of algorithmically enabled analysis such as 'social physics' and cyberbolic claims that the entire 'universe is programmable' (Axline 2014) reflect the extent to which algorithms are now understood to be 'doing things' in a variety of ways. These interests have only grown amid both the hype of the 'data revolution' (Kitchin 2014a) and the 'anxieties of Big Data' (Crawford 2014), where algorithms play a huge role in the management, analysis and visualization of massive datasets.

Recently, algorithms have become the subject of significant concern among academic researchers and media commentators alike. The revelation in 2014 that Facebook had conducted experiments on users' emotions by filtering their news feeds using its EdgeRank algorithms generated considerable worry about its capacity to 'engineer the public' (Tufekci 2014). Two years later, Facebook and other social media platforms such as Twitter were being blamed for their part in shaping public opinion during high-profile political events such as the UK referendum on membership of the European Union and the US presidential election (Howard 2016). As a consequence, a significant debate has been catalysed about the ethical implications of algorithms as the values and interests they privilege are affecting individuals as well as groups and whole societies (Mittelstadt et al. 2016).

The role of algorithms in the social world is by no means uncontested among social science researchers, but there is some broad agreement that algorithms are now increasingly involved in various forms of social ordering, governance and control (Beer 2017; Willson 2017). Algorithms have emerged as an important object of analysis in studies of surveillance, identity formation, popular culture, digital governance and algorithmic research methods, as well as more widely in debates about the apparent power and control they command (e.g. Beer 2013; Pasquale 2015; Amoore and Poitukh 2016). According to Mackenzie (2006) algorithms establish certain forms of 'order', 'pattern' and 'coordination' through processes of sorting, matching, swapping, structuring and grouping data. In this sense, algorithms appear as new kinds of 'social rules' that then can shape everyday life. Algorithms may even challenge our personal sense of identity, creating new 'algorithmic identities' (Cheney-Lippold 2011), as 'our interactions with algorithms both identify us and foster certain ways of identifying with others' (Markham 2013: 2). As Beer (2013: 81) argues, 'algorithms are an integrated and irretractable part of everyday social processes', with the potential 'to reinforce, maintain or even reshape visions of the social world, knowledge and encounters with information'.

As with code more generally, many social scientific studies of algorithms acknowledge that human intentions structure the algorithms that are programmed into computers (Neyland 2015). Software algorithms are not just neutral mathematical techniques and processes. Rather, they reflect the particular goals of those who programme them. For example, Gillespie (2016) claims that 'algorithms are in fact full of people' – programmers, designers, project managers, business managers – whose various decisions all define what the algorithm is supposed to do, what data it will collect and analyse, and how it will enact its goal. These accounts produce an image of algorithms as powerfully automated, autonomous and recursive technologies – socially produced and yet increasingly capable of producing new social formations, encounters and knowledge. Kitchin and Dodge (2011: 248) suggest that 'algorithms are products of the world' which can also 'produce knowledge that then is applied, altering the world in a recursive fashion'. As such, they argue that algorithms provide 'grammars of action' for new forms of social ordering and governance, and are endowed with the power to 'actively reshape behaviour'.

In order to reshape behaviour in such ways, algorithms require data and models to work on. Neyland (2015: 128) argues that in order for an algorithmic system to function, the world outside of the system has to be mathematically modelled in such a way that it can be built-in to 'the social world of the algorithmic system. In other words, the selection of an algorithm only comes after the formulation of a model in computational terms, a process of building 'a world out there into a world in here, in the algorithmic machine' (Neyland 2015: 129). Likewise, Amoore and Poitukh (2016) argue that the 'calculative devices' of algorithms filter what can be seen and create novel ways of perceiving and understanding the world, transforming what can be read, analysed and thought about. Algorithms are 'abstracted theories about the world' which also 'have the capacity to become active in shaping and constituting social life' (Beer 2013: 80). Algorithms are not merely neutral mathematical devices but designed to function according to particular powerful ways of perceiving the world, political assumptions and the codes of conduct to which their designers and promoters have subscribed.

Moreover, many innovations in recent algorithm design mean that algorithms are increasingly built to adapt as they interact with the world. Algorithmic processes such as machine learning, as noted earlier, consist of systems that can operate in both 'supervised' or 'unsupervised' ways. Supervised machine learning involves building models that can be trained to match inputs with certain known outputs, using exemplar 'training data' to guide the learning process; unsupervised systems, by contrast, involve models that are designed to teach themselves to identify patterns or structure in data without the need for training data (Kitchin 2014a). As Mackenzie (2015: 430) notes, machine learning techniques of recommendation, recognition, ranking, pattern-finding and prediction are increasingly 'woven into the fabric of everyday life'. In this sense, machine learning algorithms are not only social inventions capable of reinforcing existing forms of social order and organization, but have a powerfully productive part to play in predicting and even pre-empting or automatically organizing future events, actions and realities. This is important not least because in machine learning theory and practice there remain serious questions about the capacity of a given predictive model to generalize from available data to other events: modelling predictions on the 'known data' too closely can mean the model adapts to the training data and prevents effective generalization to other sources of data or the incorporation of new information (Mackenzie 2015).

Algorithmic Governance

Like the code itself in which they are written, algorithms can be understood as key techniques by which people's lives and society at large are being regulated and governed. Certain political ambitions and norms are hidden in the algorithmic structure and code that constitutes software, conferring it the power to govern and regulate behaviour:

> The notion of the algorithm is ... deployed to promote a certain rationality, a rationality based upon the virtues of calculation, competition, efficiency, objectivity and the need to be strategic. As such, the notion of the algorithm can be powerful in shaping decisions, influencing behaviour and ushering in certain approaches and ideals. The algorithm's power may then not just be in the code, but in that way that it becomes part of a discursive understanding of desirability and efficiency in which the mention of algorithms is part of 'a code of normalization'. (Beer 2017: 9)

The figure of the algorithm, then, has been conferred a certain form of authority as a concept, which has allowed it to be inserted as a technical device into all manner of social, commercial and political processes.

For example, Morozov (2013b) argues that we are now experiencing a new political era of 'algorithmic regulation' in which 'the system's algorithms do the moral calculus on their own' and people 'take on the role of information machines that feed the techno-bureaucratic complex with our data':

the commercial interests of technology companies and the policy interests of government agencies have converged: both are interested in the collection and rapid analysis of user data. Google and Facebook are compelled to collect ever more data to boost the effectiveness of the ads they sell. Government agencies need the same data – they can collect it either on their own or in cooperation with technology companies – to pursue their own programs.

These 'governing algorithms' (Barocas et al. 2013) are increasingly interwoven with the politics of the present, as the NSA surveillance regime and GCHQ's PRISM initiative demonstrate. But algorithmic forms of regulation and governance are also woven through many mundane and everyday encounters. Mager (2012) argues, for example, that search engines such as Google, Bing, Yahoo! and others have an 'ideological inner life', and that therefore it is important to understand the power relations and social practices involved in the construction of search algorithms. Taking care not to imply that algorithms act independently of social and political contexts, search engines are, she argues, socially constructed technologies mirroring and solidifying socio-cultural norms and values that are enacted and negotiated by extended networks of actors including website providers, users, marketers, journalists, and government policy makers. Search engines mirror the societies and the embedded ideologies from which they emerge. A particular kind of 'algorithmic ideology' and set of capitalist values is inscribed in the technical functioning of dominant of corporate search engines such as Google (Mager 2012).

The politics of search engines and their capacity to govern how people encounter information and gain knowledge is clearly significant. Algorithmic systems are being deployed in ways that can shape everyday lives. Influentially, the legal theorist Lessig (2000), for example, has claimed that code acts as a new kind of 'law', a form of regulation that demarcates how digital environments and platforms operate and therefore how we experience the digital world:

> This code, or architecture, sets the terms on which life in cyberspace is experienced. It determines how easy it is to protect privacy, or how easy it is to censor speech. It determines whether access to information is general or whether information is zoned. It affects who sees what, or what is monitored. ... And as this code changes, the character of cyberspace will change as well. Cyberspace will change from a place that protects anonymity, free speech, and individual control, to a place that makes anonymity harder, speech less free, and individual control the province of individual experts only.

According to this view, as programmers write code, they are designing particular values in to the software they produce in ways that regulate the lives of those that receive, experience or use it. The consequence is that coders may be able to select our values for us and potentially prioritize the interests of private technology companies over public interests and concerns.

The idea that code is law in cyberspace sounds dated as digital devices and media have thoroughly penetrated everyday life and blurred the boundaries between online and offline worlds. Kitchin and Dodge (2011) have influentially detailed how a new form of governance has been made possible within highly coded contemporary social environments. In their influential account of 'code/space', they refer to how 'software creates new spatialities of everyday life and new modes of governance':

> Code/space occurs when software and the spatiality of everyday life become mutually constituted, that is, produced through one another. Here, spatiality is the product of code, and the code exists primarily to produce a particular spatiality. ... Any space that is dependent on software-driven technologies to function as intended constitutes a code/space. (Kitchin and Dodge 2011: 16–17)

Ultimately, code/spaces are programmable environments, in that the ways in which code is programmed fundamentally alters how a software-supported space functions and is experienced. For Kitchin and Dodge, software and its spatial effects are now transforming the means by which individuals and societies are governed. They draw on Foucault's influential work on governance to show how the management of modern societies has depended on the production of systems to collect, collate and analyse information about populations, social institutions and businesses. This particular 'biopolitical' style of governance depends on viewing people as parts of larger systems, whose actions and behaviours might therefore be monitored as citizens with rights and obligations to the state, or as problems to be solved and whose behaviours might be targeted for management, intervention and alteration (Foucault 2008; Lemke 2011).

Software coded systems built around complex algorithms are now responsible for the kinds of data collection processes that have been so central to modern forms of governance and population control. The consequence of these kinds of algorithmic processes is the construction of new kinds of understandings or representations of the public:

> Methods for analysing social media data promise powerful new ways of knowing publics and capturing what they say and do. And yet access to these methods is uneven, with large corporations and governments tending to have the best access to data and analytics tools ... and a new means of controlling how publics come to be represented and so understood. (Kennedy and Moss 2015: 1–2)

The algorithms that enact data mining and analytics methods, from search engines to social networking sites, organize information according to human but increasingly automated evaluative criteria, and on that basis then tangle with users' information practices and patterns of political and cultural engagement, so that 'the introduction of algorithms into human knowledge practices may have political ramifications' (Gillespie 2014a: 168).

Moreover, as algorithms are increasingly being designed to anticipate users and make predictions about their future behaviours, users are now reshaping their practices to suit the algorithms they depend on. This constructs 'calculated publics', the algorithmic presentation of publics back to themselves that shapes a public's sense of itself:

> Algorithms ... engage in a calculated approximation of a public through their trace-able activity, then report back to them ... . [T]hese technologies, now not just technologies of evaluation but of representation, help to constitute and codify the publics they claim to measure, publics that would not otherwise exist except that the algorithm called them into existence. (Gillespie 2014a: 189)

The result of algorithmic data mining is not simply the production of individual and social profiles, but new ways of seeing and understanding social groups that then flow back into the ways in which those groups and individuals might actually relate to themselves. As such, the ways in which data mining and big data analytics are produced and programmed to function – according to their origina-tors' theories and assumptions about how the world works – are significantly consequential for ways in which individuals, groups and populations are moni-tored, profiled and acted upon. Consequently, 'we must see them as techno-economic constructs whose operations have important implications for the management of populations and the formation of subjects' (Andrejevic, Hearn and Kennedy 2015: 2)

The rise of software systems is therefore 'ideally suited to monitoring, manag-ing, and processing [data] about people, objects, and their interactions', leading to a new mode of governance that Kitchin and Dodge (2011: 85) term 'auto-mated management':

> Automated management is the regulation of people and objects through processes that are *automated* (technologically enacted), *automatic* (the technology performs the regulation without prompting or direction), and *autonomous* (regulation, disci-pline and outcomes are enacted without human oversight). Software controls ... systems that actively reshape behaviour by altering the performance of a task.

Through automated, automatic and autonomous processes, software is being mobi-lized both to transform regimes and practices of surveillance and to instil a stronger regime of discipline and behaviour change. Automated management has become a dominant reality in the governing of the present for several reasons: (1) informa-tion can be increasingly collected, processed and acted upon by software algorithms without human intervention or authorization; (2) software is becoming increas-ingly embedded in existing systems and practices, and an integral part of how any activity or tasks is both conducted and how it is measured and surveyed; and (3) automated management has been discursively normalized as part of a natural and dominant order, accepted as desirable, taken-for-granted and commonsense, and underpinning many practices of governing in important domains of everyday life such as policing, healthcare, work, travel, consumption and security. The result is that 'many aspects of social and economic life are now captured, processed, and governed to a significant degree by software (on behalf of state agencies, companies, and also individuals themselves)' (Kitchin and Dodge 2011: 110).

Predictive analytics software, crafted around machine learning algorithms, are especially significant for automated management. The nature of such technologies is that it is software operated and automated, dynamic enough to respond and regulate in real-time, and has the capacity to act predictively – bringing about the possibility of 'anticipatory governance'. These kinds of predictive algorithms ultimately function by making probabilistic associations in order to foresee or anticipate future trends. In this way, they effectively pre-empt the future, allowing decisions to be made which will act on such predictions. In a variety of practices of governing, such as border security, urban surveillance, educational testing and data comparison, urban traffic control and consumption, decisions are now routinely being delegated to software algorithms. The data derived from these algorithmic processes, rather than human discretion, then become the basis from which predictions are made about potential behaviours and actions. Anticipatory modes of governing are not so much attempts to govern the present as to govern the future.

Code and algorithms, then, are integral to a new mode of technologically enacted algorithmic governance in which software participates as an automated, automatic and autonomous actor in the surveillance and structuring of human behaviour and action. Technological environments have, in other words, become key techniques for monitoring and managing society as a whole by regulating people to comply with specific criteria and norms of behaviour.

Conclusion

In the last two chapters we have detailed how big data analytics, machine learning, visualization and so on are increasingly infiltrating society, as a new layer of social data that allows us to see society in new (but not unproblematic) ways, and also explored the sociotechnical complexity of software, code and algorithms as they increasingly infiltrate and intervene in everyday life. It is hard to understand the contemporary datafication and digitization of education without acknowledging the prominent positions that big data and software have attained in contemporary society. Together, big data, software code and algorithms in education are leading to a position where new kinds of smarter learning machines – which can learn from the data they process – are becoming imaginable, seemingly possible, and attainable, as the following chapters now detail.

4

DIGITAL EDUCATION
GOVERNANCE

Political analytics, performativity
and accountability

Education policymaking processes have been transformed by the collection, analysis and use of data in recent years. While the production of educational data is nothing new, the appearance of new technologies for its collection, analysis and use at the beginning of the twenty-first century has catalysed significant new ambitions around data-driven educational policy. Software packages, data processing platforms and infrastructures, and the imaginary that animates them, have been woven into political objectives and specific projects. This means a new software layer has been superimposed on to the political layer of education, in ways that are producing novel kinds of interventions and programs in the practice layer of the school and classroom (Lynch 2015).

The purpose of this chapter is to detail how data-based software platforms, infrastructures and projects are increasingly being stitched on to the kinds of policy work that governs education systems, institutions and practices. Data-processing software is reconfiguring, augmenting and intensifying the practices of individuals, schools, school systems and jurisdictions 'through recourse to old codes (such as accountability, efficiency, quality) that are performed in new ways' (Thompson 2016: 2). Education is becoming a site of new technologies and practices of data-driven political analytics, all of it oriented around the need to develop practical knowledge and insights for policymaking and governance (Fenwick et al. 2014).

Some exemplification of the trend toward increased datafication of education policy was provided in 2016 by the publication of a 'delivery plan' for improvement in education in Scotland. Drafted in response to a recent independent review of Scottish education carried out by the OECD, the delivery plan is part of a National Improvement Framework with ambitious plans to raise attainment and achieve equity. One of its dominant themes is 'performance information':

> We will pull together all the information and data we need to support improvement. Evidence suggests ... we must ensure we build a sound understanding of the range of factors that contribute to a successful education system. This is supported by international evidence which confirms that there is no specific measure that will provide a picture of performance. We want to use a balanced range of measures to evaluate Scottish education and take action to improve further. (Scottish Government 2016: 20)

Moreover, the plan states that current arrangements 'do not provide sufficiently robust information across the system to support policy and improvement. We must move from a *culture* of judgement to a *system* of judgement' (Scottish Government 2016: 3).

As a routemap towards the accomplishment of this new 'system of judgement', the plan emphasizes (1) an escalation in the use of standardized assessment; (2) the gathering of data about the academic progress and well-being of pupils at all stages; (3) the production of key performance indicators on employability skills;

(4) greater use of performance metrics and measurement of schools; (5) new standards and evaluation frameworks for schools; (6) more pooling of school inspection reports; (7) regular publication of individual school data; (8) the use of visual data dashboards; (9) training for 'data literacy' among teachers; (10) decentralized management; (11) comparison with international evidence; and (12) the employment of an international council of expert business and reform advisors to guide and evaluate its implementation. The relentless focus by the Scottish Government on performance information, inspection, measurement and evidence as a system of judgement is demonstrative of how education systems, organizations and individuals are now the targets of techniques of data collection, analysis and use. While the delivery plan makes no explicit mention of it, it is clear that all of these data will need to be inputted, cleaned, stored, managed, analysed and communicated, all tasks requiring advanced technical infrastructure and specialist expertise in using information technologies.

As the Scottish Government involvement of expert reform advisors and the influence of the OECD on the direction of its plan demonstrates, the datafication of education policy work is not simply the business of state governments and their official educational departments. Instead, alongside the rising use of data, education has experienced a 'governance turn' which sees authority over education redistributed from central governments and their agencies to a much wider array of private sector and civil society organizations, including businesses, consultants, entrepreneurs, think tanks, policy innovation labs, charities and independent experts, many of them tangled together in networks of relationships (Ozga et al. 2011). In contrast to central government, 'governance' is characterized by decentralization, mobility, fluidity, looseness, complexity and instability as well as by the criss-crossing of sectoral borderlines and the hybridization of ideas, discourses and materials from bureaucratic, economic, academic and media fields (Ball 2012; Ball and Junemann 2012). New practices of distributed and network governance have been described as 'government at a distance', that is, the indirect mechanisms that authorities adopt to achieve their objectives by aligning their interests, goals and ambitions with those of others, and the belief that each can solve their difficulties or achieve their ends best through shared associations, vocabularies, theories and explanations (Miller and Rose 2008).

The spatially networked and distributed nature of contemporary techniques of governance has also led to a temporal acceleration in policy development and diffusion termed 'fast policy':

> The modern policymaking process may still be focused on centers of political authority, but networks of policy advocacy and activism now exhibit a precociously transnational reach; policy decisions made in one jurisdiction increasingly echo and influence those made elsewhere; and global policy 'models' often exert normative power across significant distances. Today, sources, channels, and sites of policy advice encompass sprawling networks of human and nonhuman actors ... including

consultants, web sites, practitioner communities, norm-setting models, conferences, guru performances, evaluation scientists, think tanks, blogs, global policy
institutes, and best-practice peddlers, not to mention the more 'hierarchical' influence of multilateral agencies, international development funds, powerful trading
partners, and occupying powers. (Peck and Theodore 2015: 3)

'Fast policy' describes a new condition of accelerated policy production, circulation and translation characterized not just by its velocity but also 'by the
intensified and instantaneous connectivity of sites, channels, arenas, and nodes of
policy development, evolution, and reproduction' (Peck and Theodore 2015: 223).
It refers to the increasing porosity between policymaking locales; the transnation-
alization of policy discourses and communities; global deference to models of
'what works' and 'best practices'; compressed R&D time in policy design and roll-
out; new shared policy experimentality and evaluation practices; and the
expansion of a 'soft infrastructure' of expert conferences, resource banks, learning
networks, case-study manuals, and web-based materials, populated by intermediaries, advocates and experts (Peck and Theordore 2015).

Fast policy is becoming a feature of education policy production and circulation.
The desire for policy solutions and new forms of evidence and expertise is ultimately leading to the 'speeding up' of education policy, characterized by the
increasing rate and reach of policy diffusion from sites of policy development to
local sites of policy uptake and translation (Lewis and Hogan 2016). In other words,
policies are becoming more fast-moving, both in their production and in their
translation into action, as well as more transnational in uptake and implementation, more focused on quick-fix 'best practice' or 'what works' solutions, and more
pacey and attractive to read thanks to being packaged up as short glossy handbooks
and reports, websites and interactive data visualizations (Decuypere 2016).

Data processing software, the organizations that produce and enact it, and the
imaginaries that animate its production and use, are all now part of the networks
that allow education to be governed at a distance and at speed. Digital data
makes education knowable, governable and interveneable, via advanced data
analysis techniques and the global exchange of information between diverse
actors that can be used to make informed, evidence-based policy decisions:

Think tanks, business firms and industrial networks … [are] increasingly involved in
designing and using educational big data information technologies and applying
them in order to influence school practices, administrative organization and learning
techniques … [and to] permeate national policy-making structures. Actors producing
such big data have become more powerful in influencing not only political decisions
but also making an impact on educational practices. (Martens et al. 2016: 519)

This chapter consists of a form of 'policy network analysis' (Ball 2016) that
focuses especially on identifying and locating the connections and associations
that are being forged through software and data technologies, and their sponsors

and advocates, for the purposes of educational governance. These data-based digital technologies, the code and algorithms that enact them, and the ambitions that catalyse them, are becoming key enablers of government at a distance and fast policy for a range of joined-up actors working in flexible networks of association.

The core contention of the chapter is that new data-processing software and the actors that promote them constitute a novel kind of 'digital education governance' (Williamson 2016a) within which the enlarged scope and accelerated pace of data generation, analysis and feedback appears to make all educational problems measurable, calculable and knowable, and thereby solvable at high speed. New forms of big data are becoming especially significant to emerging techniques of digital education governance, which reach 'far beyond policy, into educational administration, school practice and individual learning activities' (Hartong 2016: 523). As a result, new 'technical policy actors' that sit outside of government bureaucracies are now performing the role of linking digital technologies of software engineering and data processing with various educational structures and processes:

> While 'mediated' data and assessment processing comprises a growing number of international organizations, it also involves global scientific or industrial networks, consulting or research institutions, philanthropic investors and private or for-profit actors, who altogether act as 'partners' within educational reform projects by providing evidence-based expertise, support or funding. (Hartong 2016: 524–5)

Likewise, the emphasis in this chapter is on the intersection of the technical actors, the software products and the policy regimes that together constitute an emerging mode of digital education governance. These actors are simultaneously working within existing policy regimes and also beyond them by extending policy expertise to new sites and spaces of authority, and by deploying technologies that might circumvent slow-paced bureaucratic policy processes and speed up the flow of data, evidence and solutions in ways that might influence school practice and individual learning activities.

The chapter is organized in a number of sections, starting with a contextual discussion of the use of numerical data for the purpose of governing the state, the emergence of big data technologies, and new claims about the possibilities of 'digital governance'. It then details how data-based technologies can be understood as specific kinds of quantitative policy instruments, and explores their implications in terms of the performance and accountability of education systems. In the following sections, an abbreviated history of the use of data in educational policy processes is provided, accompanied by a survey of contemporary digital database technologies and sites of expertise for the collection and analysis of large-scale educational data. The next section examines the emergence of school comparison website and data dashboards that exhort schools to give an 'intimate account' of themselves; the next then examines some specific emerging big data technologies; while the following section takes things even further and explores the emerging possibilities of 'real-time' policy instruments associated with automated forms of predictive and prescriptive analytics and adaptive learning software. The concluding section discusses how techniques and instruments of digital governance are now coming to play a part in the management and organization of education systems.

Political Analytics

The use of numbers in major domains of government, such as education, crime, health, trade, taxation and so on, is nothing new, and has been traced back to nineteenth-century innovations in census recording, health and crime monitoring, and myriad other bureaucratic practices of numbering and counting (Ambrose 2015; Hacking 1990). Government archives have long operated as part of the apparatus of social rule and regulation, facilitating governance through accumulated information on individuals (Bowker 2008). Archives or databases allow masses of detail from the lives of individuals to be identified, tracked, monitored, documented and stored, particularly in numerical form:

> The organization of political life in the form of the modern 'governmental' state has been intrinsically linked to the composition of networks of numbers connecting those exercising political power with the persons, processes and problems that they seek to govern. Numbers are integral to … the performance of government that characterizes modern political culture. (Rose 1999a: 199)

In other words, numbers are used to define the problems that governments might seek to solve and inform the projects devised to do so. Moreover, numbers are an essential feature of the knowledge required to govern, allowing sectors such as education, public health, trade and crime to be known, understood and therefore acted upon. In other words, the organized political machinery of the state depends on a statistical knowledge of society, and the numbering of persons, goods, activities and so on.

Statistical systems such as databases of information about populations are thus a major technique of government – the governmental operations of the state and the functional logics of databases are symmetrical:

> A good citizen of the modern state is a citizen who can well be counted – along numerous dimensions, on demand. We live in a regime of countability with a particular spirit of quantification … [and] governmentality: a modern state needs to conjure its citizens into such a form that they can be enumerated. (Bowker 2008: 30)

The potential for government departments and agencies to make use of the administrative data it holds about citizens is reflected, for example, in the establishment of the Administrative Data Research Network (ADRN) in the UK. The ADRN acts as a data intermediary that provides access to government data and potentially allows the user to track data on individuals across their entire lifetime – from birth records, through educational data, health, crime and employment details, to data on deaths – as well as to access data that might be used to inform policymaking.

With the rise of sources of big data, it is also increasingly seen as possible for governments to work with data analytics agencies to monitor its citizens through their digital traces. New forms of 'data-driven governance' are emerging that emphasize 'data for policy' and 'evidence-based policymaking' that seeks to legitimize specific forms of political action by referring to 'hard' statistical scientific evidence (Rieder and Simon 2016). The Royal Statistical Society has produced a 'Data Manifesto' to encourage government to use sources of both big data and open data in new forms of data-informed policymaking, while a 'Data for Policy' conference hosted annually by the University of Cambridge explores the opportunities and challenges of 'Policy-making in the Big Data Era'. In practice, the UK think tank Demos has established a Centre for the Analysis of Social Media (CASM), a research centre specializing in methods of 'social media science' that aims to explore the '"datafication" of social life' and 'see society-in-motion' through big data generated by individuals' social media interactions (Miller 2014). Underlying its commitment to 'social media science' is a belief that the behaviour of citizens – both individually and aggregated as a massive digital commons – can be mined, analysed and predicted through sources of big data in order to make it possible to develop new policy ideas and solutions.

Likewise, Nesta – a charity focused on government innovation – has recently partnered with the UK Government Cabinet Office to explore the idea of 'a new operating system for government'. They aim to anticipate how emerging technologies such as 'data science, predictive analytics, artificial intelligence, sensors, applied programming interfaces, autonomous machines, and platforms' might in the next five years become 'ingrained into how government thinks of itself', 'redefine the role of government, and even create a different relationship between state and public' (Maltby 2015). Nesta's chief executive Mulgan (2016a) has claimed that new governmental bodies and activities may be required to help build public understanding and trust in the algorithms and machine learning processes that underpin new big data-driven forms of governance.

Elsewhere, Mulgan (2016b: 44) has argued that governments can now benefit from many new forms of data to conduct observations, such as the use of environmental sensors and 'scraping' the Web for trends, and perform analyses, since 'computing tools, including predictive algorithms and machine learning, can help governments spot patterns. … More sophisticated machine learning can then help governments better plan for changing needs.' He notes also that governments are using techniques such as 'crowdsourcing' to 'tap brains far beyond the boundaries of the civil service or politics' and 'to help governments devise better policy options', which may 'redefine the very idea of citizenship' by making 'government more of a partnership between state and citizens':

> Some governments will use new technologies to support a centralised, all-knowing 'Big Brother' model of government, helped by CCTV cameras and traffic sensors, and techniques for pulling in vast quantities of personal data from social media. … [T]he biggest pay-offs are likely to come from finding new ways to collaborate with citizens in the creation of data, the development of options and the implementation of policy. These point to a much more appealing vision of government that is both more knowledge powered, and more people powered. (Mulgan 2016b: 44–5).

Although the data-driven vision of government as a participatory, open source platform and a form of 'collective intelligence' remains underdeveloped, organizations such as Nesta and other 'public and social innovation labs' and experimental government initiatives are slowly transforming it from an imaginary to the material practice of government (Williamson 2015a).

As a direct materialization of this vision of participatory digital governance, late in 2016, the US White House announced the launch of Code.gov to help citizens explore and improve government services by accessing the open source software code used to build government software. Code.gov is described as a:

> creative platform that gives citizens the ability to participate in making government services more effective, accessible, and transparent. We also envision it becoming a useful resource for State and local governments and developers looking to tap into the Government's code to build similar services, foster new connections with their users, and help us continue to realize the President's vision for a 21st Century digital government. (White House 2016a).

The political scientists Dunleavy and Margetts (2015: 1) have defined such visionary big data approaches as 'digital governance':

> Governments and citizens operate in a digital environment, leaving digital trails whatever they do and wherever they go. These trails generate huge quantities of information about themselves, each other and any interactions they have. In this context … most governments in the 21st century industrialised world and beyond are reliant on a large digital presence and complex network of large-scale information systems for administrative operations and policy-making.

In this reformatory model, governments are increasingly seeking to 'prioritise the interactions and feedback loops that would capitalise on the potential of the internet and digital technologies for public policy solutions and service delivery' (Dunleavy and Margetts 2015: 1).

The vision of digital governance is a response to technological developments such as analysing big data from transactional processes, peer production and network effects, and to new popular ideas of 'crowdsourcing', 'cognitive surplus', 'wikinomics' and 'democratization', and it is characterized by new automated 'zero-touch' technologies; behavioural policy and persuasive 'nudge' technologies; big data analysis; coproduction or database-led information processing; digital by default public service transactions and interactions; real-time government data-pooling; network-based communications; open data; and social web development within online government (Margetts and Dunleavy 2013). It is underpinned by the assumption that the use of big data 'offers a means of mass participation in policymaking' (Bright and Margetts 2016: 219), whilst simultaneously giving governing bodies access to huge quantities of social data captured from the actions of populations.

How individuals are to be captured, counted and classified in database systems is therefore an evolution of a particular style of governing through quantification, calculation and classification that emerged in the statistical and bureaucratic revolution of nineteenth-century record-keeping – 'first wave big data' (Ambrose 2015) – but is now amplified to real-time monitoring of the population through digital big data:

> Unlike the governance tool of statistical representations in the eighteenth and nineteenth centuries, which generally produced analyses of static (forever outdated) data sets, big data promises ultrarapid, updatable profiling of individuals to enable interventions and actions to make each individual, their thoughts and behaviours, actionable in a variety of ways. (Thompson and Cook 2016: 4)

The 'technocratic infrastructure' of this form of 'database government' represents a shift from the 'qualitative' governance of the social to the 'quantitative' governance of the 'informational', where governance is increasingly achieved through scraping statistics from society (Ruppert 2012: 117–118). The 'analytics turn' in the political landscape is enacted through experimental data science methods which enable large-scale aggregations of behavioural information about the public, collected via both administrative and social media data, to be interrogated and then used to inform political decision making (Chadwick and Stromer-Galley 2016).

These political analytics are all part of the emergence of a new 'style of government' in which a 'constant audit of behaviour' is undertaken, through techniques of big data mining, sentiment analysis and social network analysis, in order to measure and manage the conduct of individuals and thus maintain the social order as a whole (Davies 2012: 774). In other words, in digital governance, big data software has been governmentalized, although, as Dunleavy and Margetts (2015: 5) acknowledge, governments are failing to capitalise on the affordances of big data and citizens are unable to interact with governments digitally as they do with social media, as various barriers remain within government 'to using social media and embracing the digital timestream, and developing the data science skills necessary to extract public value from big data'. Moreover, big data analysis not only offers scope for understanding human behaviour, social structure and citizens' civic engagement, but can 'also be used for algorithmic and probabilistic policymaking' and 'for more coercive modes of governance' (Margetts and Sutcliffe 2013: 139).

As we shall see shortly, a new mode of data-driven political analytics and digital governance is now emerging in education, as attention is increasingly attracted to the promises of mining the digital timestream of education data for the purposes of knowing, understanding and acting upon education systems, institutions, processes and the people that enact them. The political analytics of education exemplifies how digital data are becoming key aspects of state management, governance and control.

Policy Instruments, Performativity and Accountability

The concept of 'policy instrumentation' has been influentially applied to understand the various technologies and materials that make educational policy and governance operational. According to influential conceptualization of policy instrumentation by Lascoumes and le Gales (2007), policy instruments are constituted by the different techniques, tools and methods that allow any kind of policy intervention to be put into practice. A policy instrument in this sense refers to how political aims or the solutions to government problems are made attainable through the specific choice of techniques used to address them. As with critical sociological studies of software (see Beer 2013; Lupton 2015a), this approach to policy instrumentation views devices as inseparable from both their social, cultural, political and economic processes of *production* and their socially, culturally, politically and economically *productive* effects. Policy instruments constitute 'a condensed form of knowledge about social control and ways of exercising it', and 'are not neutral devices: they produce specific effects, independently of the objective pursued (the aims ascribed to them), which structure public policy according to their own logic' (Lascoumes and le Gales 2007: 3). As such, instruments are bearers of values and interpretations of the social world that are materialized and operationalized by particular concrete techniques and tools, and that as a result have the capacity to partly structure policies, determine how actors behave, and privilege certain representations of problems to be addressed. In other words, the choice of instruments structures capacities for action, the process and its results.

In recent decades, the performance and productivity of educational systems, institutions, processes and individuals themselves have become the subject of increasing levels of measurement, inspection and auditing. This has been captured in terms such as 'governing through numbers' (Grek 2009) and 'governing by inspection' (Ozga 2016) and emphasizes how specific policy instruments and techniques of numerical measurement and evaluation have enabled the performance of education systems, institutions and even individuals to be audited and evaluated. Performance measurement and management is, however, not simply descriptive. It also brings the matter it describes into being. Captured in the term 'performativity', it has become apparent that education systems and institutions, and even individuals themselves, are changing their practices to ensure the best possible measures of performance. Closely linked to this is the notion of accountability; that is, the production of evidence that proves the effectiveness – in terms of measurable results – of whatever has been performed in the name of improvement and enhancement.

> Performativity is … a regime of accountability that employs judgements, comparisons and displays as a means of control, attrition and change. The performance of individuals and organizations serve as measures of productivity or output … [and] stand for, encapsulate or represent the worth, quality or value of an individual or organization within a field of judgement. (Ball 2008: 49)

In other words, performativity makes the question of what counts as a worthwhile activity in education into the question of what can be *counted* and of what *account* can be given for it. It reorients institutions and individuals to focus on those things that can be counted and accounted for with evidence of their delivery, results and positive outcomes, and de-emphasises activities that cannot be easily and effectively measured by numerical means.

In practical terms, performativity depends on databases, audits, inspections, reviews, reports and the regular publication of results. It tends to prioritize the practices and judgements of accountants, lawyers and managers who subject practitioners to constant processes of target-setting, measurement, comparison and evaluation (Ball 2008). Performativity and accountability are enacted through particular kinds of policy instruments, techniques and tools, such as those of data production, information storage, analysis and report production, publication, communication and display (Anagnostopoulos et al. 2013). Understood as policy instruments, data processing technologies can therefore be seen as digital policy instruments that reproduce and reinforce existing regimes of performativity and accountability. They make the performance of education systems and institutions into enumerated timestreams of data by which they might be measured, evaluated and assessed, held up to both political and public scrutiny, and then made to account for their actions and decisions and either rewarded or disciplined accordingly.

In this sense, the task of educational governance is a task of calculation – calculative both in the mathematical sense and the strategic sense. 'Centres of calculation' are those spaces described by Latour (1986) that accumulate and aggregate numbers in order to affect things somewhere else. Historically, within the education sector, government education departments were key centres of calculation that were able to collect and aggregate data on schools. These 'distant' data from schools could then be transported back to a central locale, and re-presented in order to render it 'seeable', intelligible and amenable to deliberation and decision making.

With the rise of digital forms of data collection in education by other non-state agencies and organizations, however, the centres of calculation in education have become more dispersed and distributed, with data flowing into them from schools much more quickly and flowing back out in the shape of glossy reports and data visualizations. The calculative techniques of education have been displaced to more 'distant' actors such as data analysts, educational big data specialists, data intermediaries and 'algorithmists' (Mayer-Schonberger and Cukier 2013) trained in the science of data analysis, statistics and computer science. This is not to dismiss the idea of the state being a key centre of calculation, but to acknowledge that calculations made at governmental centres like departments of education are the terminal form of a dispersed network of calculative practices enacted at distributed sites.

Data technologies of various kinds are policy instruments of performativity and accountability, and translate the logics of the technologies into the material and practical realities of educational systems and processes. Emerging big data technologies that can be used to perform a constant measure and diagnostics of individuals and organizations stand poised to accelerate and expand processes of performativity and accountability, particularly those that enable massive quantities of data to be compared in order to identify 'best practices' – and by association to locate under-performing institutions and individuals and hold them responsible for their results – and those that promise to speed up data collection and analysis to 'real-time' temporalities. Within such systems, automation plays a large role, making processes of 'automated management' (Kitchin and Dodge 2011) that can be enacted without human oversight or intervention into key policy instruments of educational governance and control. As the material form of a new practice of political analytics, however, contemporary big data-based policy instruments need to be understood in relation to the recent history of large-scale statistical data collection in education.

Large-Scale Education Data

The collection, calculation and communication of large-scale data in education has a long history. Numerical data were routinely displayed in both Europe and the USA as part of the spectacle of the great exhibitions, world fairs and scientific congresses of the nineteenth century (Lawn 2013). At these events, the visualization of large quantities of data through graphical displays such as topographical maps, tables of illustrative statistics and exemplars of student's work could be used to represent the relations between education and society directly to the viewer. These images of the data, the numerical information they represented and the statistical techniques used to generate them, were powerful explanatory and persuasive devices which made it difficult to conceive of education in any other terms – and could be used as the basis for political intervention. The exhibitions could serve as advertisements of different nations' progress, spaces in which both to 'tell' state narratives and 'sell' their successes as solutions to other national systems (Sobe 2013). In other words, the displays presented at the great expositions were themselves policy instruments.

In both Europe and America in the post-war years, an international infrastructure emerged of specialist research associations, national research centres and the formation of international organizations which together embedded data, and the skills and data processing technologies required to produce it, firmly in the governance of education (Lawn 2013). Processes of 'child collecting' have historically taken place through 'medical-social-bureaucratic networks' of interconnected agencies and hubs of information from across the state and non-state spectrum (Grosvenor and Roberts 2013). In order to enable policy decisions to be made and enacted, data have needed to be inputted, ordered, filtered and classified, all tasks requiring various skilled technical intermediaries, statistical experts and data brokers with the relevant know-how and the machinery to reconfigure it as useful knowledge. As a social institution, education has long reached for quantification and the exhibition of its numbers as an explanatory and rhetorical source, a process currently being further enabled and enhanced by digital technologies and practices of datafication.

As the scope, scale and pace of large-scale data collection in education has grown, a lively literature has developed around the idea that education is 'governed by numbers' and regulated through constant processes of audit and comparison (Grek 2009; Ozga et al. 2011; Lawn and Grek 2012). Numerical data have become a dominant political technology of governing, largely through the work of international non-governmental organizations which increasingly influence educational policymaking around the world. As educational governance has been distributed to a network of actors from across the governmental and non-governmental spheres, a vast 'web of data' is required to hold all the various agencies and actors together, since the flow of data, feedback and prediction are essential to control and steer the system (Ozga 2009). These organizations include the World Bank and UNESCO, though perhaps the most influential of these global policy actors is the OECD.

The OECD administers the Programme for International Student Assessment (PISA), which measures the performance of children from countries all over the globe in maths, literacy and science at the end of compulsory schooling, as well as the Programme for the International Assessment of Adult Competencies (PIAAC). It has also developed an early childhood testing instrument, a cross-national assessment of early learning outcomes involving the testing of 5-year-old children in participating countries (Moss et al. 2016). The results of these tests are then used as performance indicators to compare each country's potential economic competitiveness:

> Performance in these tests – along with the consequent onset of PISA 'envy' in low-performing nations and, presumably, PISA 'ecstasy' in high-performing ones – has emerged as a powerful source of governance that now serves to define the necessity for educational reform, the means to achieve it, and its ends … . [T]he simplest way to improve PISA scores is for nations to align their curricula more closely to what is measured by PISA … . If countries do this and improve their scores, we will enter into a closed and self-fulfilling system in which nations teach according to test require-ments and better scores create the illusion of improvement. (Morris 2016: 26)

As a result, national education systems can be put under pressure to improve if they fare poorly in the global comparison. This creates hierarchies of national education systems in a global policy arena (Rizvi and Lingard 2010). Countries with high-ranking performance, such as Singapore and Finland, attain iconic status within the global policy arena, and become beacons attracting policymak-ers and politicians from other countries eager to emulate their successes.

Ultimately, the ambition behind these vast techniques of data collection and analysis is the production of 'governing knowledge', the production of knowl-edge about the system that can then be used as insights to shape decisions and inform policy actions (Fenwick et al. 2014). Policy problems and their solutions are simultaneously to be found in a kind of scientific knowledge of education systems that prioritizes statistical surveillance and the comparison of data for the purposes of identifying 'best practices' of 'what works' and constructing 'refer-ence points' that other systems might emulate (Novoa and Yariv-Mashal 2014). The effects of global standardized testing undertaken by the OECD have become the particular focus for critics of performativity (Lawn and Grek 2012). For exam-ple, the effect of PISA testing in schools in England is that 'the purposes of schooling and what it means to be educated are effectively being redefined by the metrics by which we evaluate schools and pupils':

> the logic of the OECD has been internalized so that principals, teachers, pupils, and schools are now judged – and are increasingly judged by themselves – by reference to a metric based on pupils' performance in tests of academic achievement in a narrow range of subjects. (Morris 2016: 17)

This is performativity writ large, as the demands of measuring performance – dictated by international organizations like the OECD – fundamentally influence how schools go about the task of educating young people.

Sophisticated database management and data analysis technologies have been integral to these surveillance and comparison activities. The success of the OECD as an educational policy actor is that it has 'created a niche as a technically highly competent agency for the development of educational indicators and comparative educational performance measures', techniques and methods it can mobilize for 'policy construction, mediation and diffusion at a national, international and possibly global level' (Grek 2009: 25–6). The huge datasets generated by such exercises require significant technical support, with 'the governing of education systems increasingly connected to the capacity of data servers, software developments, and the use of data-mining tools' (Lawn 2013: 11–12).

An often-overlooked dimension of the production, circulation and use of educational data is the information infrastructure that underpins it. Anagnostopoulos et al. (2013: 2) have described the development of a vast 'infrastructure of accountability' (specifically in US education) that depends on computing technologies, policies and various experts:

> The performance data made ubiquitous under test-based accountability are, themselves, the products of myriad decisions about what information should be collected, how it should be encoded and processed, and how it should be inscribed in files and reports. The people who make and enact these decisions do so not only in the schools, districts and state and federal education agencies that comprise our formal education system but also in testing companies, software firms, research universities and consortia, foundations, consulting firms and newspapers. Collecting, processing, and disseminating information across these people and settings requires sophisticated computing technologies that can store and process the vast amounts of information required to produce performance measures and ratings. … The data that fuel test-based accountability are, thus, the products of complex assemblages of technology, people and policies that stretch across and beyond the boundaries of our formal education system.

Large-scale government information systems that can gather, process and disseminate information on the characteristics and performance of schools, teachers and students have become essential technologies of educational measurement and accountability. In the USA, large-scale data collection has been at the centre of efforts to hold schools and public officials accountable, with effects such as parents exiting failing schools (Holbein 2016).

Though often overlooked, the infrastructure of technologies, people and policies that underpins the production of data and accountability mechanisms is highly significant in its effects. It gives rise to new kinds of practices, new ways of conceiving of people and institutions, new kinds of interventions, and represents a new kind of 'informatic power' in education:

> Informatic power … depends on the knowledge, use, production of, and control over measurement and computing technologies … to produce performance measures that appear as transparent and accurate representations of the complex

processes of teaching, learning, and schooling. ... As they define what kind of knowledge and ways of thinking matter and who counts as 'good' teachers, students, and schools, these performance metrics shape how we practice, value and think about education. (Anagnostopoulos et al. 2013: 11)

As the material enactment of informatic power, a data infrastructure can be defined as 'an assemblage of material, semiotic and social practices' that functions to translate things into numbers; enables the storage, transmission, analysis and representation of data using algorithmic logics and computational technologies; embeds data usage into other practices; produces new kinds of spaces through practices of classification, measurement and comparison; and produces new social practices (Sellar 2015a: 770).

A significant example of the increasing size and scope of educational data collection, and of the growing requirement for an information infrastructure of technical platforms and analytical expertise to make sense of it, is provided by the National Pupil Database (NPD) in the UK. The National Pupil Database was established by the UK government in 2002 under the leadership of Michael Barber, then head of the Prime Minister's Delivery Unit (later Barber became chief education advisor of the education business Pearson, covered shortly). The NPD features extensive datasets on the educational progress of children and young people from the early years through to higher education. It includes data on seven million pupils matched over twelve years – including pupil identifiers, home addresses, test and exam results, prior attainment and progression, pupil characteristics such as gender, ethnicity, country of birth, first language, free school meals, special educational needs, absences and exclusions – and is also connected to databases holding similar information from further and higher education to produce linked data. The data are drawn from regular school censuses (usually conducted three times a year) as well as from local authorities and awarding bodies, and are processed by the Department for Education's Education Data Division and matched and stored in the NPD. The NPD is presented in Excel spreadsheet files as thousands upon thousands of rows of numbers that can be searched and analysed in myriad ways by government departments, including the Home Office and the police (as well as, controversially, by authorized third parties), and used to generate complex and sophisticated graphic displays such as charts, tables, plots, graphs and so on.

The NPD is not just a political achievement, but a technical and methodological accomplishment. Underpinning the organization of the data is the common basic data set (CBDS) database, a file containing definitions for common data items that schools and local authorities use in software systems such as management information systems. In other words, the data collected in the NPD is governed by data collection standards and definitions contained in the CBDS that regulate all the data collected in schools. The CBDS is a clear example of what has been termed a 'mundane information infrastructure', a classification system that produces and maintains standards of data collection and organization for bureaucratic purposes of measurement, comparison and evaluation (Bowker and Star 1999). The NPD is, in other words, a statistical device and a policy instrument based on a standard classification system for collecting and exhibiting large-scale educational data in order to inform governmental policy and analysis.

Such is the large scale of the NPD that an independent data analysis organization has been established to study its datasets for potential insights that might be used to inform education policies. The Education Datalab was launched in 2014 as a site of statistical expertise dedicated to the analysis of NPD datasets, which it supplements with analysis of other datasets to produce 'independent, cutting-edge research that can be used by policy makers to inform education policy, and by schools to improve practice':

> We work collaboratively with research partners and make sure that our published research is accessible to policy makers and schools. Data can't make good policy, but it can help policy-makers better understand the education system they are trying to reform. (Education Datalab 2014)

The Education Datalab has provided its quantitative expertise to the Department for Education, the Department for Business, Innovation and Skills, as well as various charitable organizations, companies, think tanks, foundations and trusts.

The availability of the NPD to third-party analysis and use has raised significant questions about trust and data privacy, particularly as its scope has expanded and sensitive individual data have been released to the media and other consulting services:

> The trustworthiness of pupil data collection ... depends on the limitation of the future scope of what purposes data will be used for and who will access them. Scope creep is not fiction, but very real, and today's use of data by government can mean that what we sign up to, does not stay what we signed up to. Data handed into schools by parents and pupils before 2012 are now used for entirely different purposes since legislation was changed to permit the release of individual pupil data. ... The release of identifiable children's confidential data without consent to companies and journalists is stunning. (Persson 2016)

In addition to its role as a key intermediary for educational data analysis, the Education Datalab is also project manager of the OECD Teaching and Learning International Survey, thus positioning itself as a key actor in the cross-sector networks of organizations and expertise that conduct the contemporary political analytics of education.

Intimate Accountability

The use of large-scale data to inform systemic policy decisions depends on schools performing a range of mundane data collection and analysis tasks (Finn 2016; Selwyn 2016). New roles for school data managers have appeared as school accountability systems designed by government education departments have made routine data collection, analysis, forecasting and reporting into an expert task requiring professional knowledge and skills in data management, statistical methods and software packages. Using data to fabricate a narrative of performance has become a key practice both of individual teachers and of the institutions they occupy. Indeed, the task of government at a distance requires individual institutions and their staff alike to take responsibility for data collection and its organization – via definitions and standards provided by databases such as the CBDS – so that it can be transported from a host of separate sites to be aggregated together within key governmental centres of calculation. As such, schools are engaged in the 'doublethink of data' (Hardy and Lewis 2016), involving teachers engaging with performative processes for purposes of compliance but without any real sense of the value of doing so.

The positioning of teachers as data collectors and data entry clerks represents the current educational instantiation of participatory collective intelligence imagined by enthusiasts for digital governance. Schools have to capture data, but are also captured through data insofar as nationally and even internationally distant pressures and agendas exert themselves in specific institutions and require practitioners to provide performance data to account for their work (Thompson and Cook 2016). As a result, schools are exhorted to provide detailed and 'intimate' data about their own institutional performances for public display and scrutiny, all requiring more 'expert handling' (Wilkins 2015), often in the shape of specialist data managers or even outsourced contractors who extend the demands of data collection.

The data that schools provide are often turned into simplified presentations. In the UK the Department for Education produces school performance tables that allow the performance of individual schools across England to be searched. The data are visually mapped with a graphic representation of England that breaks down the data by region or local authority; by school name or town; by postcode; and by type of school/college. The school performance tables permit little of the fine-grained analytical capabilities associated with the NPD, but translate the same datasets on pupil test scores and school funding into easily searchable, representable and intelligible forms that make meaning out of the data for its various audiences.

Fulfilling a similar function, the UK Office for Standards in Education (Ofsted), which has overall responsibility for inspecting and assessing schools, has produced its own School Data Dashboard package. The data dashboards consist of graphically presented accounts of school data including exam results, progress, attendance, and other contextual factors. The data dashboards are promoted as an objective and data-led augmentation to the conventional school inspection by expert inspectors embodied in their various codes of evaluation and judgement. Promoted primarily for use by school governors, Ofsted claims the data dashboards provide an analysis of performance over a three-year period and comparisons to other schools or providers.

Together, the DfE and Ofsted have also produced RAISEonline (Reporting and Analysis for Improvement through school Self-Evaluation), an interactive web portal designed to enable analysis of school and pupil performance data as part of the self-evaluation process. RAISEonline provides a common, standardized set of analyses for schools, and data management facilities providing the ability to import and edit pupil level data. It includes contextual information about individual schools including comparisons to schools nationally, reports and analysis covering the attainment and progress of pupils, and features interactive elements allowing schools to investigate the performance of pupils in specific curriculum areas throughout key stages.

The dashboard interfaces with school data are also publicly available online and are clearly aligned with shifts towards greater transparency, openness and accountability in the policy environment (Piattoeva 2015). The dashboards make visible to the public and to the media, as well as to school governors and inspectors, how well schools are progressing in terms of nationally institutionalized norms and averages, and allow schools to be identified and classified in terms of either their outstanding or deficit features. With specific regard to the Ofsted dashboard, the work of school inspection is mediated, augmented and regulated by the database software. The school data used in the process of inspection, evaluation and judgement is organized and coded by the dashboards before the embodied inspector even arrives at the school, and to a certain extent the apparently objective data displaces informed professional judgement (Ozga 2016).

Making schools amenable to public inspection by parents has also become a key driver for publishing school data in accessible and transparent formats. The commercial producer of educational technology Research Machines (RM) has produced a 'School Finder' website for use by parents. Through simple drop down menus, it allows parents to search schools in specific geographical areas, to compare those schools according to various data, and then to shortlist their preferred school choices. School Finder aggregates and combines data from school performance tables, the School Census, Ofsted data, Ordnance Survey data, and information from schools' own promotional and marketing materials. The data presented by School Finder is also augmented with an extensive set of promoted materials from RM's commercial catalogue, configuring the parent-user as an active educational consumer. As a policy instrument, School Finder is structured according to the principles of online consumer services such as Moneysupermarket.com and Gocompare.com, and combines the popular appeal of the wider online media environment with the expert judgement associated with statistical data comparison.

One of the key effects of these database instruments is to make education systems, institutions and individuals 'comparable' in ways that position them simultaneously as potential collaborators who can learn from each other but also as rivals seeking competitive advantage (Novoa and Yariv-Mashal 2014). In 2016 the Education Endowment Foundation (EEF) launched the Families of Schools Database, a searchable database that allows any school in England to be compared with statistically similar institutions in order to 'provide manageable targets on the way to closing the national attainment gap' and 'identify schools that have similar challenges that can provide support and guidance'. The database was constructed by the EEF (itself established by the philanthropic Sutton Trust with a founding grant of £125m from the Department for Education) and commissioned by the Fischer Family Trust, the non-profit parent company of the Education Datalab. Based on an interactive data dashboard format consisting of different graphs, tables and scatterplots, the database presents different indicators of any school's performance as part of a 'statistical neighbourhood' of quantitatively similar schools. It also automatically calculates and presents estimated 'future scenarios' of projected performance of each school according to past data from each of its indicators.

Scottish schools have access to a similar technology, Insight (the product of the Scottish Government), an online benchmarking tool 'designed for use by secondary schools and local authorities to identify success and areas where improvements can be made, with the ultimate aim of making a positive difference for pupils'. It provides data on national measures, including post-school destinations and attainment in literacy and numeracy, as well as information on a number of local measures designed to help users interrogate the effectiveness of their curriculum, subjects and courses. It features data dashboards that allow schools to view an overall picture of the data from their school and compare it with the national measures presented on the national dashboard. A notable feature of Insight is the Virtual Comparator, which allows users to see how the performance of their pupils compares nationally. The Virtual Comparator feature takes the characteristics of pupils in a school and matches them to similar pupils from across Scotland to create a 'virtual school' against which a 'real school' may benchmark its progress. Similarly, the Australian government has launched My School, a public website designed to enable 'like-school' comparison. Though the Families of Schools Database, Insight and My School have all been packaged up as comparative technologies of collaboration; they equally function as performative technologies of competition, encouraging schools to present themselves as positively as possible in order to bolster their league table position and market attractiveness to parents.

The development of school comparison websites like the Families of Schools Database, Insight and My School point to the increasingly fine-grained, detailed and close-up nature of educational data collection, calculation and circulation. That is, they offer a kind of numerical and 'intimate' analytics of education. One way of approaching these school comparison databases and learning analytics platforms is through the notion of 'accounting intimacy' (Asdal 2011). In this view, practices of calculation are increasingly moving away from bureaucratic practices enacted in distant offices, or governmental centres of calculation, to much more 'intimate' calculative practices that are enacted in situ, close to the action they measure. Intimacy also implies a close relationship, and practices of calculative or accounting intimacy can also be understood in terms of how numbers and numerical presentations of data can be used to build intimate relationships between different actors.

Through the presentation of school data, more 'intimate accounting' is increasingly occurring in education. For example, through the school comparison site My School in Australia, it has been documented how:

> The public, especially parents, was exhorted to make itself familiar – intimate – with the school by studying the wealth of detail about each school that was on My School. The idea was that, armed with intimate knowledge of their child's school, parents could exert pressure on schools to perform well and get the best outcomes for their children. Not only did My School become a technology through which the government entered intimate spaces of schools, schools themselves entered intimate spaces of living rooms and kitchens through discussions between parents. (Gorur 2015)

Through these techniques, schools could become available for the intimate scrutiny of the government as well as by parents. School comparison websites and data dashboards involve schools in providing highly intimate details – in the form of numbers – that can then be presented to the general public. These public databases allow the school to be known and discussed in the intimate spaces of the home, as well as involving school leaders in the intimate accounting and disclosure of their institution's performance according to various criteria. While school data certainly are collected together and transported to distant centres of calculation to allow the compilation of such databases, a certain demand is placed on institutions to present themselves in terms of an intimate account, and ultimately to share that account as a means towards possible collaboration with their numerical neighbours.

Practices of intimate accountability promoted by school data dashboards configure the school environment as a 'datascape', one whose existence in organizational reality is achieved through the calculative practices that make it 'accountable' (Lippert 2015). Different 'school realities' become visible through school comparison websites that enable the institutions represented by the data to be known, scrutinized, and then acted upon, in particular kinds of ways (Decuypere et al. 2014). Databases such as the Families of Schools Database, Insight and My School might therefore be understood as intimate datascapes, where schools' data are disclosed with the aim of building close relationships with parents and other institutions, whilst also becoming more intimately visible to government and amenable to disciplinary measures and other interventions.

The higher education sector is becoming subject to the same kind of processes. Academic research and teaching practices are increasingly monitored and assessed through the use of a variety of metrics and modes of reporting, including research excellence measures, research impact indices, student satisfaction surveys, teaching quality metrics, workload tracking instruments, and a variety of national and international league tables (Burrows 2012; Lupton 2015a). Increasingly, university managers are using new software information systems and data dashboards to visualize complex performance indicator metrics in order to inform decision making (Wolf et al. 2016). The metricization of higher education by new kinds of data-driven policy instruments, as in the schools sector, is making universities more results-oriented, performative and accountable, simultaneously inserting institutions into large-scale databases and public tables while forcing them to provide ever more intimate reports of their measurable outputs and results.

Visual Policy

Data are complex, and require new techniques to make them legible and intelligible to their intended audiences. In May 2014, the international organization OECD launched its Education GPS site as a public portal to its global PISA datasets. PISA itself generates massive datasets on educational performances that are available for download on the program website, consisting of spreadsheets, data files in ASCII format, codebooks, compendia and control files for statistical software packages such as SPSS, in order to allow users to process the data. Education GPS has been designed as a more user-friendly interface to these datasets. Publicly available on the Web, Education GPS specifically enables the user to access interactive data in order to compare countries on a 'wide range of indicators'. Through a simplified menu system, it allows the user to compile the data held by the OECD from its extensive PISA datasets in order to 'create your own, customized country reports, highlighting the facts, developments and outcomes of your choice', and to compare and review different countries' educational policies. The user can generate extensive customized datasets, and the Education GPS tools can generate maps overlaid with data representations, charts and scatterplots. Education GPS has prompted comments that 'OECD has clearly become a world leader in the big data movement in education' (Sahlberg and Hasak 2016).

With the release of the PISA 2015 results, the OECD produced an entire new Compare Your Country online tool to enable quick access to the data using an interactive world map. Users could take the country of their choice and click through for more detailed information and analysis, much of it presented in simplified charts, graphs and tables. Compare Your Country and Education GPS are database visualization technologies that demonstrate how powerful the OECD has become as a centre of calculation in global education, one that acts at arms-length to steer education systems by representing their comparative positioning in global ranks and tables. Its visualization techniques, such as maps and charts, act as a mode of 'aesthetic governance' or a visual art of political comparison (Grek 2016).

Likewise, the global educational business Pearson has become another con-tender as a centre of calculation and visualization in education, particularly since the 2012 launch of its Learning Curve Data Bank by chief education adviser Michael Barber (formerly the UK government adviser who spearheaded the National Pupil Database). Pearson's Learning Curve combines over 60 data-sets from education systems around the world in order to 'enable researchers and policymakers to correlate education outcomes with wider social and economic outcomes'. Described as providing 'lessons in country performance', the Learning Curve includes national performance data (sourced from, for example, the National Pupil Database) along with OECD PISA data and other sources such as UNESCO, in order to produce a 'Global Index' of nations ranked in terms of 'educational attainment' and 'cognitive skills'.

As an edu-business with significant commercial operations, Pearson is there-fore positioning itself through the Learning Curve to identify policy problems for national schooling systems, from which it also has the potential to profit by selling policy solutions. In other words, 'Pearson is generating knowledge about its business to produce new possibilities for profit':

> [The Learning Curve] provides Pearson with the capacity to analyse data on the performance of national systems and to present nations with a succinct statement of policy problems, linked to the creation of potential markets for its products and services. (Hogan et al. 2015: 3)

The Learning Curve is highly relational, enabling the conjoining of multiple data-sets, as well as scalable in that it can expand rapidly. New data are added frequently as new datasets from its various sources become available. In this sense, the Learning Curve provides Pearson with detailed and up-to-date knowledge about its target markets as well as 'charitably' enabling other audiences to comprehend the statistical facts of education at national, global and comparative scales.

As a public-facing policy instrument, the Learning Curve features a range of data visualization tools. It includes dynamic and user-friendly mapping and time series tools that allow countries to be compared and evaluated both spatially and temporally. Countries' educational performance in terms of educational attainment and cognitive skills are represented on the site as 'heat maps' that are colour-coded in terms of comparative performance level. It also enables the user to generate 'country profiles' that visually compare multiple 'education input indicators' (such as public educational expenditure, pupil:teacher ratio, educational 'life expectancy') with 'education output indicators' (PISA scores, graduation rates, labour market productivity), as well as 'socio-economic indicators' (such as GDP and crime statistics). The Learning Curve, like OECD's Compare Your Country and Education GPS, is a tool of global public comparison. These are powerful techniques of political visualization for envisioning the educational landscape, enabling numbers to be presented and re-presented aesthetically to function for a variety of purposes, users and audiences. Notably, the data visualizations are often spread online through social media platforms like Twitter, acting as a form of compressed visual evidence for different countries' education performance.

Data visualizations are used increasingly in the big data for policy and digital governance movement as a way of making huge and complex datasets intelligible. Practically, data visualization can help make big data more relevant and personalized for its intended audiences, to visualize and model potential scenarios, establish and cement expectations, scroll through and annotate insights, construct virtual reality models, and to create explorable explanations to complex concepts or problems (Sleeman 2016). As key sites of data visualization production in education, then, we can see key actors such as OECD and Pearson as new artful centres of calculation, whose products process and present information from far-distant locales in easy-to-use, aesthetically appealing and intelligible visual formats. A centre of calculation like the OECD or Pearson is capable of collecting vast quantities of educational data from across states and countries in order to produce a global grid of visibility in which national performance, as measured through the aggregation of pupil performance, is made comparable and public through seemingly scientific and non-political modes of measurement and graphical presentation.

Education GPS, Compare Your Country and the Learning Curve allow the OECD and Pearson to be seen as authorities with the methodological and design expertise to re-present that which has been subjected to calculation in ways that might influence their audiences. The architect of the Learning Curve, Michael Barber, has described how the Learning Curve supports 'evidence-based policy' through data visualization 'to make it easy for people … to use quickly without undermining the integrity of the data' (Barber with Ozga 2014: 77). The visualization of data is no neutral accomplishment but amplifies the rhetorical or persuasive function of data, allowing it to be employed to create arguments and generate explanations about the world, and to produce conviction in others that such representations, explanations and arguments depict the world as it really appears (Gitelman and Jackson 2013). The human eyes and hands, as well as software platforms and algorithms, involved in its display shape the interpretations that data visualization makes possible and the possible meanings that might be extracted from it. Visualization is thus socially productive, in that it directs attention to correlations between data variables and objects that might then be made actionable as insights for decision making.

A product like the Learning Curve ultimately visualizes a virtual reference space against which all education systems might measure and monitor themselves; it constitutes a virtual comparator and a global benchmark for educational evaluation, judgement and action. It is through such visual techniques that Pearson seeks to attract various publics to the insights it has extracted from patterns of learning processes in its data, and to secure consensus that the models it has constructed from the data represent the state of education as it really is rather than as it might otherwise be interpreted. One way Pearson has accomplished this is by making the Learning Curve interactive, so that the data visualizations it presents can be tweaked and modified. Michael Barber has described it as a product of 'co-creation' that allows the public to 'play' with the data and 'connect the bits together' in a way that is more 'fun' than preformatted policy reports (Barber with Ozga 2014: 84).

However, the design of the interactive interface to the data itself delimits and constrains what types of analyses can be performed. It privileges statistical country comparison over any other type of analysis, ultimately configuring the user as a comparative analyst and a data co-producer. This exacerbates what Carvalho (2014) has termed the 'plasticity' of governing knowledge, and that Piattoeva (2015) has designated as 'plastic numbers'. With the Learning Curve, public audiences rather than expert specialists are incited to become responsible for multiplying the analyses that take place, visualizing the data for different possible uses, and circulating it in different contexts. The Learning Curve promotes the public or popular plasticity of governing knowledge, simultaneously soliciting the participation of its audiences while shaping the possible analyses they can conduct, delimiting the potential interpretive yield available, and structuring what can be said and done about the data as a result. A new visual, aesthetic and interactive mode of educational policymaking and public scrutiny is made possible by these visualization products.

Real-Time Digital Datastreams

Large-scale databases such as those described above tend to emphasize country comparison or the comparison of institutions, as assessed by analysis of datasets collected at long temporal intervals through school censuses or standardized tests. However, newer instruments proposed to assist policymakers and other educational decision-makers make the flow of data and its associated feedback into a real-time process focused on the comparison of individuals. The capture, analysis and presentation of the real-time digital datastream of educational performance information has been made possible by advances in big data analytics, machine learning, and predictive and prescriptive analytics.

The commercial education organization Pearson has been one of the most visible advocates of big data-driven education reform. It has particularly promoted the continuous tracking and monitoring of 'streaming data' through real-time analytics rather than the collection of data through discrete temporal assessment events. Late in 2014 Pearson published a report (co-authored by Michael Barber) calling for an 'educational revolution' in the use of big data. The report advocates using 'intelligent software and a range of devices that facilitate unobtrusive classroom data collection in real time', and to 'track learning and teaching at the individual student and lesson level every day in order to personalise and thus optimise learning' (Hill and Barber 2014: 55). In particular, Pearson promotes 'the application of data analytics and the adoption of new metrics to generate deeper insights into and richer information on learning and teaching', as well as 'online intelligent learning systems' and the use of data analytics and automated artificial intelligence systems to provide 'ongoing feedback to personalise instruction and improve learning and teaching' (2014: 58).

Moreover, the Pearson report promotes a revolution in education policy. Its authors argue for a shift in focus from the governance of education through the institution of the school to 'the student as the focus of educational policy and concerted attention to personalising learning' (Hill and Barber 2014: 23). In short, the report seeks to make intelligent analytics into key policy instruments, through which policy will concentrate on the real-time tracking of the individual rather than the planned and sequenced longitudinal measurement of the institution or system. Along these lines, its authors note that the OECD itself is moving towards new forms of machine learning in its international assessments technologies, using 'a fully computer-based assessment in which a student interacts with a simulated collaborator or "avatar" in order to solve a complex problem' (2014: 49).

One development through which the use of big data in educational governance has been materialized is computer adaptive testing (CAT). CAT systems work by conducting a continuous, automated and real-time analysis of an individual's responses to a particular test or exam, using the data generated under test conditions to make predictions about future progress through it. The system measures whether responses to questions are correct, how long the test-taker takes to respond, and then automatically adapts the course of the test in response:

> One of the somewhat utopian promises of CAT measures is that they can operate as 'teaching machines' because they can respond far more quickly to student patterns than an individual teacher or a conventional test. In this, they clearly manifest a techno-managerialist philosophy of education. Equally, learning is constructed as

developmental, measurable and constituted through an outside knowledge, skill or performance that can become 'internalised' within the deficit student learners. (Thompson 2016: 4)

CAT systems are being mobilized in Australia specifically as part of the National Assessment Program – Literacy and Numeracy (NAPLAN). The data previously collected through pencil and paper NAPLAN tests have already been made available on the My School website as a public accountability mechanism. CAT makes NAPLAN testing ostensibly quicker and more accurate:

> It is further claimed that online testing has a range of benefits; from improved student outcomes through better data for effective teaching, improved accuracy for accountability purposes and the ability to link national testing with international testing … through interoperable digital protocols linking databases for more complete data. In short, one of the aspirations of online NAPLAN testing is creating a data infrastructure that connects databases, speeds up the feedback process and is more precise and more engaging for students – accountability and auditing as an 'invitation' to engage and be engaged. (Thompson 2016: 5)

The use of real-time CAT systems within NAPLAN is therefore part of 'a reconfiguring of intensities, or "speeds", of institutional life' as it is 'now "plugged into" information networks' (Thompson 2016: 2), making the collection, analysis and feedback from test items into a synchronous loop that functions at extreme velocity.

The use of such technologies is always catalysed by underlying ambitions, assumptions and imaginaries. Roberts-Mahoney et al. (2016: 2) have tracked the emergence of a political discourse around big data analytics in K-12 education in the US, critically analysing policy documents related to the emerging 'personalized learning technologies' of big data mining, algorithmic computation, learning analytics, and adaptive learning systems according to the values and assumptions that animate their use and define their purpose:

> Advocates for personalized learning technology … suggest that if digital platforms such as Google, Netflix, Amazon, and Facebook have transformed the way we conduct business, work, shop, communicate, travel, organize, and entertain one another, then it only makes sense to apply the operational logics of these platforms to educational systems in the name of progress and innovation.

These authors see data-driven technologies as part of a 'corporate school reform' movement that emphasizes market competition and business management as the key to educational improvement. Corporate reform processes include privatization and marketization of schools, and holding schools and teachers accountable for student academic performance through the standardization of curriculum, teacher evaluation systems and high-stakes testing. They identify 12 key reports from the USA (from government departments, commercial businesses and advocacy coalitions) that advocate the use of data-driven technologies, and trace how they produce a key discourse of human capital development that emphasizes career readiness and potential for economic productivity in high-skills technology-based sectors. These policy documents and the technical policy instruments they promote:

> position teaching and learning within a reductive set of economic goals and pur-poses that emphasize human capital development and training future workers … [and] advocate for the expansion of data-driven instruction and decision-making, while conceptualizing learning as the acquisition of discrete skills and behavior modification detached from broader social contexts and culturally relevant forms of knowledge and inquiry. (Roberts-Mahoney et al. 2016: 2)

Put simply, 'teaching and learning are increasingly being measured and quanti-fied to enable analysis of the relationship between inputs (e.g. funding) and outputs (e.g. student performance) with the goal of maximizing economic growth and productivity and increasing human capital' (Fontaine 2016: 2).

Alongside this emphasis on human capital development is a repositioning of teachers as 'coaches' or 'guides' whose professional judgement is to be at least augmented by, if not displaced to, objective forms of algorithmic assessment and evaluation. In some cases, teachers are treated by big data advocates as 'data col-lectors' who 'no longer have to make pedagogical decisions, but rather manage the technology that will make instructional decisions for them', since 'curricu-lum decisions, as well as instructional practices, are reduced to algorithms and determined by adaptive computer-based systems that create "personalized learn-ing," thereby allowing decision-making to take place externally to the classroom' (Roberts-Mahoney et al. 2016: 10).

The kind of corporate education reform movement represented by these tech-nologies and the policy aspirations that animate them, then, prioritizes the idea that curricular, pedagogical and assessment decisions should shift from public school settings to private providers of commercial technology and digital learning platforms; that it should be oriented mainly toward efficiently preparing students for the twenty-first century global economy; and that teacher professional auton-omy should be minimized as experience, expertise and deliberations are deemed less relevant, less accurate and less efficient than algorithms (Saltman 2016).

The new real-time data instruments such as CAT and personalized learning technologies shift the emphasis from the 'intimate accounting' of the institution through its historical datasets to an 'intimate analytics' of the individual through real-time digital datastreams. While much has been written on comparison in educational governance, as noted earlier, most of it has focused on the global comparability of different countries facilitated by the collection and analysis of international assessment datasets. Big data analytics platforms change the focus of such techniques of comparison by enabling the individual student's datastream to be compared with global datasets of (potentially) millions of other students in a recursive fashion. As the individual's performance on a particular task is monitored, it is continually compared with norms algorithmically inferred from a global dataset, and then used for customizing future instruction.

Equally significantly, many analytics platforms are programmed with the capacity to anticipate or predict pupils' probable future progress. Predictive analytics techniques form the basis of many contemporary social media and consumer 'recommender systems' (e.g. Amazon, Spotify) (Bulger 2016). Transplanted on to the educational context, this kind of predictive profiling provides institutions with actionable intelligence that can be used to determine appropriate pre-emptive pedagogic interventions. In addition to the predictive analytics functions, some 'adaptive learning' platforms also feature 'prescriptive analytics' capacities. Prescriptive analytics can automate actions in a feedback loop that might modify, optimize or pre-empt outcomes. The big data logics of social media are firmly articulated into the governing practices of education through such instruments, which function through the same principles of recommender systems such as those of Facebook and Trip Advisor. In this way, the governing logic of global comparison becomes a real-time event concentrated to the scale of the individual among the global masses.

Ultimately, the analytics being proposed for mobilization in the policy analysis and decision-making process anticipate a new form of 'future-tense' educational governance. They make every individual learner into the focus for a constant and recursive accumulation, analysis and presentation of data, real-time feedback, probabilistic predictions, and future-tense prescriptions for pedagogic action. These analytics capacities complement existing large-scale database techniques of governance such as those of national departments of education, statistical agencies and international organizations such as the OECD. But the deployment of big data practices in schools is also intended to accelerate the temporalities of educational governance, making the collection of data, its processes of calculation and its consequences into an automated, real-time process operationalized 'up close' from within the classroom and regulated 'at a distance' by expert centres of algorithmic calculation. While OECD data influences the conduct of national policymakers over distinct long-term temporal intervals, advocates of educational big data analytics aspire to target the conduct of the individual student in real-time and automatically, shaping performance and progress in class in ways that sculpt their conduct according to norms inferred from a growing global database. Driven by economic logics, the norms contained in the database tend to focus on the measurement, monitoring and subsequent prescriptive management of human capital development.

These developments are part of the transformation termed 'fast policy' (Peck and Theodore 2015). In the educational context, quantitative data have become especially significant for fast policy, as measurement, metrics, ranking and comparison all help to create new continuities and flows that can overcome physical distance in an increasingly interconnected and accelerating digital world (Lewis and Hogan 2016). Numbers form the evidential flow of fast policy, enabling complex social, political and economic problems to be rendered in easy-to-understand tables, diagrams and graphs that can move at speed between policymaking locales, via the advocacy of transnational actors, and influence decision making and other processes. The potential of data analytics is to accelerate fast policy processes further to the real-time temporal rhythms of the digital datastream. Real-time fast policy technologies represent a new form of active intervention in education governance.

Conclusion

Although digital governance remains an emerging form of government practice, within education specifically the current embrace of an imaginary associated with digital big data is indicative of a contemporary shift towards the digital governance of education. In this model, authorities are beginning to (or are being encouraged to) engage with the digital timestream of educational data as it is generated, and then mobilize the data extracted from it for the purposes of improved decision making in relation to policy, institutional management or even pedagogic practice within classrooms. The historical and temporally-bounded datasets associated with existing regimes of governing through data – what has been termed the 'infrastructure of test-based accountability' (Anagnostopoulos et al. 2013) – are being augmented with (or perhaps displaced by) fast policy approaches utilizing real-time datastreams that can be automatically analysed and then acted upon.

Educational governance is increasingly being practised through new digital techniques and methods of political analytics, whereby 'new governmental arrangements are created, which link the digital sphere of code, software and programming with various settings in politics, administration or school practice' (Hartong 2016: 532). The embeddedness of educational practices of many kinds in highly coded settings means that the values, worldviews and aspirations of programmers, algorithm designers, human–computer interaction designers and data scientists, alongside those of specialist educational analysts and experts from within governmental departments as well as independent data mediators from data labs, think tanks, consultancies and commercial companies, can work from a distance to govern the ways in which educational institutions, matters and persons are known and acted upon.

The term 'digital education governance', then, registers the displacement of educational governance to new digitized sites of expertise in data collection and analysis, and also acknowledges the role of digital software, code, algorithms in governing and guiding the conduct of diverse educational actors and institutions.

Increasingly, education is being governed through the knowledge gained from its digital trails and timestreams, and through the new forms of technical expertise such as data science and data analytics that make the production of knowledge about educational problems and the specification of their solutions possible. Such techniques of digital education governance are now being enacted within many government education departments, but also – and equally importantly – by other educational authorities and experts such as those of international organizations, independent data analysis agencies and commercial companies. Within all of this, existing techniques of accountability, performativity and human capital development are being reworked, reinforced and reproduced, as well as accelerated to high velocity, scaled-up to voluminous capacity, and expanded in scope to encompass a wider variety of inputs.

While digital governance remains underdeveloped as a state strategy, then, aspirations to govern significant sectors of society such as education through big data practices are growing. A shared future vision of the governmentalization of big data is emerging. In other words, digital governance is part of a larger big data imaginary being made attainable in the present through specific data practices and infrastructures. Education is in some senses acting as a beta-test site for techniques of digital governance that are set to be scaled up to state strategy.

5

THE SOCIAL LIFE OF EDUCATION DATA SCIENCE

Learning analytics, educational data mining and metrological platforms

Educational data mining, learning analytics and adaptive learning platforms have become key technologies for the imagined improvement of education. When the former Google executive Max Ventilla established a chain of new schools in San Francisco in 2013, his ambition was to transform the ways in which schools are run. The AltSchool chain he set up has become what Silicon Valley entrepreneurs call a 'full-stack' company: an organization that consists both of a digital platform and a physical service, like Uber in the public transport sector and Airbnb in hospitality. It is staffed by teachers as well as by software engineers and data analysts, with some of its staff development time dedicated to 'hackathons' where they collaborate to delegate 'robot tasks' such as routine data entry to software.

Underpinning the actual schools that constitute AltSchool is a software platform consisting of a powerful software aggregation and data analytics tool which:

> pulls in assessments from individual student work, projects, and 3rd party standards, forming a comprehensive view of a student's progress in each area. An educator can quickly see where a student has demonstrated mastery and where they need to improve specific skills. (AltSchool 2016)

The software platform, which it describes as a new 'central operating system for schools', consists of two main applications – the 'Playlist' tool for students and the 'Progression' tool for teachers – as well as a parent communication application. 'A Playlist is a customized to-do list for students to manage their work', claims the AltSchool website (AltSchool 2016). 'Educators curate a Playlist for each student. Within the Playlist, students can view their assignments, communicate with their teacher, and submit their work. Educators can then provide feedback and assess student work'. In addition, the teacher tool Progression 'provides a comprehensive portrait of a student's progress in math, language arts, and social-emotional development. It tracks a student's practice and trajectory ... and gives educators a rich view of past learning experiences, patterns, successes, and areas that need support. Insights from Progression inform how an educator plans future learning experiences and sets goals' (AltSchool 2016). These tools, AltSchool's founder has claimed, are part of 'a revised conception of what a teacher might be: "We are really shifting the role of an educator to someone who is more of a data-enabled detective"' (Mead 2016).

Allied to this, its guiding philosophy and values are drawn from student-centred progressivism. AltSchool emphasizes 'personalizing learning to student needs and passions' through 'experiential learning' and 'social and emotional learning' approaches. AltSchool is, in other words, both a private school chain run on progressivist principles of student-centred personalized learning, and a software development company with ambitions to scale its product. A recent profile of AltSchool in *Wired* magazine characterized it as:

a decidedly Bay Area experiment with an educational philosophy known as student-centered learning. … To that, however, AltSchool mixes in loads of technology to manage the chaos, and tops it all off with a staff of forward-thinking teachers set free to custom-teach to each student. … This puts AltSchool at the intersection of two rapidly growing movements in education. Along one axis are the dozens of edtech startups building apps for schools; along the other are the dozens of progressive schools rallying around the increasingly popular concept of personalized education. (Lapowsky 2015)

Notably, AltSchool's founder, Max Ventilla, was formerly head of 'personalization' at Google. He was one of the key executives responsible for Google Now, the service that tracks its users' online activities, location and communication data in order to provide algorithmically automated digital experiences. As an ideal, personalization has captured the imagination of new educational technology startup companies and venture capital investors alike, and has helped to drive massive investment in educational technology since 2010 (EdSurge 2016).

Ultimately, as a software platform, a school and an entrepreneurial company combined, AltSchool translates the social media personalization experience, and specific technical systems, into the progressivism of student-centred experiential learning. In autumn 2016, AltSchool announced it was to begin distributing its software platform to other schools, with ambitions to 'apply the company's formula to a network of private, public, and charter schools across the US' (Alba 2016). Another profile piece noted that AltSchool's founders and investors hoped it could 'help "reinvent" American education: first, by innovating in its micro-schools; next, by providing software to educators who want to start up their own schools; and, finally, by offering its software for use in public schools across the nation, a goal that the company hopes to achieve in three to five years' (Mead 2016).

AltSchool is significant because it demonstrates how a student-centred discourse of personalized learning is being deployed as a way of framing and justifying the use of big data analytics directly within the apparatus of the school. This data-driven approach to schooling is not simply being catalyzed by entrepreneurial ambitions, however. It is the product of a recent rise in data scientific ways of understanding learning and educational institutions and practices. In *Learning with Big Data: The future of education*, Mayer-Schonberger and Cukier (2014: 4) suggest that 'big data is invading all of education, with profound implications for how the world learns':

Big data gives us unprecedented insights into what works and what doesn't. It is a way to improve student performance by showing aspects of learning that were previously impossible to observe. Lessons can be personally tailored to students' needs, boosting their comprehension and grades. It helps teachers identify what is most effective … . It helps school administrators and policymakers provide more educational opportunities at lower cost.

'For the first time,' they conclude, 'we have a robust empirical tool with which to understand both how to teach, and how to learn'. As this statement indicates, all of the possibilities they list of learning with big data are fundamentally underpinned by data scientific practices, methods and ways of thinking that appeal to the technical objectivity and neutrality of empirical observation and analysis. A new educational form of data science is emerging as a way of understanding learning, one that enthuses big data commentators and also catalyses new data-analytic approaches to schooling such as those of AltSchool.

In this chapter, I provide an examination of the emergence and growth of the field of 'education data science' (also see Williamson 2016b, 2016c). Education data science is a nascent field of academic and commercial research and development focused on designing techniques and applications for the analysis of educational and learning data through techniques such as educational data mining and learning analytics (Baker and Siemens 2013; Cope and Kalantzis 2016). The emphasis for the chapter is on unpacking the 'social life' of education data science, both in terms of its social production as a field – formed from an amalgamation of data science and the 'learning sciences', along with aspects of psychometrics and metrology (the science of measurement) – and its social productivity as a toolbox of techniques and applications that are reshaping how learning is measured, known and acted upon through data. Then, I consider the implications of education data science for educational research more widely. It has been claimed that in 'the era of digitally-mediated and incidentally recorded learning, data sciences may render anachronistic (expensive, inefficient, inaccurate, often irrelevant) many of our traditional research methods', and 'require the creation of new research infrastructures' and ethics frameworks for future educational studies (Cope and Kalantzis 2015: 219, 229).

Such claims prompt an examination of the ways in which education data science is producing a 'big data infrastructure' that may confine knowledge production and theory development to well-resourced commercial settings and specialist academic labs. This raises critical questions about privacy and data protection in relation to student data. Finally, the conclusion reflects on how educational institutions such as schools, colleges and universities are being reconfigured by education data science as 'metrological platforms', where the science of measurement defines the very purposes and practices of the institution. Though education data science is primarily a field of research and development, it requires its objects of study – schools, colleges, classrooms – to be highly instrumented for data collection. Its techniques and applications are increasingly to be found built in to the digitally-mediated college course or school classroom – AltSchool is perhaps prototypical of education data science practices being embedded in the environment and functioning of the school. Fundamentally, education data science constitutes an infrastructure for big data analysis and application in education. It combines technologies and practices from across commercial R&D and academic research disciplines and produces software analytics systems that might be embedded in the administrative and pedagogic apparatus of institutions.

As with other chapters, my intention is to examine how a big data imaginary has begun to animate technical and material developments that are changing the nature and purposes of education. Much of the discussion provided in the chapter revolves around the mobilization of algorithms in the performance of education data science. This field is fundamentally algorithmic in its operations, both in the sense that it makes extensive use of algorithmic forms of calculation to undertake its analyses and also in the sense that a certain imaginative appeal to the apparent neutrality and objectivity of algorithms is made by its promoters. In this sense, education data science treats algorithms both as material things that can do productive work and as an authoritative concept:

> To understand the social power of algorithms is to understand the power of algorithms as code whilst also attempting to understand how notions of the algorithm move out into the world, how they are framed by the discourse and what they are said to be able to achieve. (Beer 2017: 10)

For that reason, my approach in the chapter is to consider the wider social and discursive framing that surrounds education data science as an algorithmic field of expertise and activity; that is, its 'social life' as an expert field of thought and action. I start by situating my examination of education data science in recent sociological debates about the 'social life of methods' and then examine the 'socialization' of education data science as it has emerged from expert settings in both academic and commercial domains of activity.

The Social Life of Methods

Education data science encompasses techniques of research on education and learning as well as the development of new applications. In this sense, it is to a large extent a methodological field, one that includes a wide range of data-based R&D activities such as big data analytics, data mining, learning analytics and adaptive learning platform development and testing. As a field of methodological expertise, education data science has focused primarily on developing analytics techniques and applications within higher education (HE). The recent proliferation of online courses such as Massive Open Online Courses (MOOCs), learning management systems and the availability of institutional analytics from the field of business intelligence have all been deployed within HE settings, leading to imaginings of the 'smart university' driven by big data (Lane 2014). For-profit vendors of these data-driven software systems have established education data science approaches within the university setting. Many offer MOOCs as part of their pedagogic apparatus and utilize management systems, analytics and data visualization tools such as data dashboards as 'automagical' decision support systems for strategic planning and management (Wolf et al. 2016).

However, education data science has begun extending its imaginary of big data-driven education to the schools sector too. For example, the New Zealand government announced a new regulatory framework for online learning which will open up a market for any private or commercial provider to get public funding to offer online education, in competition with public schools (New Zealand Ministry of Education 2016). This development not only connects online platforms that can be used to collect and analyse learner data with public schools, but suggests that conventional public schools might even be sidelined as learners are attracted to the flexibility of online course provision. Such a shift, if it occurs at scale, would certainly open the door for a massive expansion of education data science techniques beyond HE.

AltSchool provides a prototypical case of education data science applications being embedded as a kind of 'operating system' that orchestrates a school's entire administrative and pedagogic approach. Notably, by the end of 2016, with a new incoming political administration in the USA, renewed enthusiasm for the kind of data-driven approach to personalized schooling was expressed by commercial companies and non-profit foundations and campaigning coalitions. New education reform lobbying groups such as the Foundation for Educational Excellence, KnowledgeWorks, Future Ready Schools and the Technology for Education Consortium had noted new opportunities to roll out personalized learning software platforms alongside increased support for charter schools (Levy 2016; Pace 2016).

As these examples indicate, education data science as a field aspires to apply its expertise across schools *and* HE, as well as in diverse kinds of non-formal online learning environments. What it has accomplished in HE to date is merely indicative of its ambitions to go to scale in the application of big data analytics technologies across the entire spectrum of educational provision.

As a primarily methodological field, education data science needs to be situated in recent debates about the 'social life of methods'. By social life of methods, what is meant is a critical engagement with methodological devices which resists framing them simply as technical tools but makes their affordances and capacities into the object of social scientific inquiry (Savage 2013). According to this perspective, methods are social because they are shaped by the social, cultural, economic and political circumstances in which they have been produced and of which they are a part (Law et al. 2011). Methods are designed for particular purposes, through the work of advocates, as devices for examining, seeing, knowing and interpreting the world. Methods are also social because they in turn help to shape that world. The discoveries made by research conducted through particular methodological devices are not objective facsimiles of an existing world but are consequential for 'ways of knowing' and acting in it (Ruppert et al. 2013: 24).

Methods for studying big data have been the particular object for social life of methods studies. This is because big data has been widely promoted as providing a statistical window on to social realities, and have been perceived as representing an innovation in social science (Lupton 2015a). It follows from this that digital methodological devices such as big data analytics and data mining technologies are fundamentally reconfiguring the ways in which social science can be performed, and the kinds of analyses, interpretations and insights into social worlds made possible (Marres 2012). New 'digital methods' enable digital data to be explored in new ways, and also to produce novel insights that might change the ways social phenomena are perceived and then acted upon (Rogers 2013). The notion of 'socializing methods' registers a double process of socially producing and enacting methods, and of mobilizing methods to make sense of the social world and wrap new social norms around it (Ruppert et al. 2013). The next sections therefore engage with these double processes of socializing methods, first by considering the social, organizational and disciplinary origins of the field of education data science.

Socializing Education Data Science

Educational data science itself is an emerging, transdisciplinary field, building on data scientific practices as well as existing knowledges and methods drawn from the psychological and cognitive 'learning sciences' (Cope and Kalantzis 2016). As a set of practices, educational data science is being developed in both academic settings and commercial organizations, and represents a redistribution of methods across sectoral boundaries (Williamson, forthcoming). In a historical overview of the emerging field, Piety et al. (2014) have defined education data science in terms of a combination of 'Academic/Institutional Analytics', 'Learning Analytics/Educational Data Mining', 'Learner Analytics/Personalization' and 'Systemic Instructional Improvement'. These areas of research and development have begun to coalesce around shared questions, problems and assumptions over the last decade, particularly with the formation of specific professional associations, conferences and academic journals.

These authors particularly highlight how a community of researchers began to converge around educational data mining from about 2005, and from 2010 onwards joined with the learning analytics community to form a field that 'has begun to receive combined attention from both federal policymakers and foundation funders and is often seen as the community dealing with "Big Data" in education' (Piety et al. 2014: 3). They term it a 'sociotechnical movement' with shared interests that cut across the boundaries of their original communities. By sociotechnical movement what they mean is that 'the enabling conditions and key technologies emerge across sectors giving rise to multiple sets of innovations that may at times seem disconnected, but are often related and interdependent' (2014: 4–5). They also point out that a sociotechnical movement can gain traction when society's 'expectations are such that the innovations come at a time when there is other general interest in the kinds of changes that the innovations make possible' (2014: 5). Thus they note how there has, in recent years, been both increasing capability to produce data and a greater public appetite for the use of data across many areas of education. They also highlight how new forms of evidence – log files, conversational records, peer assessments, online search and navigation behaviour, and others – are raising big questions and 'disrupting' traditional ways of working in educational research, 'acting in a way similar to *disruptive innovations* that alter cultural, historical practices and activity systems' (2014: 5).

Education data science comprises a cross-sector and inter-organizational network of actors, technologies and practices. One of the key actors in this network is the Lytics Lab (short for Learning Analytics Laboratory), established at Stanford University to 'advance the science of learning through the use of data and digital technology' (Lytics Lab 2016). The Lytics Lab is an important site in the short social life of education data science. In 2011 the founders of the Lytics Lab organized a series of networking events which brought together representatives of organizations from various academic departments, philanthropic foundations, US government departments, commercial edtech companies, testing agencies and computing corporations to develop the agenda for education data science, culminating in a major report (Pea 2014).

Thanks to these efforts of the Lytics Lab's founders, a network of organizations focused on learning analytics and education data mining has grown rapidly. One of the participating organizations in the Lytics Lab workshops, the global edu-business Pearson has established a Center for Digital Data, Analytics and Adaptive Learning to practice educational data science in-house, as well as a Center for NextGen Learning & Assessment to develop new kinds of automated assessment scoring and analytics approaches. The Connected Intelligence Centre at the University of Technology Sydney, the Institute of Technology at the Open University, the LINK (Learning Innovation and Networked Knowledge) Research Lab at the University of Texas at Arlington, and the Centre for Research in Digital Education at the University of Edinburgh are key academic sites of learning analytics R&D, and there is a substantial and fast-growing body of both educational data mining and learning analytics literature (e.g. Baker and Siemens 2013; Clow 2013; Siemens 2013). The Society for Learning Analytics Research (SoLAR) and the Learning Analytics and Knowledge (LAK) conference that it has organized annually since 2011 are also key to the emergence of the educational data science field (Siemens 2016).

As well as being an inter-organizational network with its own social life, education data science also advances a highly normative agenda in relation to educational transformation. As an association linking the various organizations and actors in the education data science network, SoLAR has had explicit goals both in terms of technical R&D and pedagogic innovation:

Advances in knowledge modeling and representation, the semantic web, data mining, analytics, and open data form a foundation for new models of knowledge development and analysis. The technical complexity of this nascent field is paralleled by a transition within the full spectrum of learning (education, work place learning, informal learning) to social, networked learning. These technical, pedagogical, and social domains must be brought into dialogue with each other to ensure that interventions and organizational systems serve the needs of all stakeholders. (Siemens 2016)

Education data science is constituted, therefore, through a network of organizations and associations, events and publications through which knowledge, techniques and normative aspirations can be shared, and is enacted through a range of expert technical practices of data mining and analytics.

Educational data science demands advanced technical and methodological expertise. It has been claimed that 'while the learning analytics and educational data mining research communities are tackling the question of what data can tell us about learners, relatively little attention has been paid, to date, to the specific mindset, skillset and career trajectory of the people who wield these tools' (Buckingham Shum et al. 2013). Educational data scientists are required to be experts in both learning analytics and educational data mining, as well as in a host of related techniques. Its disciplinary origins have been traced to computer science techniques of computational statistics, data mining, machine learning, natural language processing and human–computer interaction (Piety et al. 2013).

In order to grow the expertise of the field as a 'big data infrastructure' for education, the Lytics Lab founding director Pea (2014) has called for much more support from governments for this sector, and details the need for new undergraduate and graduate courses to support its development. His report establishes the need for a new kind of 'professional infrastructure in the field of learning analytics and education data mining, made up of data scientists (straddling statistics and computer science) who are also learning scientists and education researchers' (Pea 2014: 17). Specifically, he identifies 'several competencies for education data science' that would contribute to this professional infrastructure, including: (1) computational and statistical tools and inquiry methods, including traditional statistics skills as well as newer techniques like machine learning, network analysis, natural language processing, and agent-based modelling; (2) general educational, cognitive science, and sociocultural principles in the sciences of learning; (3) principles of human–computer interaction, user experience design, and design-based research; and (4) an appreciation for the ethical and social concerns and questions around big data, for both formal educational settings and non-school learning environments (Pea 2014).

Expert techniques in psychometrics and educational measurement, cognitive neuroscience, bioinformatics, computational statistics, and other computational methods have also been promoted as education data science has sought to establish itself as a distinctive field. These disciplinary practices and competencies offer a clear sense of the style of thinking underpinning educational data science, particularly its computer science and data science origins twinned with primarily psychological, cognitive and neuroscientific theories of learning – or 'learning science'.

Likewise, Cope and Kalantzis (2016: 9) point out that education data science repositions researchers of education as 'data collaborators' who can work alongside instructional software designers, teachers and learners, since 'the division of instruction and assessment is blurred in the era of big data' and 'so also is the division blurred between the data used for pedagogy and the data used by researchers in the educational data sciences'. They further note how massive quantities of educational big data will require education data scientists to: (1) develop techniques and methodologies appropriate to dealing with whole 'census' data rather than 'sample data'; (2) adopt 'multiscalar' perspectives whereby 'scaling up or down, zooming in or out, offers a range of viable perspectives on a shared data source'; (3) adopt 'short time frames, feeding small incremental changes back into the learning environment', as well as 'longitudinal time frames as a consequence of data persistence'; (4) trace 'heterogeneity in data, e.g. different paths in adaptive learning environments, salient activities of outliers'; (5) conduct 'microgenetic causal analysis, e.g. learning progressions for different students, differential effects traceable in varied learning paths'; and (6) integrate 'quantitative and qualitative analyses; increasing importance of theory in data analyses' (Cope and Kalantzis 2016: 10). As this list demonstrates, education data science is a highly technical field of emerging knowledge production, as well as led by highly normative aspirations in relation to improving learning outcomes.

Education data science depends on the parallel discourses and practices of both data science, with its promises of algorithmic calculability and objectivity, and learning science approaches which treat learning as psychological processes that can be measured through computable processes. In this sense, education data science is an evolution of psychometric forms of expertise and disciplinary practice. As a field of psychological measurement, psychometrics has been at the very centre of educational assessment techniques such as large-scale standardized testing (O'Keeffe 2016). Psychometrics combines psychological theories with instruments, methods, materials and tools of data production that appear to provide a scientifically objective test of psychological traits, abilities and learning.

In the big data context, psychometrics is now additionally combining with real-time data analytics and machine learning systems to produce a new subdiscipline of 'psycho-informatics', which has been presented as an epochal shift in the science of psychological measurement. Psycho-informatics, it is claimed, is:

about to induce the single biggest methodological shift since the beginning of psychology or psychiatry. The resulting range of applications will dramatically shape the daily routines of researchers and medical practitioners alike. Indeed, transferring techniques from computer science to psychiatry and psychology is about to establish Psycho-Informatics, an entire research direction of its own. (Markowetz et al. 2014: 405)

Based on 'the vision of a transparent human' (Markowtez et al. 2014: 410), psycho-informatics makes use of wearable sensors that can track movements and smartphones to trace online activities, and then deploys data mining and machine learning in order to detect, characterize and classify behavioural patterns and trends as they change over time. Like psycho-informatics, education data science rests on a technological vision of unprecedented tracking of student behaviours and actions through big data and their analysis through algorithmic techniques of data mining and machine learning. This psycho-informatic approach treats mental life and learning as if they could be known mathematically and computationally, and, having been made measurable, as if they could then be enhanced or optimized.

These notes on the social life of education data science indicate how its origins lie in an organizational mix of academic and commercial research centres, linked by associations and affiliations into a global network of R&D and advocacy work. It combines data science methods and epistemologies with those of the psychological sciences, especially psychometrics and emerging psycho-informatics of behaviour tracking through big data analytics. Ultimately, education data science acts as a new kind of data-driven metrological field that is committed to the scientific measurement of learning, and that also aspires to a normative vision of how teaching and learning processes can be improved via big data.

Data Science Pedagogy

In summer 2016, the social media company Facebook announced that it was partnering with Summit Schools Network, a charter schools network headquartered in Silicon Valley, to introduce a new 'student centred learning system'. The Summit Personalized Learning Platform developed by the partnership is a data-driven learning system with built-in courses made up of projects and focus areas vetted by Stanford University's centre for assessment and learning (Summit Learning 2016). By tracking students' engagement and progress on each of the courses, the system automatically adapts to allow students to 'work through playlists of content at their own pace and take assessments on demand' and enable teachers to 'use that data to personalize instruction and provide additional support through mentoring and coaching'. Available for free online, the Summit Personalized Learning Platform is highly indicative of how educational data science approaches such as educational data mining, learning analytics and adaptive learning platforms have migrated from the R&D lab to the pedagogic apparatus of the school. Schools outside of the official Summit Schools Network can also join as part of a Summit Basecamp program which 'provides teachers and schools across the US with the resources they need to bring personalized learning into the classroom' (Summit Basecamp 2016). At the core of the Summit Personalized Learning Platform is a powerful suite of learning analytics techniques and applications.

Learning analytics is perhaps the most prominent application of education data science for personalized learning. Learning analytics software is designed to enable individual students to be tracked through their digital data traces in real-time, to provide automated predictions of future progress, and thus to optimize learning and the environments in which it occurs (Siemens 2013). An international review of learning analytics has identified a number of key rationales:

> By merging information known about individuals in advance, such as their prior qualifications, with data accumulated about their educational progress, learners likely to withdraw can be identified earlier than in the past. Personalised interventions such as advice from a tutor can then be taken to help to try to retain those students. ... [E]ducators are likely to have an interest in maximising the academic performance of their students and enhancing the overall experience of attending their institutions. ... Learning analytics can furnish teachers with information on the quality of the educational content and activities they are providing, and on their teaching and assessment processes. Some analytics are used ... to monitor the performance of their students while the module is taking place; they can then adapt their teaching. (Sclater et al. 2016: 12)

The report highlights how learning analytics platforms have been mobilized for purposes of efficiency and accountability, to identify at-risk students, to review course content and improve pedagogy, and also to give learners 'more control' over their learning by 'providing analytics-based systems to help students to select future modules, building on data about their career choices, aptitudes and grades for previous modules to provide optimum pathways through their studies' (Sclater et al. 2016: 9).

Learning analytics is also described as an 'enabler for the development and introduction of adaptive learning – i.e. personalised learning delivered at scale, whereby students are directed to learning materials on the basis of their previous interactions with, and understanding of, related content and tasks' (Sclater et al. 2016: 5):

> Adaptive learning systems are emerging to help students develop skills and knowledge in a more personalised and self paced way. These too may depend on data about a student's aptitude and performance, together with fine grained details of their clickstream, enabling the educational content to be tailored to their level of understanding as they progress through it. (Sclater et al. 2016: 13)

Together, learning analytics and adaptive learning platforms appear to promise to provide a fine-grained analysis of learner performance, progression and behaviour, largely in line with the psycho-informatic approach to understanding behaviours from big data traces, and also to transform the provision of content.

Learning analytics is often described in terms of both its techniques and applications. Techniques involve the specific algorithms and models for conducting analytics; applications involve the ways in which insights generated from analytics are then codified into software products designed to impact and improve teaching and learning. For example, 'an algorithm that provides recommendations of additional course content for learners can be classified as a technique. A technique, such as prediction of learner risk for dropout, can then lead to an application, such as personalization of learning content' (Siemens 2013: 1386). Through the development of specific learning analytics applications, data scientific ways of approaching education have been translated into powerful pedagogies which are designed to support the 'personalization' and 'optimization' of learning through being embedded in courses and institutions.

Underpinning the pedagogic aims of education data science, though, are techniques such as model construction. Through advances in machine learning, artificial intelligence techniques and statistical analysis, 'new data-based discoveries are made and insight is gained into learner behavior … where discovery occurs through models and algorithms' (Siemens 2013: 1386). Likewise, 'a pre-eminent objective' in educational data science is that of:

> *creating a model of the learner.* What characteristics are important as predictors for what is appropriate to support the learner's personalized progress? What are the classes of variables and data sources for building a learner model of the knowledge, difficulties, and misconceptions of an individual? (Pea 2014: 24, italics in the original)

Learner modelling, cognitive modelling, behaviour modelling, probability modelling and 'knowledge domain modelling' (the mapping of the knowledge structure of a discipline) are crucial predictors in any learning analytics platform. Once these models are combined, they can then be used to produce predictive models of learner progressions, and to automatically prescribe changes in a course or test that might be required by the individual.

The techniques and applications of education data science are being translated into practice across HE and the schools sector by increasingly powerful and wealthy commercial providers. The start-up company Knewton has become one of the world's most successful learning analytics platforms, providing back-end support to educational content produced by Pearson (the world's largest educational publisher and e-learning provider) as well as many others. In one of its technical white papers, the Knewton platform is described as 'a flexible, scalable system for delivering adaptive learning experiences and predictive analytics across arbitrary collections of content in different learning environments' (Wilson and

Nichols 2015: 4). Knewton claims to support the learning process through three core services: personalized recommendations for students, analytics for teachers and students, and content insights for application and content creators.

For Knewton, the value of big data in education specifically is that it consists of 'data that reflects cognition'; that is, vast quantities of 'meaningful data' recorded during student activity 'that can be harnessed continuously to power personalized learning for each individual' (Knewton 2013: 13). The collection and analysis of this 'data that reflects cognition' is a sophisticated technical and methodological accomplishment. As stated in scientific documentation on the Knewton website:

> The Knewton platform consolidates data science, statistics, psychometrics, content graphing, machine learning, tagging, and infrastructure in one place in order to enable personalization at massive scale. ... Using advanced data science and machine learning, Knewton's sophisticated technology identifies, on a real-time basis, each student's strengths, weaknesses, and learning style. In this way, the Knewton platform is able to take the combined data of millions of other students to help each student learn every single concept he or she ever encounters. (Knewton 2013: 2)

The analytics methods behind Knewton include 'sophisticated algorithms to recommend the perfect activity for each student, constantly' (Knewton 2013: 8). Knewton works by collecting a variety of different educational attainment data combined with psychometric information and social media traces to produce a kind of 'cloud' of data on each individual that can be used as a quantitative record for data mining and predictive analytics. Though much of its activity has previously been confined to HE, by partnering with Pearson the two companies aspire to take learning analytics and adaptive learning systems into the schools market.

Through their partnership, Knewton combines the power and potential of its adaptive learning platform with Pearson's content and distribution, promising to 'usher in a new era of personalized and customizable education products':

> The Knewton Adaptive Learning Platform™ uses proprietary algorithms to deliver a personalized learning path for each student ... . 'Knewton adaptive learning platform, as powerful as it is, would just be lines of code without Pearson', said Jose Ferreira, founder and CEO of Knewton. 'You'll soon see Pearson products that diagnose each student's proficiency at every concept, and precisely deliver the needed content in the optimal learning style for each. These products will use the combined data power of millions of students to provide uniquely personalized learning.' (Knewton 2011)

This partnership is perfectly aligned with Pearson's current ongoing attempts to reposition itself as a major source of expertise in relation to big data analytics in education. Its Center for Digital Data, Analytics & Adaptive Learning was established in 2012 to use data science methods to 'capture stream or trace data from learners' interactions' with learning materials; enable computer analysis to detect 'new patterns that may provide evidence about learning'; and 'to take a learner's profile of knowledge, skills and attributes and determine the best subsequent activity' (DiCerbo and Behrens 2014). Pearson's ongoing ambition to mine students' data for patterns is based on the understanding that 'faced with a very large number of potential variables, computers are able to perform pattern identification tasks that are beyond the scope of human abilities ... not only to collect information but also detect patterns within it' (DiCerbo and Behrens 2014).

The computational method of pattern recognition enacted by Pearson and Knewton operates by taking trace data of a user's activity and then subjecting it to detailed analysis using various measures; data captured from a single individual can then be aggregated with other users' data to see if they can be combined into generalizable indicators of aspects of learning. To do this, Pearson's report details how pattern recognition analysis can be used to trace and match patterns in learners' activities:

> Learner interactions with activities generate data that can be analysed for patterns. ... Performance in individual activities can often provide immediate feedback ... based on local pattern recognition, while performance over several activities can lead to profile updates, which can facilitate inferences about general performance. (DiCerbo and Behrens 2014)

The ambition of the centre is to promote the application of data analytics to generate insights into teaching and learning, but also to provide a constant stream of feedback that might be used to personalize the learning experience for each student and thereby improve their measurable learning outcomes.

Framed by the discourse of personalized learning, education data science is destabilizing the idea that school knowledge should be contained in standardized curricula, and proposes instead that students' access to knowledge should be determined by automated, algorithmic processes and techniques. Algorithmic machine learning techniques make it possible to predict students' probable future progress through predictive analytics processes, and then, in the form of prescriptive analytics, to personally tailor their access to knowledge through modularized connections that has been deemed appropriate by the algorithm. For example, in Knewton's scientific documentation, it is stated that all content in the platform is:

> linked by the Knewton knowledge graph, a cross-disciplinary graph of academic concepts. The knowledge graph takes into account these concepts, defined by sets of content and the relationships between those concepts. Knewton recommendations steer students on personalized and even cross-disciplinary paths on the knowledge graph towards ultimate learning objectives based on both what they know and how they learn. (Knewton 2013: 6)

The Knewton platform's 'knowledge graph' treats knowledge in terms of discrete modules of content that can be linked together to produce differently connected personalized pathways. In this sense, knowledge is treated in terms of a network of individual nodes with myriad possible lines of connection, and the Knewton platform 'refines recommendations through network effects that harness the power of all the data collected for all students to optimize learning for each individual student' (Knewton 2013: 8). For Knewton, knowledge is nodal like a complex digital network, and constantly being refined as machine learning algorithms learn from observing large numbers of students engaging with it: 'The more students who use the Knewton platform, the more refined the relationships between content and concepts and the more precise the recommendations delivered through the knowledge graph' (2013: 7).

Through techniques of personalization such as the knowledge graph, powerful educational data science companies such as Pearson and Knewton are increasingly seeking to control educational data, which impacts on what school knowledge is made to 'count' and how it is organized and encountered by students through being rearranged for them as personalized learning pathways by adaptive learning analytics platforms. Instead of schools transmitting official school knowledge via curricula and subject arrangements, adaptive learning analytics platforms automatically curate students' encounters with knowledge by conducting a constant diagnostics on their learning progressions, predicting outcomes, and then prescribing personalized learning pathways which route them through a networked knowledge graph of 'nodalized' and modularized content.

Productive Predictive Methods

Metric systems such as learning analytics can exert productive effects on people's lives. In the broader social context, 'the way that people are *measured*' then '*circulates* through the data systems of the organizations collecting it', which 'shapes the *possibilities* for the treatment of that individual. This will also then have implications for how people live – as they come to live a predictive life in which they adapt to the measures' (Beer 2016a: 8). A particular issue is raised by learning analytics developments concerning the predictive algorithms that determine the personalization of content and its acquisition. Notably, the machine learning algorithms that underpin most analytics packages – particularly those, like learning analytics, of the predictive variety – need to be trained to learn from:

> a data sample that has already been classified or labelled by someone. The existence of the classifications is crucial to the work of the techniques. The classification becomes what the data mining techniques seek to learn or model so that future instances can be classified in a similar way. (Mackenzie 2015: 433)

Data analytics platforms, including adaptive learning analytics, produce algorithmically-learned knowledge that can be deployed to shape future activities, though this is dependent on the classificatory labour of the algorithm designers. Even advanced machine learning systems require feedback to confirm that they are processing and organizing data as their developers intended.

The practical activities of training and classifying data have been recognized explicitly by some in the educational data science community:

> Statistical patterns in machine learning data are to a significant extent creatures of patterns already built into supervised training models. In the case of unsupervised machine learning, the statistical patterns make sense only when they are given explanatory labels. (Cope and Kalantzis 2016: 11)

In this sense, how machine learning systems are designed to learn from data become highly significant to the ways in which insights are generated from the data or how students might be targeted for future intervention. For example, Knewton, as noted above, relies on a knowledge graph and on techniques of content classification and taxonomization for its functioning. Without such processes of categorization taking place, content cannot be fitted into the knowledge graph. Once the classification of content has taken place, it can then be:

> organized in a graph-like structure, which means that the student flow from concept-to-concept can be optimized over time, as Knewton learns more and more about the relationships between them through data. Every student action and response around each content item ripples out and affects the system's understanding of all the content in the system and all the students in the network. (Knewton 2013: 14)

The human act of training the algorithm to identify and learn from things that have been classified or labelled for inclusion in the knowledge graph indicates how machine learning is both a form of automated knowledge production, but also one shaped by people working in specific labour conditions, within institutional frameworks, according to professional commitments, worldviews and disciplinary theories about the ways in which the world works. These contextual factors are consequential to the ways in which machine learning is trained, re-trained and checked to ensure the accuracy and generalizability of its models, and have significant implications for how data may be communicated and visualized for the apprehension, interpretation and meaning-making practices of people.

Beyond being trained on data selected by their engineers, adaptive learning analytics platforms also have their own algorithmic and mathematical rules. Previous studies have shown how great effort needs to be put into the kind of calculative practices that generate educational data from standardized tests and assessments, which demonstrate how mathematical promises of 'objectivity' are ultimately produced in social contexts, and in turn change perspectives on the very things they enumerate (Sellar 2015b). Turning something into numbers – such as a learning task – transforms it because it alters how that object can be understood and how it might be acted upon. Extending such claims to learning analytics, key algorithmic techniques such as 'cluster analysis' work according to operational properties that do not merely discover patterns in data, but actively constitute them.

Cluster analysis, in basic terms, consists of mathematical or algorithmic techniques for organizing data into groups of other similar objects. It is often used in quite exploratory stages of data analysis and research, as a way of seeking patterns in masses of disorganized information. The fundamental rule of cluster analysis is that it groups together objects that appear to have a high degree of similarity and association. It is concerned with finding structures between data points:

> The algorithm starts by establishing a number of clusters, each with its own centre, it then takes data points and assigns them to clusters using distance from the centres as a criterion. Centres are then recalculated and the process starts again until distance is minimised, so that stable results can be obtained. (Perrotta and Williamson 2016: 9)

Clustering techniques are put to work in the analysis of student data in many learning analytics platform – as they are in Knewton's heirarchical agglomerative clustering (HAC) method. The key point here is that for data to be fitted into a cluster or group of other similar data, certain parameters and criteria have to be set in advance. Cluster analysis does not necessarily 'discover' patterns in data, but can actively construct a structure as it calculates distance between data points according to pre-established criteria. Certain operational impositions and mathematical formalizations are therefore made to stabilize the results into a 'best fit' solution:

> In data mining, hierarchical clustering is a method of analysis which aims to construct a hierarchy or structure of clusters. At Knewton, the technique is used to detect latent structures within large groups and build algorithms that determine how students should be grouped and what features they should be grouped by. (Knewton 2013: 5)

Through learning analytics, such cluster algorithms therefore impose upon the ways that optimal learning pathways are prescribed for student users of the system. These algorithmic rules produce personalized learning pathways as patterns that dictate how students encounter content and information, and structure the ways they form knowledge. In short, the numbers and the calculations performed on them change the learning process that has been enumerated.

Learning analytics platforms proceed from specific kinds of calculative practices that are, therefore, socially produced but also socially productive. Their internal processes rely on human practices such as the design of cluster algorithms and the training and classification undertaken to make machine learning algorithms perform 'in the wild'. Taking this further, Ruppert et al. (2015) have detailed that big data come into being through social and technical practices in specific expert settings, practices which do not just generate those data but also 'order, manage, interpret, circulate, reuse, analyse, link and delete them' according to 'the normative, political and technical imperatives and choices ... [of] the actors and institutions that shape big data'. But these processes are not merely the product of human practices; they exceed human capacities and enable work to be undertaken automatically that would be impossible with human hands. The classification of content into a knowledge graph by Knewton, and the structuring of clusters of both students and content by cluster analysis algorithms, are in this sense consequential in terms of both 'what is known' *about* learners as their participation is tracked, measured and analysed by the system, and 'what is known' *by* learners as they are steered by algorithmic means through knowledge that has been 'unbundled' into modularized nodes within content networks.

Knowledge, Theory and Ownership

The dominance of the learning analytics and adaptive learning market by companies like Pearson and Knewton raises significant issues about data ownership and control in education. This further raises the question 'who owns big data?' (Ruppert 2015) as digital data is being used by increasingly powerful technical organizations to produce knowledge and drive decision making:

> It has become profitable to build a database containing the entire world's knowledge. The few for-profit companies that own the data and the tools to mine it – the data infrastructure – possess great power to understand and predict the world. (Nielsen 2015)

Such knowledge-producing technologies and techniques pose distinctive challenges for education, not least as new kinds of educational analytics platforms are mobilized to generate constant real-time streams of learner data and then transform them into predictive knowledge that might be used as actionable and practical intelligence to shape pedagogic intervention. For companies such as Knewton and Pearson, it has become desirable to build a database containing huge quantities of educational data, and they own the data and tools to analyse it and so understand and make predictions based upon it. Pearson and Knewton in this sense 'own' educational big data, and stand to benefit from generating novel insights from it.

Underpinning the work of Pearson and Knewton is a powerful disciplinary apparatus associated with data scientific knowledge work, one that valorizes a 'big data epistemology' (Kitchin 2014b) of scientific objectivity – which seeks to use numerical insight to inform new practices of educational management – but also theory generation. For example, John Behrens, the founding director of

Pearson's Center for Digital Data, Analytics & Adaptive Learning, has claimed that data mining 'the billions of bits of digital data generated by students' interactions with online lessons as well as everyday digital activities' will challenge current theoretical frameworks in education, as 'new forms of data and experience will create a theory gap between the dramatic increase in data-based results and the theory base to integrate them' (Behrens 2013). Pearson is claiming to be opening up a 'theory gap' in existing understandings of effective education and learning, and at the same time working on new digital methods and data scientific approaches that might produce new knowledge to fill that gap. As a global educational media company and increasingly a policy influencer, it is then very well positioned to use the insights it gains from the data to come up with new kinds of solutions in the shape of new software products for schools, or even new policy solutions for governments (Hogan et al. 2015).

What these developments illuminate is the ongoing construction of a data infrastructure for knowledge production and theory generation in education, one orchestrated by powerful technology companies and their technical experts, and increasingly enacted by calculative practices encoded in algorithms that exceed human capacities. Knewton is up-front about being 'education's most powerful data infrastructure platform' (Knewton 2013). The concept of a data infrastructure is particularly important as infrastructures are the physical, material and organizational structures that underlie and orchestrate social, political and economic life (Bowker and Star 1999). Others have proposed the notion of a 'knowledge infrastructure' as 'enormous transformations have occurred over the last 20 years in our systems for generating, sharing, and disputing human knowledge' (Edwards et al. 2013: 1). New infrastructures for the production and communication of knowledge associated with the Internet, big data and social media have proliferated widely, leading to 'a world where knowledge is perpetually in motion. Today, what we call "knowledge" is constantly being questioned, challenged, rethought, and rewritten' and 'norms for what can count as "knowledge" are clearly changing' (2013: 6–7). These authors note that new knowledge infrastructures, beyond being technical systems, reinforce or redistribute authority, influence and power by advancing the interests of some and displacing the prospects of others, while simultaneously exerting effects on the shape and possibility of knowledge in general.

In the above examples from education, the infrastructures of data generation and knowledge production are changing as education data science organizations like Pearson and Knewton enter the scene and populate them with their data scientific practices and accompanying business plans. The dominance of education data science by a small number of connected organizations means that knowledge production in the field of education itself is being redistributed, often to commercial settings where the specialist technologies and the expert technicians are available. Educational theory is also being generated in these settings. In a review of education data science methods, it is noted that 'theory is needed more than ever to frame data models, to create ontologies that structure fields for data collection, and for model tracing' (Cope and Kalantzis 2016: 11). This point about increasing the importance of theory in big data analysis raises significant questions about the sites of expertise where such theory generation might occur.

As the examples of the Stanford Lytics Lab and the Pearson Center for Digital Data, Analytics & Adaptive Learning indicate, educational data science is being concentrated in well-resourced and highly-financed research centres and labs. Because they have access to a technical, professional and financial infrastructure for collecting and analysing big educational data, these organizations are increasingly able to generate new insights and knowledge from those data. They can mine the data for patterns, and in so doing seek to formulate new explanations and theories for the learning processes that those data indicate or reveal. With governments increasingly keen to mobilize big data for purposes of educational research, Pearson, Lytics Lab, Knewton and so on are positioning themselves as leading centres of data-driven intelligence, with the infrastructure in place to conduct data-driven educational analyses. Owning the databases, in other words, is a prerequisite for knowledge production and theory generation, and puts powerful education data science organizations at a competitive advantage over other sites of educational research.

In this sense we can see educational data science as an increasingly influential and powerful field of knowledge production and theory generation in education. The fact that this field is being concentred in the hands of significantly well-resourced labs and centres such as those associated with Stanford and Pearson raises real questions about the generation of new theories that might themselves reshape the ways in which processes of learning are known, understood and accepted more widely in the educational research field. Few education departments in universities have the big data infrastructure to conduct the kinds of advanced data scientific studies that Pearson or Stanford can. In other words, there is a political economy dimension to educational theorizing as it seems to be migrating toward well-resourced commercial research centres like those of Pearson or academic institutions with close industry and governmental connections such as Stanford. How learning is understood, conceptualized and theorized looks increasingly to be led by actors with access to the technical, professional and financial infrastructure to generate insights from big data. Some of them, like Pearson, might then stand to gain commercially by designing and patenting e-learning software resources on the basis of the theories they have generated – essentially a case of locking-in a theory to a specific technical innovation. The technological future of education is one where software 'patents *become* the theory', which 'does not guarantee that these companies have developed technologies that will help students learn. But it might mean that there will be proprietary assets to litigate over, to negotiate with, and to sell' (Watters 2016).

As big data practices increasingly infuse educational research, and educational analyses are performed by profit-making companies with ownership of the relevant big data infrastructure and proprietary machine learning algorithms, the question of who owns educational theory, and how it becomes patented into edtech products, is becoming one of serious concern. The ownership of educational big data, the generation of educational theory, and the application of such theories within proprietorial systems and software patents may then be leading to a near-future scenario where private companies with market imperatives and proprietorial systems become government-approved sites of expertise into learning and teaching processes. In this context, how learning is conceptualized and understood looks likely to become a kind of intellectual property for privately-resourced research centres.

Data Protection and Privacy

The rise of education data science as an infrastructure for big data analytics in education raises significant issues about data privacy, protection and the responsible use of student data. In a recent news article, it was reported, for example, that the company Blackboard had conducted a massive data mining exercise on student data from 70,000 courses hosted on its learning management platform. In response to this study, one commentator said:

> We've entered a world in which many of the most data-rich organizations about student teaching and learning are not schools – they're learning-management systems, they are MOOC providers, they are other instructional-service providers ... . We have to start thinking about how to govern data and research in this new plural domain ... . We have every reason to think that the proprietary sector should be taking leadership in building that science, but how we architect and govern that science is the frontier. (Young 2016)

These comments ultimately amount to an agenda to regulate and govern education data science, in particular to ensure that it maintains strict codes of conduct and policies related to data privacy and protection as increasing numbers of studies occur outside of the academic research context with its ethical boards and frameworks.

Others have suggested that educators in universities and schools need to develop 'data literacy' to be able to 'make decisions and to develop skills to analyse student needs and adjust practices using student performance data':

> Data literacy for teaching is the ability to transform information into actionable instructional knowledge and practices by collecting, analyzing, and interpreting all types of data (assessment, school climate, behavioral, snapshot, longitudinal, moment-to-moment, etc.) to help determine instructional steps. It combines an

understanding of data with standards, disciplinary knowledge and practices, curricular knowledge, pedagogical content knowledge, and an understanding of how children learn. (Mandinach and Gummer 2016: 44)

Teacher data literacy includes the responsible use of student data, taking full account of privacy and data protection, though it is complicated by the fact that the majority of student data is collected and analysed by proprietorial systems that are beyond the control of classroom teachers in schools or lecturers in universities and colleges. Wider recognition is emerging that the collection and analysis of student data, particularly among commercial vendors and their proprietorial systems, may even cause harm.

The legal scholar Solove (2006) has produced an influential taxonomy of 'privacy harms' associated with information systems. He has organized such harms into four categories: (1) *data collection*, which refers to how businesses, people and governments collect information about an individual 'data subject'; (2) *information processing*, which is conducted by those that collect the data – the 'data holders' – who then process, store, combine, manipulate, search and use it; (3) *information dissemination*, in which the data holders transfer or release the information, and move the information away from the control of the individual; and (4) *invasions*, which refers to impingements directly on the individual.

Under the first heading, data collection, are included specific techniques of *surveillance*, or the watching, listening to or recording of an individual's activities, and *interrogation*, consisting of forms of questioning or probing for information. In the examples provided earlier, it is clear that students are increasingly the data subjects of surveillant analytics activities that allow their personal information to be probed and investigated, often without their knowledge and often performed automatically by algorithmic techniques. The second category, information processing, includes *aggregation*, the combination of different pieces of information about an individual; *identification*, or the linking of information to individuals; *insecurity*, carelessness in protecting stored information; *secondary use*, or the use of information collected for one use for a different purpose without the data subject's consent; and *exclusion*, concerning the failure to allow the data subject to know about the data held about them, or its handling and use. Again, learning analytics platforms proceed by aggregating students' data to provide a detailed digital timestream of their lives, raising significant concerns about insecurity and secondary use of their data. The third category, information dissemination, includes *breach of confidentiality*, breaking an assurance to keep an individual's data confidential; disclosure, the revelation of information that can affect how others judge an individual; *increased accessibility* and amplification of one's data availability; *appropriation* of a data subject's identity to serve another's interests; and *distortion*, which consists of the dissemination of misleading or false information about an individual data subject. The growth of a serious commercial industry around student data suggests that their information is now being appropriated for commercial gain. Their data are also open to unintended data breaches and hacking attacks. While distortion may not be occurring explicitly, it is also clear that the aggregation of student data traces can lead to the formation of digital identities – or 'data doubles' – that are only partially representative of their lives, and may be used as an informational substitute to account for their subjective, embodied and sensory experiences.

Finally, in the fourth category, invasions, are the privacy harms of *intrusion* into one's life, disturbing daily activities and altering routines; and *decisional interference,* which refers to attempts to intervene in an individual's decision making. Rather than engaging students in their right to involvement in decisions about important matters that affect their own lives, many analytics systems appear to distribute decision making to automated, proprietary systems where students have little opportunity for involvement in the handling or use of their own data. The collection, processing and dissemination of student data may be intrusive, as it is used to inform decision making by others that might impact upon their own lives, or it may even interfere in their own decision making, persuading students to make decisions about their lives on the basis of information that has been shaped through multiple layers of human and technical intervention. The use of predictive machine learning techniques in learning analytics platforms is perhaps the paradigmatic example of decisional interference, as algorithms are programmed and optimized by their designers to pre-empt students' decisions and nudge them to change their lives according to norms inferred from calculations performed automatically by algorithmic assemblages within massive databases.

As a result of growing recognition of the kind of privacy harms and risks associated with big data in education, the protection of student data has become a major concern. For example, in 2016 the educational consultancy Ithaka S+R and Stanford University's Center for Advanced Research through Online Learning (CAROL) launched a collaborative project on 'Responsible Use of Student Data in Higher Education'. It included the publication of a report reviewing new uses of student data for research (whereby data are used to conduct empirical studies to advance knowledge in the field), application (to inform changes in institutional practices, programs or policies) and reporting (to report on the educational experiences and achievements of students to internal and external audiences), and the major practical and ethical questions surrounding these uses (Alamuddin et al. 2016). The report's authors note in particular the challenge of controlling the use of student data when it shifts between educational institutions and digital platforms that are in commercial ownership:

> Many of the new uses rely on the integration of data from multiple systems within institutions, each of which has a different business owner. Moreover, third-party providers are embedded throughout the process of generating, collecting, and analyzing student data. ... In part because of the boundary-defying nature of their

work, researchers, institutions, and other organizations engaged in these areas often struggle to define who owns the data, who has authority to use them, in what ways, and for what purposes. ... In an environment with unclear ownership and governance, the most prominent risk is overreach – that someone will take action that crosses an ethical line. (Alamuddin et al. 2016: 3–4)

In response to these concerns, the Responsible Use of Student Data project has defined 'responsible use' in a way which encompasses questions of data privacy and protection, but also captures values such as transparency, student autonomy and the obligation to take action to reduce adverse effects or privacy harms. Nonetheless, considerable unresolved concerns remain about the adequacy of contemporary student privacy and data protection policies and frameworks in relation to the rise of educational data science practices of big data analytics and data mining (Zeide 2016).

Conclusion

Educational data science and its applications are turning educational institutions – schools, colleges and universities alike – into metrological platforms that perform a constant scientific form of measurement of learning processes. AltSchool is perhaps the prototypical metrological platform for schools, a 'full-stack' service that juxtaposes advanced data science techniques and applications on to the physical space and the pedagogic apparatus of the school. The sociologist of statistics Desrosieres (2001) has described 'metrological realism' as the assumption that statistics provides a more or less accurate reflection of reality. Educational data science is, arguably, a field of metrological realism, one that proceeds by assuming that big data can reveal human behaviours, psychological traits and mental processes such as learning through constant scientific measurement and quantification. As a consequence, education data science – like similar new fields such as psycho-informatics – is enthusiastically pursuing the production of new knowledge and theory generation along metrological realist lines.

Yet as Desrosieres (2001) insists, to enumerate something is to change it as its quantitative representation circulates into decision making and other activities. Thus what is known as learning is becoming the subject of potential transformation as it is quantified in learning analytics systems. Before it can even be counted, learning has to be framed and classified in such a way that it can be included in a database. What particular behaviours or signals from the student can indicate that learning is taking place? Education data science has set itself the task of addressing such questions. In the effort to do so it is seeking to generate novel theorizations and understandings that might transform the ways in which educational institutions are organized and pedagogic practices are conducted.

In effect, through education data science a new process of active 'infrastructuring' (Edwards et al. 2013) is occurring in education. Through building a new big data infrastructure for education, the organizational network that constitutes education data science is generating data about educational practices and processes in ways that allow them to exert a number of effects. First, they are making digital big data into a new form of expert knowledge and actionable insight that can inform educators' decision making, but which might also be utilized by autonomous machine learning systems to generate prescriptions for pedagogic intervention. Second, they are using insights from 'data that reflects cognition' to shape how students access, encounter, experience and receive knowledge through algorithmically-defined personalized learning pathways rather than the pedagogic pathways through school knowledge defined by teachers.

Third, in so doing, these organizations are reworking school knowledge itself, redefining the shape of knowledge as a nodal network of contents and concepts that can be connected up into optimal pathways for each individual. Much of the school knowledge contained in a curriculum would need significant reshaping and reorganization to fit a database, thus repositioning education according to a 'narrow conception of learning as the acquisition of discrete skills ... detached from broader social contexts and culturally relevant forms of knowledge and inquiry' (Roberts-Mahoney et al. 2016: 1). And fourth, they are constructing a new organizationally networked infrastructure of knowledge production and theory generation, one with the economic resources and social networks required to become a powerful source of influence in educational research. They are producing new kinds of evidence about learning and education according to a big data epistemology of metrological realism and methodological techniques of psycho-informatics that are increasingly attractive to policymakers and governments.

The massive reach of proprietorial systems that have been programmed to make sense of student data is now raising serious concerns about privacy, data protection and the potential harms associated with its collection, processing and dissemination. Perhaps most notably, education data science brings with it the capacity for student data to be used for decisional interference, by algorithmically delimiting opportunities and pre-empting individuals' learning pathways under the guise of 'personalized learning'. The metrological approach to quantifying learning is ultimately changing the ways in which students might view themselves, allowing algorithmic systems to make decisions about the direction of their learning on their behalf, and even interfering in their own embodied decision making as they are encouraged to measure themselves in metrological terms. The capacity for data to be used for decisional interference is especially pronounced through the use of new technologies of emotional and behavioural data analytics, to which we turn our attention in the next chapter.

6

THE CompPsy
COMPLEX

Non-cognitive learning, psychological enhancement and behaviour change

I s it possible to data-mine the embodied, behavioural and emotional aspects of learning? In the science-fiction novel *The Red Men* by Matthew de Abaitua (2007), a wealthy commercial organization named the Monad undertakes to construct a detailed simulation of a British town by training its artificial intelligence system with data about its environment and inhabitants. Through a massive and detailed data mining of the intimate personal details, emotional lives and behaviours of each of its inhabitants, the Monad aspires to create the ultimate simulated focus group, a testbed on which new government policies can be run to predict and model their outcomes in real-time. The simulated data analogue to the town it is modelled on eventually becomes a complex psychological laboratory for political experimentation, through which the feelings and behaviours of the population can be predicted and ultimately pre-empted. While *The Red Men* is a fictional account, it represents well a current sociotechnical imaginary which envisions a future in which populations can be subjected to intimate emotional measurement and behavioural auditing, for the purposes of making predictions about their future feelings and thus designing pre-emptive strategies that might serve governmental ambitions while impacting positively on individual and collective behaviours.

Already, new technologies are being designed to make emotional measurement and management possible in educational institutions. While educational data mining and learning analytics have demonstrated the attainability of gaining new insights into academic learning from big data sources, other forms of digital data collection and analysis propose that the non-academic and non-cognitive aspects of learning can also be mined, known and understood. As we saw in the last chapter, great excitement is already being generated around the promises of 'psycho-informatics', or the application of computer science methods to the psychological tracking and analysis of behaviours. In this chapter, the focus is on the development and application of new kinds of devices and platforms that can measure and intervene in the body, behaviour and mood of the learner. As with many of the emerging big data technologies encountered in other chapters, the attempt to capture – and act upon – non-cognitive learning through digital data systems is animated by a powerful shared imaginary that is in turn catalysing applied technical development projects.

At the core of the chapter is the contention that psychological forms of expertise are interweaving with educational practices and associated computational methods of big data analysis. New psychological vocabularies for understanding children and learning are being produced, and reinforced through the design of specific technologies of psychological data collection and analysis. In the first part of the chapter I articulate the concept of the 'CompPsy complex' (Williamson 2016c) to delineate the emerging interdependencies of computation and psychology ('CompSci' + 'Psy'), and its 'biopolitical' goal to reshape the behaviours of citizens as governable subjects of digital capitalism. I then describe how 'non-cognitive learning' has become a significant concern in education, part of a new scientific knowledge of the mind that has been translated into education policy and practice.

Following that, the chapter focuses on specific examples of the CompPsy complex being enacted in specific educational projects and initiatives. Sections focus on emerging biometric techniques of mood detection and engagement measurement; on new kinds of body analytics that measure physical activity as an indicator of health and well-being; on the emergence of 'emotional learning analytics'; and then on behaviour monitoring and management devices that firmly locate the school classroom as the target for strategic psychological governance techniques of 'behaviour change'. In the discussion I explore how psychological measurement of non-cognitive learning is situated among emerging 'psycho-policies' that could hold schools accountable for students' affective development and personal qualities in ways that amount to a biopolitical strategy of psychological 'character' enhancement.

As with the simulated town of *The Red Men*, education is being positioned as a psychological laboratory for measuring and experimenting on children's minds, moods and embodied behaviours as citizens of contemporary states characterized by big data mining. Underpinning the big data imaginary of the CompPsy complex is the belief that the emotional states of students can be decoded scientifically from reading the body, rather than by eliciting students' voices.

Psychological Computation

Psychology has long been influential in the organization and governance of modern societies. Rose (1999b) has influentially argued that psychological forms of knowledge, expertise and authority, or the 'psy-sciences', have played a major role since the late nineteenth century in shaping how people can conceive of themselves, speak about themselves and conduct their lives in particular ways. In particular, he argues that a 'psy complex' of affiliated forms of psy science and psy expertise have had a key role in constructing 'governable subjects' and in contemporary forms of political power. By this he means that psy has made it possible to understand human conduct, and therefore to develop practical techniques and 'know-how' for managing and acting upon human capacities for specific objectives. Psy, in other words, has made it possible to govern and administer individuals and wider populations.

The rise of psychological expertise over the last century is part of what Michel Foucault has influentially described as 'biopolitics'. The term 'biopolitics' signifies 'the entry of phenomena particular to the life of the human species into the order of knowledge and power, into the sphere of political techniques' (Foucault 1990: 141–2). Disciplines such as statistics, demography, epidemiology, psychology and biology have become the basis for new strategies of 'bio-power' which have brought human life into 'the realm of explicit calculation' (1990: 143) and made both individuals and populations amenable to social control and management:

> These disciplines make it possible to analyse processes of life on the level of populations and to 'govern' individuals and collectives by practices of correction, exclusion, normalization, disciplining, therapeutics, and optimization. ... The discovery of a 'nature' of the population ... that might be influenced by specific incentives and measures is the precondition for directing and managing it. (Lemke 2011: 5–6)

The concept of biopolitics, then, articulates how distinctive disciplinary practices, authoritative forms of knowledge, and historical truths about human lives have been developed by specialist fields such as the life science and psychological sciences, all of which might then be translated into specific practices for intervening in and governing human lives (Rabinow and Rose 2006). In other words, human life has been anatomized in terms of its biological and psychological features in ways that allow people to be measured, compared, evaluated and then acted upon by various psychological, medical and bureaucratic authorities.

Biopolitical practices of 'psychological governance' have become especially pronounced in recent years with the rising influence of behavioural economics. As an expert psychological discipline, behavioural economics is increasingly contributing its insights into the roots of human behaviour to governmental 'behaviour change' agendas around the world. This new psy-science has ascertained that humans are susceptible to unconscious emotions and sentiments, and can therefore be 'nudged' to change their behaviours, choices and decision-making processes towards healthier lifestyles and more emotional fulfilment (Jones et al. 2013). Behavioural economics has become a 'new policy knowledge' that has been translated into diverse domains of governmental intervention (McGimpsey et al. 2016). As such, 'nudge theory' assumes that:

> everyday decisionmaking can and should be framed in particular ways to encourage ('nudge') people to choose in advantageous ways. This idea recasts the design of large-scale systems (such as savings, health care and education) as 'choice architectures' designed for the production of optimum outcomes (from the perspective of the system designer) without removing freedom of choice from the individual. (Bradbury et al. 2013: 247)

Behaviour change approaches assume that public policy (in education, for example) can be designed to recognize the irrational and emotional components of human behaviour. It is premised on a psychological view that humans routinely make 'bad' decisions that are poor for their health and well-being, and focuses on the design of social and economic systems that can stimulate 'good' decisions and choices and lead to positive outcomes. Policy designs can then change people's behaviours in the direction of greater emotional fulfilment, happiness and well-being, while simultaneously serving governmental ambitions and commercial objectives (Davies 2015).

Behavioural economics and nudge techniques have now been installed in the dominant operating model of many governments. In 2008 the UK Government Office for Science produced a report entitled *Mental Capital and Wellbeing* that claimed the future prosperity and well-being of society in an increasingly interconnected and competitive world would require greater policy attention to mental and material resources (Foresight 2008). The mental capital report represents how the psychological improvement of individuals in order to 'correct' their behaviours and feelings has become the target of government efforts to secure social order and economic productivity and prosperity through citizens' happiness and well-being. Subsequently, the UK government has begun measuring the well-being and happiness of the population through the Office for National Statistics' annual Measuring National Well-being survey; charitable organizations and think tanks have launched initiatives such as the Action for Happiness campaign; and there has been a rapid translation of psychological expertise – via intermediaries such as think tanks – into public policies designed to encourage people to change their lives and their behaviours in the direction of happiness and well-being. This new expertise of well-being centres on 'the self as a site of intervention, whereby the … subject is articulated in terms of the abstracted measurement of emotional states and capacities … with strong echoes of the logic of "smart investment"' (McGimpsey et al. 2016: 8). Through this logic of smart investment, citizens are exhorted to turn their lives 'into an exercise in wellness optimization' as part of an emerging 'biomorality' that demands individuals act to become more happy and healthy even as governmental austerity has cut into welfare and social services provision (Cederstrom and Spicer 2015: 3). In other words, the sciences of happiness and well-being have now ascertained how to measure the emotions, and nudge theory can be applied to help the 'suboptimal citizen' make choices that better serve their own and society's well-being.

These psychological techniques and aspirations are now being implanted in everyday life through digitized technologies of persuasive computing, sentiment analysis and emotional analytics. The psy-sciences have begun to embrace 'psycho-informatic' big data analyses (Markowetz et al. 2014), face-reading software, sentiment analysis and 'more emotionally intelligent computers' that can be taught how to interpret human emotional behaviours and produce social trend data on population mood (Davies 2015). The commercial sector has already seen a surge in the development of 'machine emotional intelligence' applications that are designed to detect human sentiment and feelings through facial, speech and text analysis. Face-reading technologies often consist of facial detection, eye tracking, and specific facial position analytics; textual sentiment analysis can be performed through natural language processing, tone analysis and linguistic analysis; while speech analysis applications can detect emotion from common biological signals in the human voice through sonic algorithms. Such technologies are based on a synthesis of data analytics technologies and psychology, and most perform emotion detection based on seven main categories of human emotion: joy, sadness, anger, fear, surprise, contempt and disgust. For example, the classification of the emotions contained in facial detection technologies relies on techniques such as the physio-psychological facial action coding system (FACS) developed in the 1970s. It is used to describe how faces express emotion through muscle movements. Other emotion classification systems developed since then are similarly designed to correlate physiological indexes to their emotion explanation (Rose et al. 2016).

These technologies are captured in the term 'affective computing', and have significant consequences:

> The broader concerns of affective computing involves not only identifying human emotions and responding appropriately but also potentially ... to simulate human emotions such that the intended emotion might be recognizable to a human. Affective computing might potentially influence the human user, increasing persuasiveness, and in some cases deliberately generating a particular emotional response in the user. (Rose et al. 2016: 23)

Machine-based forms of emotional intelligence or affective computing, then, are intended not just to perform emotion-detection functions, but also to simulate emotions and by doing so to influence and persuade people through the affective register.

The field of 'persuasive computing' in particular represents the close-knit relationship between psychological behaviour change techniques and computational, data-driven methods. Researchers and developers of persuasive computing aim to create and apply psychological insight into how computing products – from websites to mobile phone software – can be designed to change what people believe and what they do (Fogg 2002). Persuasive computing demonstrates how the psychological theories underpinning the behaviour change agenda in the political domain have been translated into the design of digital products that are intended to influence long-term habitual behaviours and persistent routines towards particular objectives. Such persuasive technologies can be designed to exert 'hypernudges' whereby the individual's decision-making processes can be directed or guided in ways identified by the underlying software algorithm as 'optimal' by offering suggestions intended to prompt the user to make decisions and therefore modify their behaviours (Yeung 2017).

The availability of big data and persuasive computing technologies to commercial companies and government agencies is giving rise to a new form of 'digital capitalism', where the exchange of digital information over data networks is becoming the centre of many economic and social activities (Schiller 2015). Digital capitalism proceeds by making the creation and exchange of information and data – including that made and shared by consumers – into the source of commercial gain. Social media platforms have become especially significant to this shift, giving rise to 'platform capitalism', whereby platforms enrol users through a participatory culture and mobilize code and data analytics to realize a business model that prioritizes rapid up-scaling and the extraction of revenues from users' data trails (Langley and Leyshon 2016: 1). A similar model for government underpins approaches to 'digital governance', or the design of the state in the era of social media and big data (Dunleavy and Margetts 2015). Digital governance assumes that the activities, behaviours and sentiments of citizens – as well as their transactions with organizations and interactions with each other – can be mined in real-time from the datastreams available via platforms, and that new kinds of digital designs for government services can be created that might nudge and shape their behaviours towards desired outcomes, such as enhanced emotional health and well-being.

The datastreams of citizens' behaviours available from commercial social media platforms and the big data resources they collect are therefore valuable to governments wishing to understand and shape citizens' sentiments and actions. The emotional data available from all of these approaches and technologies are becoming key to a new style of government in which a constant audit of public mood and citizen sentiment can be used to inform new policy interventions. The sciences of nudge theory, happiness and well-being indicators, and the mobilization of techniques of sentiment analysis, represent the mass psychological surveillance of population mood being carried out by scientific experts on behalf of governments. These technologies enable unprecedented psychological tracking and gauging of the emotions of individuals and populations, but can also be programmed to judge and nudge feelings through techniques of persuasive computing. As a consequence, 'the truth of our emotions will, allegedly, become plain, once researchers have decoded our brains, faces and unintentional sentiments' and 'society becomes designed and governed as a vast laboratory, which we inhabit almost constantly in our day-to-day lives' (Davies 2015).

Within the parallel approaches of digital capitalism and governance, then, a new form of 'soft biopolitics' is emerging, one that functions through algorithmic sorting of users' data and is 'embedded and integrated within a social system whose logic, rules, and explicit functioning work to determine the new conditions of possibilities of users' lives' (Cheney-Lippold 2011: 167). In other words, the datafication of everyday life enables powerful social, commercial and political actors to conduct a constant algorithmic diagnostics of patterns of human life, emotional sentiments and behaviours, and to use the insights gained from those data to derive new models, classifications and theories of both individual and social behaviours (Ruppert 2012). This leads to the design of particular technologies to maximize those behaviours deemed appropriate by psychological expertise, shaping individuals with the correct behavioural and affective comportment for a desired social order. In this sense, the 'lines of code' that constitute many emotion-sensing and persuasive, behaviour-changing technologies are also 'codes of conduct', particular ways of conducting one's life that users are encouraged to inhabit, internalize and embody in the ways they comport and express themselves behaviourally and emotionally. Data-driven persuasive technologies are therefore ideal means to confer upon citizens particular ways of thinking and behaving – in other words, for educating citizens to participate in the dominant governing styles of society.

In the term 'CompPsy complex' what I am trying to capture is how computer science (CompSci) has amalgamated with the psy-sciences as a biopolitical strategy of psychological citizen optimization under digital capitalism and equivalent modes of digital governance. By analyzing citizens' sentiments via machine emotion intelligence applications and psychologically enhancing individuals via data-driven technologies of nudge and persuasion, various authorities are now involved in the attempt to build the mental capital, happiness, emotional health and well-being of citizens as a way of ensuring the smooth functioning and prosperity of society as a whole. Individuals and populations alike are increasingly amenable to a constant psychological and emotional analytics, producing an affective audit trail that can be mined for purposes of governmental prediction and pre-emption via new kinds of 'psycho-policies' (Friedli and Stearn 2015). This emerging political rationality of mood measurement and behaviour management via digital data analytics is manifesting in education through the merging of psychological expertise with educational technologies and governmental agendas about maximizing children's emotional well-being and other aspects of non-cognitive learning.

Non-Cognitive Learning

The role of psychological strategies in measuring and then shaping the behaviour of young people in schools is widespread, and has long historical origins (Popkewitz 2012). Through psychological techniques developed over the last century, children have been made visible and assessable through scales, charts, visual displays and other inscriptions pertaining to norms of posture and move-ment, personal habits, personality, and diverse forms of conduct (Rose 1996).

At least partly as a consequence of psy scientific forms of knowledge, expertise and authority, since the 1990s schools have become increasingly focused on the monitoring and management of children's emotional health, well-being and other non-cognitive or non-academic personal qualities and affective factors of learning. Major international organizations such as the World Economic Forum (WFE) have begun to promote the development and measurement of social and emotional skills, particularly through technological means (WEF 2016). The international organization the Organization for Economic Cooperation and

Development (OECD) has established its Education and Social Progress project to develop specific measurement instruments for social and emotional skills such as 'perseverance' and 'resilience'. The project is intended to generate evidence about children's emotional lives 'for policy-makers, school administrators, practitioners and parents to help children achieve their full potential, improve their life prospects and contribute to societal progress' (OECD 2015). These reports promote the idea that educational outcomes are dependent upon students developing social and emotional skills and other indicators of 'character', and are supporting the growth of new techniques of social and emotional measurement.

Policy proposals introduced in the US are now making the measurement of children's social and emotional skills in schools into a significant governmental agenda (Zernike 2016). Prominently, a report for the US Department of Education in 2013 promoted a 'shift in educational priorities to promote not only content knowledge, but also grit, tenacity, and perseverance' (Schechtman et al. 2013: v). As a result, new instruments have been developed to measure 'personal qualities' such as self-control, grit, character, growth mindsets and many others (Duckworth and Yeager 2015). In 2015, the US government initiated the Every Student Succeeds Act, a federal law requiring all states to collect information on at least one 'non-cognitive' or 'non-academic' aspect of learning. As a result, new ways of measuring social and emotional learning have been proposed (Fontaine 2016). New initiatives such as the Character Lab have been established to develop the science and practice of social and emotional measurement and character development; it promotes several distinctive 'character strengths': curiosity, gratitude, grit, growth mindset, optimism, purpose, self-control, social/emotional intelligence and zest (Character Lab 2016). The US state of California is leading the way in practice by trialing instruments to collect social-emotional data. These data will be used to evaluate the performance of schools in much the same way that academic test scores are used as a metric of performance. With Californian schools now under pressure to provide measurable evidence of progress on the development of students' personal qualities, this 'new accountability system is thought to be the largest effort to focus on and evaluate students' habits of mind' (Adams 2014).

Meanwhile, in the UK 'therapeutic education' has been increasing in both policy and practice through an emphasis on the social and emotional aspects of learning, well-being, happiness, self-esteem, psychological resilience and so on (Ecclestone and Hayes 2009). Campaigns such as Action for Happiness have sought to introduce 'well-being' and 'character development' into school curricula, which have been variously taken up by government. New careers for psychological experts have been made possible by the therapeutic turn, all informed by the view that the problem that needs to be addressed is some type of psychological deficit in the individual, rather than focusing on social, environmental or material causes of emotional problems (Furedi 2009).

The therapeutic trend in education is associated with the emergence of positive psychology in schools and the focus on teaching children happiness and well-being since the 1990s. Such initiatives are the product of psychological experts and gurus, whose theories and techniques of well-being optimization have become highly attractive to governments as ways of offsetting escalating trends in anxiety and depression among young people:

> Much of the interest in 'character', 'resilience' and mindfulness at school stems from the troubling evidence that depression and anxiety have risen rapidly amongst young people over the past decade, resulting in heightened rates of self-harm. It seems obvious that teachers and health policy-makers would look around for therapies and training that might offset some of this damage. ... In the age of social media, ubiquitous advertising and a turbulent global economy, children cannot be protected from the sources of depression and anxiety. The only solution is to help them build more durable psychological defences. (Davies 2016)

Such developments reinforce how psychological conceptions have had major impacts on many governmental policies in relation to the measurement and management of children's minds, while policies focusing on wider social, political and environmental determinants of children's engagement have diminished. The consequence is that children and young people are viewed not as individuals, 'but as an abstracted measurement of emotional development, as a quantitative point in a statistical correlation with projected future outcomes' (McGimpsey et al. 2016: 9).

As an exemplification of this therapeutic trend in education, at the time of writing, a great deal of attention is being paid to 'mindfulness' in education. School-based mindfulness initiatives are largely based on the assumption that young people are stressed and vulnerable, and can benefit from meditative practices that focus their energies on present tasks rather than longer-term anxieties caused by uncontrollable external social processes. But from a more critical perspective, mindfulness represents 'a biopolitical human enhancement strategy' to insulate youth from pathologies that stem from 'digital capitalism' – 'an exercise in pathology-proofing them in their capacity as the next generation of unpaid digital labourers' (Reveley 2015: 804). In other words, mindfulness is seen as a psychological cure for problems caused by wider changes in the social and environmental landscapes of a form of capitalism that derives value from the constant mining and analysis of information and data about people's everyday lives and behaviours.

The rise of a 'happiness industry' in recent years is a commercial, profit-seeking response to the pathologies and anxieties originally caused by contemporary capitalism, economic austerity and governmental priorities around performance measurement combined (Davies 2015). Instead of targeting the causes that underlie children's anxieties and concerns, initiatives such as mindfulness – and associated well-being schemes – represent a biopolitical technique that focuses on ensuring that children are adequately adapted and emotionally moulded to be able to cope psychologically with a demanding social and technical environment, and which requires the constant measurement of their emotional development to project future outcomes.

Ultimately, the therapeutic turn in education and the emphasis on non-cognitive learning, character development and so on, amount to a new psychological vocabulary for classifying, measuring and intervening on children. These developments are continuous with previous techniques invented by the psychological sciences which have provided ways of describing, representing and visualizing human mental capacities and behavioural characteristics. Psychology has made the human individual 'calculable and manageable' by turning spaces such as classrooms into 'mini-laboratories' for 'quantifying all the qualities of the human soul' (Rose 1996: 112). A range of new psychological ideas, concepts, initiatives and techniques is now being implanted in education, via new kinds of analytics, affective computing techniques and educational technologies, in ways that are intended to reshape behaviours, optimize emotional and embodied wellness, and enhance measurable 'mental capital' to fit with the demands of digital capitalism. In the rest of this chapter, I document how a CompPsy complex derived from juxtaposing computer science methods of data collection and analysis with psychological theories and governmental aspirations is now being enacted through specific technological products and projects targeted at schools.

Biometric Mood Detection

Biometric technologies play an increasingly substantial role in education, through technologies such as fingerprint scanning, finger-vein scanning or iris scanning (Patton 2016). Sources suggest that around one million pupils in UK secondary schools have had their data collected via automated biometric recognition system, which includes recording pupils' biometric data; storing pupils' biometric information on a database system; or using that data as part of an electronic process, for example, by comparing it with biometric information stored on a database in order to identify or recognize pupils (Big Brother Watch 2014). Such technologies are part of the steady rise of 'surveillance schools' and represent an advance on existing forms of educational surveillance such as CCTV security camera networks (Taylor 2013).

Biometric technologies are advancing quickly beyond simple techniques of video surveillance to encompass facial recognition and wearable technologies designed to collect biometric data from the skin. Many such biometric technologies have been developed specifically as part of the 'quantified self' movement, a global trend that involves people monitoring and measuring their physical activity, emotions, sleep, and so on (Lupton 2016). These technologies rely on miniature biosensor devices that combine a biological element (sweat, saliva, blood sample or CO_2) with a physiochemical detector that converts it into an electrical signal that can from there become part of a larger platform where it can be transformed into data and visualizations to be displayed on a screen (Nafus 2016).

As part of the broader field of affective computing, biosensor and biometric technologies for measuring children's moods have been developed for schools, though many remain prototypical to date. One prototype device, called EngageSense, consists of a computer-mounted webcam connected to facial recognition software and computer vision algorithms that have been designed to measure and monitor children's levels of emotional engagement through eye-tracking and facial expression. EngageSense is intended to provide teachers with an automated metric of student engagement throughout the day, which can then be used to tailor subsequent pedagogic routines to heighten positive emotional responses, such as motivation, attention and engagement, and minimize negative emotions such as confusion, distraction or anxiety. Machine vision is becoming a major industry as images shared on social media and surveillance systems enable faces and their emotions to be identified by algorithmic processes, such as Facebook's DeepFace and Google's TensorFlow (Paglen 2016). EngageSense is prototypical of how such algorithmic facial identification systems could be rolled out into schools.

Another prototype technology has been designed to detect excitement, stress, fear, engagement, boredom and relaxation directly through the skin. Student sensor bracelets or 'engagement pedometers' have been designed to send a small current across the skin and measure changes in electrical charges as the sympathetic nervous system responds to stimuli. Originally developed by affective computing researchers at the Massachusetts Institute of Technology (MIT) in 2010 with funding from the Bill & Melinda Gates Foundation, these electrodermal skin response bracelets – known as Q Sensors – measure how well the skin conducts electricity, which varies with its moisture level; sweat glands are controlled by the nervous system so skin conductance can be used as a physiological indicator of an emotionally aroused response (Simon 2012).

Though the Q Sensor was never commercially marketed for use in schools, its developers at MIT have evolved the technology into the Embrace watch-style sensor (Picard 2016). The Embrace watch has been enthusiastically endorsed in the WEF report on using technologies to foster social and emotional learning:

> The Embrace watch … is a wearable device that tracks physiological stress and activity. It can be programmed to vibrate when stress reaches a specific level, giving someone time to switch to a more positive response before stress gets out of control. Combining the functionality of the Embrace watch with coaching from parents and teachers may further enhance opportunities to build a child's social and emotional intelligence. (WEF 2016: 14)

More broadly, the WEF has advocated the use of wearable biometric sensor devices to track physical responses to learning situations, such as fluctuations in stress and emotion, and to 'also provide a minute-by-minute record of someone's emotional state, potentially helping to build self-awareness and even empathy, both of which are critical components of social and emotional skills' (WEF 2016: 14). The US Department of Education report *Promoting Grit, Tenacity and Perseverance* (Schechtman et al. 2013) also features a strong emphasis on the use of biometric technologies for the measurement of the affective aspects of learning. The report outlines how new biometric sensor systems can be used to measure non-cognitive factors and student dispositions such as grit, tenacity and perseverance that involve measuring physiological processes, and to measure and collect data on dispositions and engagement such as levels of frustration, motivation, confidence, boredom and fatigue.

Biometrics, biosensor and face-reading technologies record biophysical signals from the body of the child as indicators of underlying emotional processes, as defined by psychological forms of emotion classification and modelling. Such technologies consist of an amalgamation of technical expertise in affective computing, biomedical science, and biometric techniques of electrodermal monitoring, along with the psychology of emotional engagement. The underlying logic driving the promotion of these devices in education is to detect and measure the feelings of children, and to then target them for mood modification.

Emotional Learning Analytics

The analysis of children's emotional data has become a core concern in the emerging field of educational data science. For example, the leading educational data scientist Pea (2014: 28) has proposed using data scientific methods to engage with '"non-cognitive factors" in learning, such as academic persistence/perseverance (aka "grit"), self-regulation, and engagement or motivation' that are 'improvable by appropriate practices'. Various techniques of measuring the 'emotional state' of learners include collecting 'proximal indicators that relate to learning' through such techniques as 'facial expressions detected by a computer webcam while learning', plus other data sources like 'video, eye tracking, and skin temperature and conductivity' (2014: 32, 46).

The computational measurement of the emotional state of the learner is a clear manifestation of affective computing within the field of education. The WEF report on developing social and emotional learning through technology, for example, explicitly details the possibilities for affective computing in education:

Affective computing comprises an emerging set of innovations that allow systems to recognize, interpret and simulate human emotions. ... [T]his technology holds great promise for developing social and emotional skills such as greater empathy, improved self-awareness and stronger relationships. ... [A]rtificial intelligence and multimodal social computing could help improve cognitive, social and emotional skills. (WEF 2016: 15)

The identification and measurement of psychological indicators through content analysis, natural language processing, emotion questionnaires, as well as big data techniques of sentiment analysis and 'machine emotional intelligence' systems are all emerging expert techniques for mining children's emotions. As a consequence, it has been claimed that 'with increased affordances to continuously measure facial and voice expressions with tablets and smartphones, it might become feasible to monitor learners' emotions on a real-time basis' (Rienties and Rivers 2014: 15).

Similarly, education data scientists Piety et al. (2014: 3) also promote data science methods to measure 'student characteristics' such as 'differences in levels of academic motivation, attitudes toward content, attention and engagement styles, expectancy and incentive styles ... persistence through adversity ... [and] tenacity or grit'. The vocabulary of non-cognitive student characteristics of motivation, engagement, grit, self-regulation, emotional state and so on is highly indicative of the strongly psychological genealogy of the education data science field. It particularly points toward the possibility of using digital devices to collect and calculate data about children's emotions during educational experiences in real-time, and then offer psychologically defined prescriptions towards emotional maximization.

The wider field of learning analytics is itself underpinned by psychometric modes of psychological measurement and emerging techniques of psycho-informatics. The subfield of 'emotional learning analytics' takes psychometrics and associated forms of psychological monitoring and profiling to a much more fine-grained and intimate scale. Emotional learning analytics platforms are designed to capture real-time data about children's affective and non-cognitive experiences during learning programs, making extensive use of psychometrics, sentiment analysis and natural language processing, in order to enable the automatic detection, assessment, analysis and prediction of emotions through measurable behavioural indicators. The aim of emotional learning analytics is:

to integrate automatic emotion analysis ... into learning analytics measures in order to achieve a holistic view of the learners' progress and uncover any potential risks due to negative emotions ... [and] the use of the automatic detection, assessment and analysis of emotions to provide further assistance, personalised feedback and guidance in online courses. (Montero and Suhonen 2014: 165)

Automated forms of emotional learning analytics are assumed by their promoters to provide teachers with the relevant information required to decide on appropriate pedagogic intervention, enable educational data scientists to gain new insights into the affective dimensions of schooling, enable school administrators to access visualizations of pupils' affective experiences, and help children themselves to understand their emotions.

Significantly, emotional learning analytics and related applications depend on expert techniques that can classify human emotion. Rienties and Rivers (2014) have reviewed over 100 different measurable emotions that might be captured by emotional learning analytics platforms, each linked to different methods of identification, classification and measurement. Research on the emotions in education is rooted in different branches of the psy-sciences which have translated positive emotional concepts such as joy, satisfaction, motivation, pride and happiness, as well as negative emotional concepts such as frustration, boredom, confusion, stress and anxiety into measurable classification systems. Specialist psy expertise and knowledge about the affective dimensions of human life is coded in to emotional learning analytics platforms, providing automated ways to survey, codify, calculate, predict and maximize the emotional functioning of the learner. Such mood-detecting and behaviour-changing technologies are clearly continuous with the longer history of psychological surveillance, measurement and inscription of the young person as an 'object-child', rendered in 'manipulable, coded, materialized, mathematized, two-dimensional traces, which may be utilized in any procedure of calculation' (Rose 1996: 112). But they also make young people's emotional data 'actionable' so that the insights derived from it can be used to inform (and potentially automate) immediate intervention via new forms of affective computing.

Body Analytics

Closely related to data-driven devices of emotion detection and affective computing are devices designed to measure the physical activity of the body as a series of proxy indicators for one's overall health, fitness and well-being. Wearable devices for young people to measure their physical activities are now being marketed to schools, particularly for physical education. These devices closely resemble mainstream products used as part of the broad 'quantified self' movement, such as the Fitbit. The quantified self has become a cultural phenomenon, not just a technical fad, and the practices, meanings, discourses and technologies associated with self-tracking are the product of broader social, cultural and political processes and the role of particular experts of the body and health (Lupton 2016). As these technologies have been promoted for use in education, they have also been invested with specifically pedagogic aspirations and political agendas concerned with children's health and well-being (Williamson 2015b). These technologies constitute an emerging form of digitally enacted 'biopedagogy', or a pedagogy focused on the conduct of the body itself, which conveys knowledge, competencies, skills and moral codes relating to what the body is and ought to be, and what 'body work' needs to be done to make it 'fit' both in terms of health and the social order (Evans and Rich 2011).

An emerging market in wearable physical activity monitors is now being promoted to schools that combine tracking and biosensing capacities with built-in algorithms for calculating and estimating health and fitness levels. These technologies combine smartphones, tablet and wearable computing devices with online platforms for health and fitness analysis, and are capable of collecting and disseminating large amounts of personal biophysical data. Many health-tracking apps for children are designed to encourage healthy lifestyles, aid dietary planning and encourage physical activity. Popular features of health-related apps for children include the concept of caring for virtual creatures by fulfilling their dietary and fitness needs, often combined with various gaming and competition elements and online social media platforms.

One fitness app for kids launched in 2016, Monsuta Fitness, combines the popular appeal of augmented reality games such as Pokémon GO (which requires players to locate virtual characters in the real-world through a smartphone) with a fitness regime. Designed for use in physical education in schools, Monsuta Fitness allows teachers to place virtual monsters around the school, which students then need to hunt down using their smartphones and battle against by performing increasingly strenuous fitness workouts. Understood as a biopedagogy, Monsuta Fitness is more than simply a game, but the product of 'particular knowledges and truths about the ways in which individuals should conduct their lives for the betterment of self and society' (Vander Schee 2009: 558).

The task of improving the health of both self and society is one of the animating aims of FitnessGram, 'the most widely used youth physical fitness assessment, education and reporting tool in the world'. As a fitness software platform, FitnessGram consists of a range of tests, instruments and data presentation tools that enable schools to collect and aggregate data and generate reports on children's body composition, health and fitness. In its most recent iterations, FitnessGram has been redesigned for use on mobile devices, and is able to supply educators and school administrators with immediate data on individual student activity, performance and fitness through a dynamic data dashboard interface:

> Based on Healthy Fitness Zone® standards, created by the FitnessGram Scientific Advisory Board, FitnessGram uses criterion-based standards, carefully established for each age and gender.

> FitnessGram assesses the five components of health-related fitness: Aerobic Capacity, Muscular Strength, Muscular Endurance, Flexibility, and Body Composition.

> Personalised reports provide objective, feedback and positive reinforcement which are vital to changing behavior. (FitnessGram 2016)

FitnessGram consists of a combination of scientific standards, medical expertise, age-referenced norms, reinforcement techniques, the objective reporting of biophysical data on children's health and fitness, and a commitment to behaviour modification. FitnessGram is a big data technology of the body that combines numerical knowledge about the individual body with societal imperatives around well-being and the maintenance of a healthy social order, and has the capacity to structure and shape pedagogical decisions about how to intervene in young people's lives and health (Pluim and Gard 2016).

Other biopedagogic platforms can be worn on the body. Zamzee, the 'game that gets kids moving', combines accelerometry technologies, game design and 'motivation science' (Zamzee 2016). It consists of a wearable 'meter' device to 'measure the intensity and duration of physical activity'; an online 'motivational website' featuring challenges and lesson plans; and 'group analytics' to enable educators and school administrators to 'track individual and group progress with real-time data'. The original strapline for the product was 'Motivate. Measure. Manage.', and Zamzee is entirely consistent with current governmental priorities around behaviour change and behaviour modification programs which target people's unhealthy lifestyles for active intervention. The promotional video for Zamzee explicitly makes the case that the device is based on 'behaviour change science'. Similarly, Sqord, 'your online world, powered by real-world play', consists of a wearable data logger, an online social media environment and a personalisable onscreen avatar (Sqord 2016). Sqord is marketed as 'one part social media, one part game platform, and one part fitness tracker', and the blurb for the device and app claims it is 'Motivating real-world activity and building life-long healthy habits with an online world full of friends, challenges, characters, points and awards'.

Sqord, like Zamzee and FitnessGram, provides an administrative reporting tool for educators to access metrics on the physical activity levels and participation of each child player. These examples demonstrate how physical activity trackers and biosensors can enable educators to subject young people to a surveillant gaze through the enumeration and visualization of their physical activities. These streams of observed student data can then be used to make decisions and shape specific pedagogic interventions that accord with societal well-being imperatives. The children's charity UNICEF has even promoted its initiative UNICEF Kid Power as a way of linking mobile self-tracking with global citizenship and responsibility. Kid Power combines a wearable activity wristband and digital platform with issues of global citizenship and responsibility along with a competitive appeal inspired by motivation science:

UNICEF Kid Power gives you the power to save lives. By getting active with the UNICEF Kid Power Band, you can go on missions, earn points and unlock therapeutic food packets for severely malnourished children around the world. (UNICEF Kid Power 2016)

It makes physical fitness into a key indicator of global responsibility. The design of biosensor devices has therefore turned complex social phenomenon with deep-rooted structural causes into personal deficits to solve (Nafus 2016). Embedding techniques of biosensor surveillance in physical education in schools via platforms such as Zamzee or Kid Power is one way in which wider societal problems of health, well-being and fitness are being translated into the personal responsibilities – and the continuous evaluation – of children and young people.

Moreover, these health tracking and surveillance devices demonstrate how the well-being of young people is the subject of expert calculation across a range of psy and medical disciplines. Many wearable devices depend on existing mathematical formalizations about the energy costs of physical activities calculated in terms of metabolic rate, such as those contained in the Compendium of Physical Activities (2011). Zamzee, for example, is specifically based on this resource. In other words, strapping a wearable physical activity monitor on to a child involves subjecting their bodies to specific mathematical calculations pertaining to physical intensity and metabolic rate. It should be noted, though, that resources such as the Compendium of Physical Activities are the products of particular forms of scientific expertise and knowledge.

The biomedical scientific expertise and knowledge that underpins the design of wearable activity monitoring devices is a major influence on what the devices measure, how they measure and present the data, and how the human subject that is the object of the measurement is understood and treated. Health informatics, physiological analytics, bioinformatics and digital medicine also provide the expert knowledges on which physical activity monitors are programmed. Other psy fields such as motivation science and the behavioural sciences are additional influences. These knowledges are then entwined with expertise in algorithms and data analytics in the design of health tracking devices, so that the devices can approximate or predict users' future health and automate prescriptive pedagogic recommendations on exercise and diet. Expert scientific forms of knowledge such as those of the medical profession and biomedical research have therefore become tools of social control by subjecting the body to quantification (Nafus 2016). These 'self-mediation interfaces with health' are now becoming 'inextricable from the manner in which people learn about health' and conduct their lifestyles (Rich and Miah 2014: 301).

Health tracking devices and platforms can be understood as technological extensions of the body, augmenting it with data and motivational nudges that urge citizens to change their healthy behaviours in the direction of greater over-all well-being. Lupton (2015b) terms the idealised figure of such techniques a 'socially fit biocitizen' who accepts the duty of self-responsibility and the entre-preneurial management and optimization of one's life, including promoting and maintaining good health, emotional well-being and physical fitness, as a means toward securing societal wellness. A socially fit biocitizen is therefore an individual who has been taught by health tracking systems to comport his or her body according to the expert medical knowledge and normative moral codes of behaviour that have been coded in to the devices.

Mindset Monitoring

Interest is growing in the psychological determinants of student behaviour in schools, and particularly in the use of new technologies to capture data about students' behavioural characteristics. One of the most high-profile psychological concepts to have emerged in education on both sides of the Atlantic in recent years is that of 'growth mindsets' (Reynolds and Birdwell 2015). Associated chiefly with the Stanford University psychologist Carol Dweck, the concept of growth mindsets focuses on the ways people differently perceive their intelligence. According to this theory, while some people have an 'entity theory of intelligence', as something that is fixed and unchangeable, others possess an 'incremental theory of intelligence' whereby they perceive intelligence as subject to change, which can be improved through hard work and effort (Dweck 2015). People with an incremental theory of intelligence, or a growth mindset, are more likely to seek out intellectual challenges and respond positively to complex tasks:

> Teaching people to have a 'growth mind-set,' which encourages a focus on 'process' rather than on intelligence or talent, produces high achievers in school and in life. Parents and teachers can engender a growth mind-set in children by praising them for their persistence or strategies (rather than for their intelligence), by telling success stories that emphasize hard work and love of learning, and by teaching them about the brain as a learning machine. (Dweck 2015)

In 2013 the US Office of Educational Technology strongly promoted Dweck's findings on growth mindsets in the recommendations of its report *Promoting Grit, Tenacity and Perseverance*, in which she was listed as a 'key informant' (Schechtman et al. 2013).

Growth mindsets research is also associated with behavioural economics. According to a recent report on behavioural economics implications for education, the field attempts to integrate research from psychology, neuroscience and economics to help develop policies that address shortcomings in individuals' decision-making processes, and acknowledges that 'our brain's architecture may lead to suboptimal outcomes' (Lavecchia et al. 2014: 4). The report highlights Carol Dweck's work on growth mindsets, linking her notion that 'the brain is malleable and that through hard work, intelligence can be improved' to the idea that students might be 'nudged' through small interventions aimed at 'decreasing the likelihood that small failures cause students to believe that academic success is unachievable' (2014: 67). The focus of such behavioural economics approaches is on nudging individuals to invest in self-optimization through hard work.

Growth mindset theory and its association with nudge theory has been assisted into classroom practice by ClassDojo, the most successful educational technology in history. At its core ClassDojo is a simple application designed for teachers to collect, store and visualize data about the behaviour of children in the classroom. Launched as a beta product in 2011 and as a full platform in 2013, by early 2016 ClassDojo's founders reported over 3 million subscribing teachers, serving 35 million students across 180 countries worldwide. Its rapid successful growth has been supported by enthusiastic venture capital funding, with over US$31million invested in the ClassDojo company by mid-2016 (Kolodny 2016). Available as a free mobile app that allows teachers to award or deduct points for individual children's behaviour and participation in the classroom, ClassDojo can be operated on a variety of desktop and mobile platforms. The promotional video on the website shows it used on a smartphone and tablet, with the teacher awarding points on-the-move and in real-time. Behavioural targets can be set for both individuals and groups to achieve positive goals. Based on time series analysis, the awarding and deduction of points becomes a kind of behavioural data timeline, with teachers able to produce visualizations for each child to show their progress over time, or display relative progress against each other to a whole class.

In addition, parents are able to receive messages, photographs and video content from the classroom posted by teachers, and can log in to the website to see their child's points and updates. In 2016, ClassDojo announced 'school-wide' features to allow whole schools to sign up for accounts, which allow 'teachers and school leaders to safely share photos, videos, and messages with all parents connected to the school at once, replacing cumbersome school websites, group email threads, newsletters, and paper flyers', while also launching features to allow schoolchildren to create their own digital portfolios (ClassDojo 2016a). The capacity for teachers to observe and reward behavioural points in such a way that they are visible to both parents and school leaders has been described as normalizing surveillance in schools through the constant assessment of behaviour (Soroko 2016).

At the same time, ClassDojo has aligned itself with a number of prominent behaviour management initiatives led by different governmental and for-profit commercial organizations, including PBIS and 'The Leader in Me'. PBIS stands for 'Positive Behavior Interventions and Supports' and is an initiative of the US Department of Education's Office of Special Education Programs which aims to support the adoption of the 'applied science' of positive behaviour support in schools. 'The Leader in Me', meanwhile, is a project of the for-profit FranklinCovey company, an international provider of educational leadership programs and 'transformational processes'.

Also in 2016 ClassDojo announced a partnership with the Project for Education Research that Scales (PERTS), an applied research center at Stanford

University that is the intellectual home of the theory of growth mindsets and is led by Carol Dweck. The partnership between ClassDojo and PERTS takes the form of a series of short animations that help explain the growth mindsets idea for teachers and learners themselves. The press release stated:

> Because it is already used in half of U.S. schools, ClassDojo provides an unprecedented opportunity to seamlessly bring breakthrough, evidence-based educational practices to millions of teachers and classrooms.

> 'Growth mindset is a phenomenally important idea that's been proven to benefit children well into the future,' said Liam Don, co-founder and Chief Product Officer at ClassDojo. 'In developing our "Big Ideas" series we wanted to make these transformative ideas easy for teachers to incorporate into their classroom, and delightful for students. Our partnership with Stanford PERTS is a good example of how technology can help make big ideas accessible and exciting for students in every classroom. We're thrilled to share this "Big Idea" with our community of teachers – the first of more to come!' (ClassDojo 2016b)

The partnership with PERTS also positions ClassDojo as a large-scale site for growth mindsets research. PERTS' executive director Dave Paunesku has claimed that because ClassDojo can track engagement with their videos and tools, the PERTS researchers can gather new insights into how the growth mindset message changes student engagement levels, claiming that '"We want teachers to think about the kind of norms they want to set in the classroom so that growth mindset is integrated in it"' (van Dijk 2016). In practice, this means that the PERTS partnership is intended to encourage schools to align the ways they award points for specific kinds of behaviours through ClassDojo with the behvioural norms defined by growth mindsets experts.

In addition to Dweck and PERTS, many of the influences listed by the original designers of ClassDojo are also strongly associated with behavioural economics, non-cognitive learning and the development of 'character'. Its founding director Sam Chaudhary has explicitly described the purpose of ClassDojo as promoting 'character development' in schools:

> 'Education goes beyond just a test score to developing who the student is as a person – including all the character strengths like curiosity, creativity, teamwork and persistence. … We shouldn't just reduce people to how much content they know; we have to develop them as individuals.' (Chaudhary, cited in Mead 2013)

Chaudhary has also listed the 'people whose example shapes our work', including:

> 'thought leaders in the field of behavior and building character: James Heckman and his work on the power of building character early in life; Angela Duckworth's work on persistence and grit; Carol Dweck's work on the growth mindset and the praise we give kids.' (Chaudhary, cited in Mead 2013)

These thought leaders represent a mishmash of behavioural economics, behaviour management expertise, and non-cognitive learning theory. James Heckman is a professor of behavioural economics at the University of Chicago. Angela Duckworth is a professor of psychology at the University of Pennsylvania, and has also established the Character Lab to investigate and promote character qualities such as grit, growth mindset and self-control. Together, these thought leaders, as ClassDojo's founder describes them, represent an alliance of psychological and economic conceptualizations of teaching and learning.

The central mechanism of awarding and deducting points based on behaviour acts as a crude behaviourist nudging technique that is designed to compel young people to comply with specific behavioural and psychological norms derived from the work of these thought leaders. Burger (2015: 186) has found that when ClassDojo is used in practice,

> students are influenced by the results associated with their behaviors. … [W]hen a student receives a positive point, the other students in the classroom recognize what that student did to earn the positive point. They then think about what they have to do to replicate that behavior in order to receive the same reward/benefit.

Understood as a technique of nudge, ClassDojo represents the partial resuscitation of behavourist theory in education, one that encourages teachers to reward observable behaviours and by doing so to reinforce behaviours that are observably compliant with the psychological norms scripted into the device. Through its reward-and-reinforce mechanism, it is designed to inculcate children into habitual behaviours and persistent routines in ways that are entirely aligned with the emphasis of behavioural economics, and which also align well with governmental behaviour change programmes such as the US Department of Education's PBIS and its 'grit' agenda.

ClassDojo therefore represents a successful instantiation within education of the behaviour change agenda which has become part of many aspects of public policy and state strategy in recent years, and that has been termed 'psychological governance' (Jones et al. 2013). Furthermore, as behavioural economics has influenced the development of persuasive computing, new computer-based techniques of 'hypernudge' have emerged whereby behaviours of individuals are targeted for intervention through social media platforms (Yeung 2017). The combination of the behaviour change agenda with persuasive technology represents the abandonment by technical designers of the image of social neutrality, as they have 'set themselves the task of "nudging" their users toward the "right" behaviors' and ultimately become enforcers of psychological intervention who see individuals, and not institutions or social arrangements, as in need of changing' (Nafus 2016: xvii). Through involvement in technologies such as ClassDojo, key figures such as Carol Dweck have become the expert enforcers of nudge and hypernudge for education, exerting massive influence on how the 'psychological gaze' (Rose 1999a) perceives children.

With government policies increasingly targeting children's personal qualities, characters and mindsets, ClassDojo is part of the wider governmentalization of behaviour change. It is an educational application of an emerging governmental 'nudgeocracy' that is committed to behaviour change and management, as governmental initiatives such as PBIS (to which ClassDojo has aligned itself) demonstrate. By normalizing and even gamifying key messages of the behaviour change agenda, ClassDojo is becoming a technology for government at a distance, one that translates and aligns the aspirations of departments of state with the commercial ambitions of persuasive technology companies, the scientific expertise of psychologists, the institutional goals of schools, and the individual practices and projects of teachers, children and parents alike. It invites schools to classify and treat children according to new psychological definitions of behavioural development and social-emotional learning. Teachers then enforce and reproduce this classification system by measuring children against those psychological categories on the device and its dashboard.

Affective Accountability and Psycho-Policies

As with other areas of education where digital data now appear, it is important to note that the educational adoption of affective computing, body analytics and behaviour monitoring devices is both animated by imaginaries of desired futures and intersecting with existing practices. ClassDojo, emotional learning analytics, wearable biosensors and the like do not represent a decisive break from the past, but are now working to reinforce, amplify and alter the ways in which the emotions, feelings and the non-cognitive and behavioural aspects of learning are treated in education. Psychological definitions of the behavioural, social, emotional and other non-cognitive aspects of learning are being simultaneously commercialized, through applications like ClassDojo, and also governmentalized via key reports, projects and policy proposals. Psychology, commerce and government of education are becoming interdependent.

The measurement and monitoring of the affective dimensions of learning is now well established in government departments and initiatives. In Scotland, for example, a new national improvement framework launched in 2016 made the collection of data on learners' well-being into a key priority (Scottish Government 2016). In England, the Department for Education has actively funded policy research by the Centre for Understanding Behaviour Change to investigate the application of behavioural economics 'to promote desired behavioural changes amongst young people' (Bradbury et al. 2013: 251). Likewise, in the US, recent policies in some states – following the introduction of the Every Student Succeeds Act in 2015 – are putting pressure on schools to demonstrate data on students' well-being as a measure of institutional performance. New measures of growth mindsets and other personal qualities are rapidly becoming new accountability tools, with the success of schools measured by 'quantifying growth in non-cognitive skills' (Adams 2014; also Zernike 2016).

As reports and initiatives by the WEF and the OECD demonstrate, there is increasing global policy advocacy and political appetite for these psychological techniques of mood measurement and behaviour modification in schools. Just as the quantification of the emotions has become a desirable ambition in the commercial domain, the measurement and management of students' social and emotional skills is becoming a key target of education authorities around the world.

These new accountability mechanisms for schools represent 'an ideology that welds together pre-modern ideas of "flourishing" with an uber-modern obsession with metrics and performance ranking', whereby policymakers are anxiously 'wrestling to make the world conform to their numerical understandings' (Davies 2016). The key point here is that commercially developed devices and platforms such as ClassDojo, emotional learning analytics, wearable well-being monitors, affective computing and so on are intersecting with and reinforcing existing and emerging state strategies that are making the measurement of the emotions into a technique of affective accountability. Schools are being made responsible for the measurement, management and numerical reporting of children's well-being, character development, happiness and other personal qualities. Yet these developments simultaneously threaten to exacerbate the existing stresses and anxieties brought about by the political culture of performance measurement. Instruments that assist in both capturing data on young people's non-cognitive learning and improving it – specifically by 'nudging' them to perform the 'correct' behaviours – are therefore becoming valuable tools for schools, and part of a governmental apparatus of constant performance management at institutional and individual scales.

Furthermore, the datafication of children's non-cognitive learning is part of a biopolitical strategy designed to shape citizen subjectivities as pathology-proofed individuals endowed with the personal capacities to deal with the stresses and anxieties themselves caused by contemporary government policies and capitalist culture combined. With the increasing production of governmental policies around measuring 'mental capital', 'national well-being' and so on, children and young people are being targeted for continuous psychological surveillance and wellness optimization in order to contribute to state-defined well-being and happiness targets. A biopolitical strategy of the calculation and transformation of the emotional life of the child – as a 'smart investment' – is proposed by these government initiatives, and then enacted through the production of specific devices and their implantation in schools. This strategy is aimed at producing emotionally maximized characters whose personal well-being is understood to be the prerequisite for the development of productive human capital under conditions of digital capitalism.

At least in part, data-driven techniques of emotional enhancement and affective accountability mechanisms in education reflect wider governmental 'psycho-policies' that highlight 'psycho-compulsion' or 'the imposition of psychological explanations ... together with mandatory activities intended to modify beliefs, attitude, disposition or personality' (Friedli and Stearn 2015: 42). Schools are increasingly becoming sites of psycho-compulsion, responsible for ensuring that their students are healthy and emotionally well 'characters' with resilience, growth mindsets and grit as contributors to national 'mental capital'. Individual learners, likewise, are subject to psychological compulsion as they are increasingly required to demonstrate that they are sufficiently resilient and emotionally well to cope with the demands of academic learning and assessment.

The therapeutic turn toward social and emotional learning in schools is premised on the assumption that young people are emotionally vulnerable and require psychological intervention to develop the emotional resilience required of the high-performance model of schooling – or 'psychology first, education later' (Ecclestone and Hayes 2009). Those deemed emotionally fragile, at risk or lacking in self-esteem and so on, are more likely to receive a curriculum high in emotional intervention and the development of non-cognitive skills before being subjected to the cognitive challenge of academic learning (Furedi 2009). The collection of psychological data about young people is therefore important for schools and learners alike as they are required by governmental psycho-policies to demonstrate high psychological performance in exchange for access to academic content. New technologies of behaviour change and emotional modification can then be mobilized to compel them to perform to high emotional standards.

Conclusion

The CompPsy complex in education represents a juxtaposition of psychological knowledges and computational methods with educational imperatives, governmental health and well-being agendas and associated psycho-policies, plus innovations in affective computing, surveillance techniques and the political demands of behavioural economics as a new source for state strategy, smart investment and social control. It is part of the surveillance, management and government of human feelings that has now become a key biopolitical strategy of states, well-being experts and the commercial 'happiness industry' alike. The political analytics and modification of citizens' sentiments, and the shaping of their behaviours toward greater emotional well-being, is thus a key priority in emerging techniques of digital governance, and is enabled by the commercial media and big data companies of digital capitalism. These digitized techniques of psycho-compulsion are being ushered into educational spaces by international organizations such as the WEF and the OECD, as well as through government agendas regarding social and emotional skills, public health priorities around well-being, and commercial ambitions to sell products that promote wellness. Underpinning these efforts, and the imaginary that animates them, is a belief that the emotional lives of students can be read from their bodies and observable behaviours, rather than by eliciting students' voices through dialogue.

Ultimately, the ambitions of the CompPsy complex are to produce behaviourally optimized citizens, who actively pursue psychological well-being and physical health through self-surveillance; who understand, are mindful about, and care for their emotional development and resilience; demonstrate fitness of character as pathology-proofed inhabitants of digital capitalism; and contribute to the 'mental capital' of society at large. Through the interventions of experts and technologies of behavioural economics and psychology, education is being reimagined as a laboratory of emotional experimentation, measurement and manipulation, all imbued with aspirations to shape young people as the governable citizens of the future state in the era of big data and persuasive computing.

7

REWIRING BRAINS

Artificial intelligence, cognitive
systems and neuroeducation

In 2011, the Royal Society published a report on the implications of neuroscience for education as part of its major Brain Waves project. One of the key claims and recommendations of the report was that insights from neuroscience about the lifelong adaptability of the human brain could be used to help inform the design of 'adaptive technologies for learning and cognitive development':

> The brain changes constantly as a result of learning, and remains 'plastic' throughout life. Neuroscience has shown that learning a skill changes the brain and that these changes revert when practice of the skill ceases. ... Thus, neuroscience has a key role in investigating means of boosting brain power. ... [I]nsights from neuroscience are relevant for the development and use of adaptive digital technologies. These technologies have the potential to create more learning opportunities inside and outside the classroom, and throughout life. (Royal Society 2011: v)

These intertwined claims about the 'plasticity' of the learning brain, and the potential of adaptive technologies for learning, cognitive enhancement and 'boosting brain power' form the launchpad for this chapter.

As the Royal Society Brain Waves report demonstrates, the human brain has become the focus of significant scientific and political interest in recent years. The brain has become the concern of policymakers, pharmaceutical companies, learned societies, think tanks, scientists, engineers and designers, as well as experts working in law, social work and education among other sectors. In particular,

> efforts to map the brain, to capitalise on the vast datasets emerging from contemporary neuroscience, and eventually to develop the computing power to simulate neural functioning are the latest indications of a culture in which the brain is privileged in its explanatory power for all manner of human experiences, decisions, capabilities, actions and relationships. (Pykett 2015: ix)

Neuroscience has, in other words, 'left the lab' and begun to inhabit the imaginations and initiatives of experts and practitioners in all sorts of diverse spaces, all of whom are seeking to govern, shape and manage human conduct through 'cerebral knowledges' (Rose and Abi-Rached 2013).

Moreover, the intersections of neuroscience and sophisticated new forms of computing have animated significant research and development, much of it characterized as a new frontier in artificial intelligence (AI). A recent 'foresight' report produced by the massive European Human Brain Project (HBP) documents many recent developments in neuroscience, AI, cognitive computing, and their implications. Entitled *Future Computing and Robotics* (Rose et al. 2016), it focuses on 'machine intelligence', 'human-machine integration' and other 'neurocomputational' technologies that use the neural networks of the human brain as inspiration:

The power of these innovations has been increased by the development of data mining and machine learning techniques, that give computers the capacity to learn from their 'experience' without being specifically programmed, constructing algorithms, making predictions, and then improving those predictions by learning from their results, either in supervised or unsupervised regimes. In these and other ways, developments in ICT and robotics are reshaping human interactions, in economic activities, in consumption and in our most intimate relations. (Rose et al. 2016: 5)

Growing interest in AI has been amplified by the publication of the White House report 'Preparing for the Future of Artificial Intelligence' (White House 2016b), a report by the think tank Center for Data Innovation on *The Promise of Artificial Intelligence* (Castro and New 2016), the launch of the Leverhulme Centre for the Future of Intelligence at the University of Cambridge and the establishment of an Intelligence and Autonomy Initiative focused on robots, algorithms and machine intelligence at the Data & Society Research Institute, New York. In the autumn of 2016, a Partnership on AI was announced by Facebook, Amazon, Google, IBM and Microsoft. The central tenet of the Partnership on AI is that 'artificial intelligence technologies hold great promise for raising the quality of people's lives and can be leveraged to help humanity address important global challenges such as climate change, food, inequality, health, and education' (Partnership on AI 2016).

Together, these developments point to a growing contemporary concern with forms of machine intelligence that are sometimes described as 'weak' or 'narrow' forms of AI. That is, weak or narrow AI includes techniques such as cognitive computing, deep learning, genetic algorithms, machine learning and other automated, algorithmic processes, rather than aspiring to 'strong' or 'general' models of AI which assume computers might become autonomous superintelligences (Floridi 2016). The underlying rationale behind many claims and debates about machine intelligence is that because the brain can now be scanned, imaged and understood at greater and greater levels of sophistication, it is possible then to build computing technologies that are inspired by its neural architectures and processes.

The focus for this chapter is on the intersections of neuroscience with big data analytics and machine intelligence applications in relation to education, with particular emphasis on emerging aspirations to employ brain-inspired technologies of AI and cognitive computing as a new form of brain-targeted digital education. This is an emerging field of technical development with significant social consequences for how the actions of young people are to be governed. For example, the US Department of Education has proposed the creation of an advanced R&D program to explore how AI technologies, such as digital tutors, might improve student outcomes (White House 2016b). These aspirations to insert machine intelligences into educational spaces reinforce and reproduce the earlier claims of the Royal Society Brain Waves project that adaptive technologies might be designed to help 'boost brain power' by stimulating the neural plasticity of the learning brain.

Another strand of the emerging big data imaginary for education is evident in the increasing claims that neuroscientific insights and data about the brain can be mobilized in the design of artificially intelligent educational technologies. Advocates and developers of these brain-inspired and brain-inspiring technologies advance on existing developments in the field of education data science such as learning analytics, adaptive learning platforms and emotion management platforms to focus on human neurology and the neural basis of cognitive processes. The emerging neurocomputational variant on the big data imaginary for education sees the brain itself as the target for measurement, management and modification.

In outline, the chapter first provides some theoretical contextualization in emerging 'biosocial' concepts and debates, before discussing the emergence of neurocomputation as an important field of technical development, and then the growth of neuroeducation where neuroscientific insights have been deployed in relation to learning and cognitive development. After that I provide two detailed examples of how brain-based technologies are being advanced for use in education, focusing first on claims about AI made by the edu-business Pearson and then second on the global computing company IBM's aspirations to build cognitive systems for learning. I follow the examples with a discussion of the implications for how learning processes may be understood and acted upon, and conclude with some emerging critical issues and questions about the emerging neurocomputational imaginary of education and its potential to create new hierarchical striations of neurobiological capacity, hybrid intelligence and enhanced cognition. To be clear, the object of the chapter is not to provide a critique of the neuroscientific enterprise, but rather to query the purposes to which neuroscientific claims are being put specifically in relation to new brain-targeted educational technologies, and to tease out the underlying sociotechnical imaginary that animates these efforts.

THE BIOSOCIAL LIFE OF THE BRAIN

Neuroscience has become the subject of feverish excitement in recent years. The 'neuro-' prefix has been attached to neuromarketing, neuroeconomics, neuropolitics, neurorobotics, neurolaw, neuroeducation and neurotechnology, amongst others, and given rise to critiques of neuromania, neuromyths, and even neurobollocks. All of these neuro-prefixed domains add up to a 'neuro-complex' of competing brain claims, whereby the brain is variously understood as an 'orchestrator of our thoughts, feelings, behaviours, desires; object of scientific investigation and intervention; and an endlessly elaborated cultural resource and point of reference. ... Hence the "neuro-" is a complex field of contested truths, claims, and counter-claims' (Williams et al. 2011: 135–6).

Beyond being a diversifying discipline that is being applied in all kinds of domains, neuroscience has become the object of serious critical study as a field of scientific knowledge production that claims explanatory power over the complexities of the human brain. Critically nuanced sociological and geographical scholarship has begun to engage seriously with the implications of neuroscientific claims and expertise as they have been applied in diverse domains of knowledge production, consumer services and public policy (Pickersgill 2013; Fitzgerald and Callard 2014; Pykett 2015). The increasingly prominent application and popularization of 'neuro knowledges' in public policy – those formalized disciplines related to the brain sciences with their own styles of thinking, explanations, modes of expertise, and application – represents how the brain has become the subject of governmental concern and strategic intervention (Pykett 2013). Policy interest in brain science stems from the belief that it is possible to understand 'social problems through understanding the brain' and to correlate 'outcomes (crime, addiction, health behaviour, educational attainment) with brain structure' (Friedli and Stearn 2015: 42). Brain-based policymaking – the attempt to solve social problems by understanding how they are linked to brain structure – is taken increasingly seriously by governments engaged with behaviour change techniques.

The translation of neuroscience into public policy is part of an emerging debate about the influence of neuroscientific thinking in addressing societal challenges and shaping human subjectivity (McGimpsey et al. 2016). The 'cerebral knowledges' of neuroscience are coming to play a significant role in contemporary techniques of governance:

> it is the experts of the brain, rather than of 'psy' or society, who will enable us to address the 'grand challenges' facing our societies in the future. ... [T]he problems of governing living populations now seem to demand attention to the brains of citizens. ... [G]overning the conduct of human beings [has] come to require, presuppose and utilize a knowledge of the human brain. (Rose and Abi-Rached 2014: 3–5)

Neuroscientific developments have become entwined with strategies designed to govern human conduct by drawing upon the growing availability of empirical knowledge of the brain. Such approaches acknowledge a connection between the biological substances of the brain and the dynamics of society, and have led to the emergence of new kinds of 'biosocial' studies. The permeability of the body and the brain to their social, material and technical surroundings is at the core of biosocial studies.

Biosocial studies emphasize how social environments are now understood to 'get under the skin' and to influence the biological functions of the body, whilst also acknowledging how biology extends 'outside the skin' through human actions that impact upon the social environment (Fitzgerald and Callard 2014).

In other words, 'neural structure and functioning may have a profound role in shaping the social environment, just as the latter reciprocally influences individual brain development throughout the life course' (Bone 2016: 245). There is some attempt in such studies to challenge the historically constructed divisions between nature and nurture, and biology and culture, and instead to acknowledge bio-cultural or bio-social syntheses (Keller 2016). For biosocial and biocultural theorists, it is now accepted that the existing separation of the social and the biological is the contingent effect of a specific history of disciplinary segregation between the social and life sciences, which has removed society from nature and vice versa (Meloni et al. 2016). Thus there has been a 'social turn' in (some aspects of) biology as well as a 'biological turn' in (some) social science, with calls for new kinds of interdisciplinary biosocial research involving experts from both the life and social sciences.

Concepts such as 'neuroplasticity' and 'epigenetics' emerging from biology have been key to this biosocial synthesis of the social and biological sciences. Simply put, neuroplasticity recognizes that the brain is constantly adapting to external stimuli and social environments while epigenetics acknowledges that social experience modulates the body at the genetic level (Chung et al 2016; Rose and Abi-Rached 2013):

> With respect to neural plasticity, the notion that brain development is not fixed but is shaped by an ongoing process of connecting and pruning of neural/synaptic connections in response to experience has been recognized for several decades, indicating that a non-deterministic biosocial model was possible. Moreover, the recognition in the emerging sub-discipline of epigenetics that even gene expression (rather being a straightforwardly constitutive process) is also highly environmentally sensitive, has further supported the position of those who have begun to view brain/self construction as being very much an ongoing bi-directional biosocial process. (Bone 2016: 244)

Methodological inquiries inspired by the concepts of neuroplasticity and epigenetics within neuroscience itself have ascertained that the brain is open to environmental input, with the environment shaping the neural architecture and functional organization of the brain through the formation, strengthening and trimming of synaptic connections, and also through the modification of genes and associated proteins. Conceptualizations of neuroplasticity and epigenetics therefore instantiate the social within the neurobiological, with new understandings of 'the social life of the brain' being used to catalyse policies and practices in healthcare, education and other social domains (Pickersgill 2013: 322). Biosocial studies therefore acknowledge that 'the brain is a multiply connected device profoundly shaped by social influences' and that 'the body bears the inscriptions of its socially and materially situated milieu' (Meloni et al. 2016: 13). But such critical biosocial studies also subject to detailed scrutiny the ways in which specific biological and neuroscientific claims are put to practical and political use.

One of the most contentious uptakes of epigenetics insights is in the field of 'educational genomics'. Educational genomics makes use of massive databases of information about the human genome to identify particular traits that are understood to correspond with learning. Large-scale genetic studies on education-related traits such as learning ability, memory and academic achievement now suggest that understanding genetic variants could be used to identify individual differences in learning, including the controversial notion of 'learning styles'. Educational genomics also recognizes, in keeping with epigenetics, that social environments play a role in human genes. As a result, it takes seriously the idea that specific environmental conditions can be created that might maximize learners' potential. As a consequence, it has been suggested that by 'considering DNA differences among people in the future, educational genomics could provide the basis for a more personalised approach to education', even that specific learning environments and conditions could be engineered to 'personalize' the learning experience and enable 'educational organisations to create tailor-made curriculum programmes based on a pupil's DNA profile' (Gaysina 2016). The language of personalized learning used in educational genomics resonates clearly with the emphasis on personalization in relation to learning analytics and adaptive learning software discussed earlier, indicating a key point of overlap in biological and technical imaginings of the future of education.

Emerging biosocial studies are now increasingly taking seriously, but also critically, the reciprocal connections between biological processes and social, environmental, technological and other material influences. As a result, calls have been issued for:

> greater attention to the ways in which social experience is lived biologically, as well as the need to develop concepts and methods for understanding and describing biological forms of human life that emerge within, and are reproduced by, specific kinds of social, political, and economic relations. (Fitzgerald et al. 2016: 16)

Such studies, then, point to the need for biosocial accounts of the life of the human brain as it adapts to its environment, while simultaneously taking account of how biology can also get outside the skin to affect behaviours, choices and outcomes.

However, critical biosocial studies also attend to the social shaping or social production of neuroscience and genomics rather than taking its claims at face value as objective 'brain facts' (Williams et al. 2011). From this critical perspective, the important task is to trace how the expert knowledges and claims of biology and neuroscience have come to be (Meloni et al. 2016). The discoveries of the 'cerebral knowledges' of neuroscience are themselves products shaped by specific social, political, cultural and economic contexts such as funding arrangements, methodological developments, technical innovations, political support, industrial involvement and so on (Rose and Abi-Rached 2013). Critical biosocial studies, then, take seriously the ways in which neuroscientific expertise, concepts, arguments and claims are produced, circulated, used and sometimes abused.

A key aspect of critical biosocial research is to examine the technologies that are involved in the production of neuroscience, the organizations and other actors that promote and mobilize them, and the sectors in which they are put to use. Neuroscience has itself become a big data enterprise through massive brain imaging and high-resolution simulation projects such as the Human Brain Project. Such projects – sometimes categorized as computational neuroscience – are producing torrents of brain data, which are being used both to transform the ways the brain is understood as a multiply-connected, dynamically neuromorphological and socially adaptive organ, and to inspire the development of new brain-based computing technologies and processes (*Nature Neuroscience* 2014). Neurocomputation is a key field in which the plasticity and epigenetic nature of the brain has been deployed in ways that connect neuroscientific expertise with technical development, commercial ambitions and governmental objectives.

Neurocomputation

Much advanced research and development in big data analytics is replete with references to the brain as a 'big data processor', 'brain-like computations', 'neuromorphic' hardware, 'neural computation', 'machine learning', 'algorithms that learn', 'neural network learning algorithms', 'brain-inspired algorithms', 'deep learning algorithms', 'cognitive computing' and 'machine intelligence'. Increasingly, the human brain is being treated as a model and metaphor for the design of neurobiologically plausible computer systems that act in brain-like ways. Neuroscientific accounts of the brain understood in terms of its plasticity and malleability to adapt to environmental stimuli have been at the centre of this emerging hybridity of the neural and the computational.

The result of the emerging 'imaginary of plasticity' (Rose and Abi-Rached 2013) is that new computational techniques are now being devised which recognize and manage the processes involved in shaping and reshaping the brain. Based on insights about neuroplasticity and epigenetics, these approaches promote the idea that the brain is flexible, mouldable, able to be trained, rewired, improved and ultimately optimized. In particular, the field of neurocomputation focuses on the possibility of computation in computers that is modelled on the computation that occurs in neurons in the brain.

The recent Foresight report on future computing and neurotechnologies from the Human Brain Project details many of these emerging developments (Rose et al. 2016). Its authors foreground how neuroscientific explanations are increasingly informing the design of information-processing technologies that are designed to act in brain-like ways, and to bring about greater human–machine integration. Such neurotechnologies use the brain as an inspiration. As such they are animated by the desire to synchronize machines with 'biological time' and to enable computers with 'brain-like intelligence' to perform functions that human brains excel at while current computers running hard-programmed routines cannot. However, approaches to brain–machine integration 'can entail conceiving of humans as mere components in complex ICT [information and communications technology] and robotics systems, components which might be optimized and interfaced in the same terms as the silicon parts', raising critical questions about 'how "the brain" is conceived and mobilized as an inspiration in ICT and robotics' (Rose et al. 2016: 22). There is a risk that developments in human–machine integration ignore the affective, interpersonal and social capacities of the human brain and instead treat it in rationalistic terms as an information processor, with the aim to model essential aspects of mental processes to eventually replace them in a quest for optimization.

If we take seriously the contention from critical biosocial studies that social environments can get under the skin to affect biological and neurobiological structures and functions, then the implantation of intelligent machines in social environments where they can interface with humans raises significant issues. For example, it has been argued that neurocomputational technologies such as brain-based or brain-related devices 'harbour the potential to take us far beyond the poles of normality and abnormality, health and illness, to a new era of "augmentation," "enhancement," "optimization" or "upgrades" of various kinds, which promise to make us "better than well" or "better than humans," if not "better than human"' (Williams et al. 2011: 137).

Claims about the social life of the brain, and its collapsing of taken-for-granted distinctions regarding biology and society, have been taken up by critical media scholars to explore how they might imply a shift in understanding of human subjectivity. If, as neuroscience has claimed, humans develop through 'epigenetic changes – changes initiated and transmitted through the environment rather than through the genetic code' – then epigenetic changes might also be associated with, and accelerated by, changes in the environment instantiated by digital technologies (Hayles 2013: 10). From this perspective, the code that constitutes digital media might become encoded in brains as it increasingly permeates social environments and interweaves with human actions and mental tasks:

> As digital media ... embedded in the environment, become more pervasive, they push us in the direction of faster communication, more intense and varied information streams, more integration of humans and intelligent machines, and more interactions of language with code. These environmental changes have significant neurological consequences. (Hayles 2013: 11)

According to this view, sophisticated digital technologies that extend human capacities to deal with more intensive and pervasive media are exerting considerable influence on the structuring of neural pathways, synaptic connections and brain morphology and functioning. This is now being exacerbated by the development of artificially intelligent, cognitive computing devices that can employ learning processes modelled like those of embodied biological organisms, using their experiences to learn, achieve skills and interact with people. When these non-human cognitive systems penetrate into human systems, they can then potentially change the dynamics of human behaviours by moulding and sculpting the plastic brain (Hayles 2014). The potential of non-human neurocomputational techniques based on the brain, it now appears, is to become legible as traces in the neurological circuitry of the human brain itself, and to impress itself on the cerebral lives and identities of learners.

Neuroeducation

Within education itself, neuroscientific expertise and new neurotechnologies have become the objects of increasing interest in recent years. For example, broadly biosocial explanations of the reciprocal connections between social environments and the neurobiological aspects of learning derived from epigenetics and brain science are beginning to be applied in the conceptualization of learning processes:

> [A]n emphasis on the biosocial determinants of children's learning, educational outcomes and life chances resonates with broader calls to develop hybrid accounts of social life which give adequate attention to the biological, the nonhuman, the technological, the material, ... the neural and the epigenetic aspects of 'life itself'. (Pykett and Disney 2015: 2)

In addition, recent proposals for critical biosocial studies of education suggest that such conceptualizations might change our existing understandings of processes such as learning altogether. From this perspective, learning is understood as a highly diverse and complex set of overlapping social, cultural, biological and neurological processes:

> as the interaction between a person and a thing; as embedded in ways of being and understanding that are shared across communities; as influenced by the social and cultural and economic conditions of lives; as involving changes to how genes are expressed in brain cells because it changes the histones that store DNA; as provoking certain parts of the brain into electrochemical activity; as relying on a person being recognised by others, and recognising themselves, as someone who learns. Shared meanings, gene expression, electrochemical signals, the everyday of the classroom and a sense of self are all ... parts of the phenomenon that is learning. (Youdell 2016a: 5)

From this perspective, both biological and sociological accounts might be applied to education, such as through analyses of how learning environments interact with neuronal composition and functioning; how epigenetics is involved in learning and memory formation; and how characteristics such as intelligence and healthiness 'emerge over many years as bodies interact with and are shaped by environments' (Youdell 2016b: 791). Rather than seeing the figure of the human learner 'sealed off from the world' (Youdell 2016b: 797), a critical biosocial approach to education would highlight the porosity and movement between the body and its milieu, viewing learners and learning as being constituted through a matrix of biological and sociocultural processes that shape each other.

One significant area of education requiring critical biosocial examination is 'neuroeducation', part of 'the dispersal of neurobiological language, imagery, symbolism and rhetoric within formal and informal learning environments' (Busso and Pollack 2015: 169). From the perspective of neuroeducation, recent neuroscientific insights into brain plasticity mean that education is seen as playing a crucial role in shaping 'the shifting balance of strengthening and weakening of connections in the brain' (Sharples and Kelley 2015: 127). For researchers of neuroeducation, it is seen as desirable to study the brain-based nature of learning through advanced brain scanning and imaging techniques. Such techniques include electroencephalography (EEG), which can allow the researcher to detect 'cognitive load' while undertaking a task; functional magnetic resonance imaging (fMRI), which allows activity in specific brain regions to be identified; and electrodermal activity (EDA) monitoring, which can be used to detect the effects of emotional arousal on cerebral activity (Howard-Jones et al. 2015).

Based on insights into the brain-based nature of learning generated from these scanning and imaging methods, a range of technical applications has been produced. These include computer-based brain-training programs, multi-modal forms of virtual reality designed to stimulate regions of the brain associated with learning, and the design of 'human-like' artificial tutoring agents:

> New learning technologies that embody key elements of individual human tutoring are likely to exploit insights about human neurocognitive processes of imitation, shared attention and empathy. ... When we 'communicate' with non-human technology we may recruit brain regions usually involved with communicating face-to-face with each other. (Howard-Jones et al. 2015: 142)

Some applications of neuroscience to educational technology development include wearable fMRI brain scanning devices that use optical topography and neuroimaging techniques to measure and visualize changes in blood flow to different areas of the brain during learning activities, and robotic systems that can adapt to the mental state of their human controllers. Some have argued there is potential for 'neurosensing' devices to be used to measure students' brain activity in real-time:

> Neurosensors ... could provide insight into students' cognitive activity using ... technology that measures brain activity ... . Identifying which students are expending a higher amount of cognitive energy on an exercise ... teachers could send a 'haptic' vibration – similar to silent notifications on mobile devices – to a student's wearable or tablet, redirecting her attention or behavior. (Meyers 2015)

Enthusiasm for connecting neuroscience with educational technology is the main animating force of the Royal Society Brain Waves project mentioned earlier. This project proposed that artificial tutors based on brain science might be able to 'boost brain power', since 'adaptive programmes emulate a teacher who constantly adapts to current learner understanding. Thus they enable far more practice than is often possible through one-to-one teaching' (Royal Society 2011: 14). The report continues that 'digital technologies can be developed to support individualised self-paced learning and highly specialised practice', which 'means interactive technologies can provide personalised help on a daily basis in a way that is difficult to achieve in a demanding classroom environment' (2011: 15).

Commenting specifically on this report and its recommendations, one critic of recent technological developments in neuroeducation has pointed out, however, that:

> the emphases that are developed from this way of thinking, in, for instance, ... 'adaptive learning technology' or ... a 'robot tutor,' risk confounding teaching with learning. By instrumentalising teaching instruments, by focusing on the brain and not the child or student, these advocates seem oblivious to the fact that both teaching and learning are not timeless and isolated activities but in their very essence socioculturally embedded. (S. Rose 2013).

Nonetheless, in the years since the Brain Waves project, significant efforts have been made to apply neuroscience insights to educational technology development, particularly adaptive learning technologies that utilize analysis of student data for the purposes of personalizing the learning experience. One example suggests, for example, that as 'adaptive educational computer programs are being developed in tandem with imaging studies of how such innovations drive changes in brain activity, new possibilities may emerge for educational and cognitive neuroscience research efforts to inform one another in increasingly rapid cycles' (McCandliss cited in Howard-Jones et al. 2015: 140). The assumption here is that 'EEG can be processed in real-time, supporting applications that require . . . online measurement of neural response (e.g., as part of an adaptive system)' (2015: 136). Real-time brain scanning and data analysis connected to adaptive learning software platforms are the ultimate ambition of neuroeducation, a key part of the sociotechnical imaginary that animates technical development in the field.

With the recent development of technologies that can process huge quantities of big data, the plasticity of the human learning brain is being positioned in two ways. On one hand, it is being taken as the inspiration for brain-based computing, such as in the development of deep-learning and machine-learning algorithms based on the dynamic morphological nature of neural networks. On the other, the plasticity of the brain is seen as the target for strategic intervention and enhancement. If the brain is plastic and constantly adapting to environmental input, stimuli and social experience, it appears, then, new digitally enhanced, adaptive environments might be designed that can stimulate the brain toward improvement and optimization, and to exceed its supposed cognitive capacity.

Artificial Intelligence In Education

A key area in which neuroscience, education and adaptive technology have been combined is in the emergence of artificial intelligence (AI) applications for education. Although the idea of applying AI to education will doubtless meet firm resistance from those who see education as a fundamentally relational process, its advocates are growing across government and industry. The 2016 White House (2016b) report on AI promotes its use in education, as does the Center for Data Innovation's survey of existing AI applications (Castro and New 2016). Exemplifying this growth of interest is the education business Pearson, which has sought to firmly establish itself as a central authority on AI in education.

Pearson has been promoting itself as a new source of expertise in educational data analysis since establishing its Center for Digital Data, Analytics and Adaptive Learning and its global Learning Curve databank in 2012, as seen in previous chapters. The ambitions of the Center for Digital Data, Analytics and Adaptive Learning are to make sense of the masses of data becoming available as educational activities increasingly occur via digital media, and to use these data and patterns extracted from them to derive new understandings of learning processes, cognitive skills and the social-emotional dimensions of learning. More recently Pearson has published *Intelligence Unleashed: An argument for AI in education* (Luckin and Holmes 2016).

Pearson's report proposes that AI can transform teaching and learning. Its authors state that:

> Although some might find the concept of AIEd alienating, the algorithms and models that comprise AIEd form the basis of an essentially human endeavour. AIEd offers the possibility of learning that is more personalised, flexible, inclusive, and engaging. It can provide teachers and learners with the tools that allow us to respond not only to what is being learnt, but also to how it is being learnt, and how the student feels. (Luckin and Holmes 2016: 11)

Rather than seeking to construct a monolithic AI system, Pearson is proposing that a 'marketplace' of thousands of AI components will eventually combine to 'enable system-level data collation and analysis that help us learn much more about learning itself and how to improve it' (Luckin and Holmes 2016: 12). In technical terms, what Pearson terms 'AIEd' relies on a particular form of AI. This is not the AI superintelligence of sci-fi imaginings, but AI reimagined through the lens of big data and data analytics techniques – the 'ordinary artefacts' of algorithmic machine learning systems (Floridi 2016). Notably, the report refers to advances in machine learning algorithms, computer modelling, statistics, artificial neural networks and neuroscience, since 'AI involves computer software that has been programmed to interact with the world in ways normally requiring human intelligence. This means that AI depends both on knowledge about the world, and algorithms to intelligently process that knowledge' (Luckin and Holmes 2016: 18).

Pearson's brand of AIEd requires the development of sophisticated computational models of the learner, models of effective pedagogy, and models of the knowledge domain to be learned, as well as models that represent the social, emotional and meta-cognitive aspects of learning:

> Learner models are ways of representing the interactions that happen between the computer and the learner. The interactions represented in the model (such as the student's current activities, previous achievements, emotional state, and whether or not they followed feedback) can then be used by the domain and pedagogy components of an AIEd programme to infer the success of the learner (and teacher). The domain and pedagogy models also use this information to determine the next most appropriate interaction (learning materials or learning activities). Importantly, the learner's activities are continually fed back into the learner model, making the model richer and more complete, and the system 'smarter'. (Luckin and Holmes 2016: 19)

Based on the combination of these models with data analytics and machine learning processes, Pearson's proposed vision of AIEd includes the development of intelligent tutoring systems (ITS) which 'use AI techniques to simulate one-to-one human tutoring, delivering learning activities best matched to a learner's cognitive needs and providing targeted and timely feedback, all without an individual teacher having to be present' (Luckin and Holmes 2016: 24). It also promises intelligent support for collaborative working – such as AI agents that can integrate into teamwork – as well as intelligent virtual-reality environments that simulate authentic contexts for learning tasks, with teachers supported by their own AIEd teaching assistants and AIEd-led professional development programs.

Pearson's vision of intelligent, personalized learning environments is based on new understandings of 'how to blend human and machine intelligence effectively', and assumes specific kinds of understandings of human intelligence and cognition that are derived specifically from the expert disciplinary knowledges of neuroscience and psychology:

AIEd will continue to leverage new insights in disciplines such as psychology and educational neuroscience to better understand the learning process, and so build more accurate models that are better able to predict – and influence – a learner's progress, motivation, and perseverance. … Increased collaboration between education neuroscience and AIEd developers will provide technologies that can offer better information, and support specific learning difficulties that might be standing in the way of a child's progress. (Luckin and Holmes 2016: 37)

These points highlight how the design of AIEd systems will embody neuroscientific insights into learning processes. Such insights can then be translated into models that can be used to predict and intervene in individuals' learning processes. This reflects the recent and growing interest in neuroscience in education, and the adoption of neuroscientific insights for 'brain-targeted' teaching and learning. Such practices target the brain for educational intervention based on neuroscientific knowledge.

In particular, it highlights how an ambition for Pearson is to mobilize AIEd applications in the development of 'human capital'. Through its AIEd ambitions, Pearson is seeking to construct models, predict and influence learners' progress as a means toward the development of their measurable cognitive skills. Cognitive skills is the proxy category used by Pearson's own global databank of 'country performance' in education, the Learning Curve. The Learning Curve databank mobilizes national measures of cognitive skills as a way of ranking education systems in a global league table. By emphasizing the measurement of cognitive skills and their comparison across countries, these technologies are part of contemporary policy preoccupations with building, measuring and comparing 'human capital', which position metric accounts of learners' cognitive skills as proxy indicators of national progress and future economic productivity (Roberts-Mahoney et al. 2016). These cognitive skills are calculated from input:output indicators from diverse sources of global educational comparison, and produce league tables that can be used by policymakers as a measure of their country's pool of human capital, and as a catalyst to compete for comparative advantage in a globalizing policy space.

The brain-based techniques and applications of AIEd are thus seen by Pearson as ways of modelling learners' cognition and building human capital through boosting brain power. As a consequence, in Pearson's imaginary of AIEd, machine intelligence applications are understood as potential contributors to the whole-scale reform of education systems:

Once we put the tools of AIEd in place as described above, we will have new and powerful ways to measure system-level achievement. … AIEd will be able to provide analysis about teaching and learning at every level, whether that is a particular subject, class, college, district, or country. This will mean that evidence about country performance will be available from AIEd analysis, calling into question the need for international testing. (Luckin and Holmes 2016: 48)

In other words, Pearson is proposing to bypass the cumbersome bureaucracy of mass standardized testing and assessment – the kind of 'country performance' data that is contained in its own Learning Curve databank – and instead focus on real-time intelligent analytics conducted up-close within the pedagogic routines of the AI-enhanced classroom. This will rely on a detailed and intimate analytics of individual performance, which will be gained from detailed modelling of learners through their data. These data, analysed by AI applications that are based on neuroscientific insights, will make the measurement of individual performance into a metric of country performance, in ways that reflect biopolitical strategies of rendering individuals calculable as a means of monitoring and modelling larger populations. As such, Pearson's AIEd ambitions for education policy represent an emerging form of 'bio-edu-policy' that seeks to manage designed, enhanced and optimized populations in efforts to govern more efficiently (Gulson et al. forthcoming).

Pearson is proposing to turn educational systems at large into neurocomputational networks where brain-based technologies will perform a constant measurement and management of learning environments and of all those individuals who inhabit them. It emphasizes the role of neurocomputation in the performativity of education systems, as brain-inspired technologies that can optimize human capital development and simultaneously enact intelligent real-time measurement at large scale.

Cognitive Systems For Learning

One of the world's most successful computing companies, IBM has recently turned its attention to educational data analytics and the potential of brain-inspired computing to inform the development of 'smarter schools' (Williamson 2017). An emerging development in IBM's data analytic approach to education is 'cognitive learning systems' that are based on neuroscientific methodological innovations, technical developments in brain-inspired computing, and artificial neural networks algorithms. In recent years, IBM has positioned itself as a dominant research centre in cognitive computing. It has built huge teams of engineers and computer scientists working on both basic and applied research, with its own neuroscience experts providing insight about the brain for these developments. Its varied R&D activities have involved new developments in computer architecture, programming languages, artificial neural network algorithms, and has finally culminated in the production of cognitive system applications, all underpinned by its own models of the human brain's synaptic structures and functions. It thus claims that cognitive computing aims to 'emulate the human brain's abilities for perception, action and cognition' (Modha 2013). It has even produced its own visionary book, *Smart Machines: IBM's Watson and the era of cognitive computing* (Kelly and Hamm 2014).

Two main technical innovations have enabled IBM to position itself as a market leader in cognitive systems – its Watson supercomputer and its 'neurosynaptic chips', or computer chips modelled on real brains. 'Watson' is a massively advanced cognitive supercomputer promoted by IBM for its capacity to process and learn from natural language and other unstructured data in ways that emulate human cognition but at much higher speed and distributed scope. This sets it apart from conventional machine-learning processes that depend on being training using selected 'example data'. In addition IBM has dedicated extensive R&D to the production of neurosynaptic chips that can emulate the neurons and synapses in the human brain. In 2014 IBM announced in *Science* magazine a 'one million neuron brain-inspired processor', a 'brain chip' that is 'capable of 46 billion synaptic operations per second, per watt – literally a synaptic supercomputer in your palm' (Modha 2014; also Merolla et al. 2014). The neurosynaptic chips could also be tiled together into 'scalable neuromorphic systems' of several millions of neurons and billions of synapses, referred to as 'computing brains', 'systems that can perceive, think and act', or even a 'brain-in-a-box' (Modha 2013).

Brain-inspired cognitive computing has quickly moved to the core of IBM's business model and marketing campaigns. In a recent high-profile promotional white paper entitled *Computing, Cognition and the Future of Knowing*, IBM defines its cognitive systems as 'systems that learn at scale, reason with purpose and interact with humans naturally. Rather than being explicitly programmed, they learn and reason from their interactions with us and from their experiences with their environment (Kelly 2015: 2). This powerful imaginary of 'naturally' cognitive computing systems has been developed further in IBM's vision for personalized education:

> Until recently, computing was programmable – based around human defined inputs, instructions (code) and outputs. Cognitive systems are in a wholly different paradigm of systems that understand, reason and learn. In short, systems that think. What could this mean for the educators? We see cognitive systems as being able to extend the capabilities of educators by providing deep domain insights and expert assistance through the provision of information in a timely, natural and usable way. These systems will play the role of an assistant, which is complementary to and not a substitute for the art and craft of teaching. At the heart of cognitive systems are advanced analytic capabilities. In particular, cognitive systems aim to answer the questions: 'What will happen?' and 'What should I do?' (King et al. 2016: 9)

Rather than being hard-programmed, cognitive computing systems are designed like the brain to learn from experience and adapt to environmental stimuli. These cognitive technologies are specifically brain-based, utilizing expert knowledge about brain plasticity 'to learn dynamically through experiences, find correlations, create hypotheses and remember – and learn from – the outcomes, emulating the human brain's synaptic and structural plasticity (or the brain's ability to re-wire itself over time as it learns and responds to experiences and interactions with its environment)' (IBM Research 2011). In other words, just as IBM's in-house neuroscientists have conceived of the human brain as a dynamic system with the capacity for 'rewiring', it conceives of cognitive systems as computers with capacity to reprogram themselves in response to environmental input.

IBM has initiated a large marketing campaign around its new cognitive technologies, producing glossy and seductive imaginaries of 'cognitive business', 'cognitive healthcare' and 'cognitive education' among others. To apply its cognitive computing applications in education, IBM has developed a specific Cognitive Computing in Education program, which explicitly combines neuroscientific insights into cognitive learning processes with neurotechnologies. Its program director has presented its intelligent, cognitive systems as able to:

> learn and interact with humans in more natural ways. At the same time, advances in neuroscience, driven in part by progress in using supercomputers to model aspects of the brain ... promise to bring us closer to a deeper understanding of some cognitive processes such as learning. At the intersection of cognitive neuroscience and cognitive computing lies an extraordinary opportunity ... to refine cognitive theories of learning as well as derive new principles that should guide how learning content should be structured when using cognitive computing based technologies. (Nitta 2014)

Under the banner Cognitive Computing in Education, IBM has begun developing and trialing prototype innovations including automated 'cognitive learning content', 'cognitive tutors' and 'cognitive assistants for learning' that can understand the learner's needs and 'provide constant, patient, endless support and tuition personalized for the user' (Eassom 2015).

IBM's latest report on cognitive systems in education proposes that 'deeply immersive interactive experiences with intelligent tutoring systems can transform how we learn', ultimately leading to the 'utopia of personalized learning' (King et al. 2016: 9). This is the vision IBM claims it is able to realize through its Watson Education program, launched in 2016:

> These intelligent tutoring systems will be able to interact autonomously with learners and deliver personalized learning experiences using aspects of interactive dialogue, visual and speech recognition, and natural-language-based understanding of the learners' responses. These systems can help students understand their own knowledge gaps and offer tutoring help to remediate those gaps. (IBM Watson Education 2016a)

Instead of seeking to displace the teacher, IBM sees cognitive systems as optimizing and enhancing the role of the teacher, as a kind of cognitive prosthetic or machinic extension of human qualities. As such, the larger promise of cognitive computing for IBM is not just of more 'natural systems' with 'human qualities', but a fundamental reimagining of the 'next generation of human cognition, in which we think and reason in new and powerful ways':

> It's true that cognitive systems are machines that are inspired by the human brain. But it's also true that these machines will inspire the human brain, increase our capacity for reason and rewire the ways in which we learn. (Kelly 2015: 11)

A recursive relationship between machine cognition and human cognition is assumed in this statement. It sees cognitive systems as both brain-inspired and brain-inspiring, both modelled on the brain and remoulding the brain through interacting with users. The figure of the teacher in its imaginary is one whose capacities are not displaced by algorithms, but are algorithmically augmented and extended. Similarly, the student enrolled into a cognitive learning system is also part of a hybrid system, cognitively augmented and enhanced to perform tasks that might otherwise be beyond human capacity.

IBM's R&D in cognitive computing fundamentally depends on its own neuroscientific findings about neuroplasticity, and the translation of the biological neural networks that are studied in computational neuroscience into the artificial neural networks used in cognitive computing and AI research, as evidenced in the development of both Watson and its neurosynaptic brain chip. It is deploying its own kind of biosocial explanations about the functioning of the brain, the possibility of emulating the brain in silicon, and about the amenability of the brain to be 'rewired' through interaction with non-human cognitive systems. Supported by evidence about the plasticity of the brain from its own in-house neuroscientists, IBM's cognitive computing engineers have constructed systems that emulate the brain as a networked device constantly adapting to environmental input. In these ways, technologies such as cognitive systems for education can be seen as techniques of governance, insofar as they are based on claims to an objective knowledge about human embrained nature that can be used to underpin interventions. Moreover, IBM proceeds from a rather deficit view of cognition, maintaining that human cognition and intelligence can and should be enhanced and extended – by being rewired – through its integration with machine-based cognitive systems.

Like Pearson, IBM is mobilizing knowledge about the plasticity of the brain as a way of making the argument that human capacities can be augmented, strengthened and optimized via intelligent machines in order to deal with technical and economic demands. As stated in the introduction to IBM's report on cognitive systems in education:

> There is a growing disconnect between what education delivers and the skills being demanded in today's ever-changing global marketplace. The net result is that upon leaving full-time education, many young people are ill-prepared for the world of work.

At the same time, we are seeing unprecedented levels of change across industries and professions, with digital technologies serving as agents of transformation. (King et al. 2016: 2)

For IBM, the capacity for human capital development and the production of labour for this technological context lies in the brain itself. By mapping the brain, it is claiming authority to know and be able to intervene in cognitive processes by activating the brain using advanced cognitive systems that have been designed to integrate themselves into human cognition and from there to enhance and optimize it as appropriate to contemporary demands. Caution is required, however, about these claims:

> There is clearly an 'elective affinity' ... between this emphasis on plastic, flexible brains and more general sociopolitical changes that prioritize individual flexibility across the life span to accommodate to rapidly changing economic demands, cultural shifts, and technological advances – and that demand a constant labor of self-improvement on the part of today's citizens. (Rose and Abi-Rached 2013: 223)

IBM, like Pearson and other edu-businesses, is thoroughly engaged in a reimagining of the capacities, skills and dispositions required of young people – as well as of professional teaching practitioners – in a period of significant technological and economic change.

Late in 2016, IBM and Pearson joined forces in a new global partnership to take forward the shared vision contained in each of their cognitive computing and AIEd projects. The core of the partnership involves embedding IBM's Watson technologies in Pearson's digital courseware content. One of the key applications IBM has developed is the data-based performance tracking tool IBM Watson Element for Educators, which is 'designed to transform the classroom by providing critical insights about each student – demographics, strengths, challenges, optimal learning styles, and more – which the educator can use to create targeted instructional plans, in real-time' (IBM Watson Education 2016b). Designed for use on an iPad so it can be employed directly in the classroom, Element can capture conventional performance information, but also student interests and other contextual information, which it can feed into detailed student profiles. It can also track whole classes, and automatically generates alerts and notifications if any students are off-track and need further intervention. Another, complementary application is IBM Watson Enlight for Educators, which has been designed to support teachers with 'curated, personalized learning content and activities aligned with each student's needs. ... Teachers can optimize their time and impact throughout the year using actionable, on-demand insights about their students ... [and] craft targeted learning experiences on-the-fly from content they trust' (IBM Watson Education 2016b).

The partnership with Pearson will allow Watson to penetrate into educational institutions at huge scale, thanks to the massive reach of Pearson's courseware products. Pearson's press release stated it would 'make Watson's cognitive capabilities available to millions of college students and professors' by 'innovating with Watson APIs, education-specific diagnostics and remediation capabilities' (Pearson 2016). In practice, this means that Watson will become a 'flexible virtual tutor' enabled to 'search through an expanded set of education resources to retrieve relevant information to answer student questions, show how the new knowledge they gain relates to their own existing knowledge and, finally, ask them questions to check their understanding' (Pearson 2016). The IBM press release added that Watson would be 'embedded in the Pearson courseware':

> Watson has already read the Pearson courseware content and is ready to spot patterns and generate insights. Serving as a digital resource, Watson will assess the student's responses to guide them with hints, feedback, explanations and help identify common misconceptions, working with the student at their pace to help them master the topic. (IBM 2016)

What Watson will do, then, is commit the entirety of Pearson's content to its computer memory, and then, by constantly monitoring each individual student, cognitively calculate the precise content or structure of a learning experience that would best suit or support that individual. The partnership is ultimately the material operationalization of a shared imaginary of machine intelligences in education that both IBM and Pearson have been projecting for some time. But this imaginary is slowly moving out of the institutional enclosures of these organizations to become more widely perceived as desirable and attainable in the future.

Computing Brains

To some extent, Pearson and IBM are mobilizing their own biosocial explanations and imaginaries in the development of their cognitive and AI techniques and applications. Models of neural plasticity and epigenetics emerging from neuroscience have inspired the development of cognitive computing systems, which are then used to activate environments such as Pearson's AIEd intelligent learning environments or IBM's cognitive classroom. These are reconfigured as neurocomputationally 'brainy spaces' in which learners are targeted for cognitive enhancement and neuro-optimization through interacting with other non-conscious cognitive agents and intelligent environments. In this way, brain-based machine intelligences are proposed to meet the human brain, and, based on principles of neuroplasticity and epigenetics, to influence brain morphology and cognitive functioning.

In this context, the emphasis of Pearson and IBM on using neurocomputational technologies to activate the capacities appropriate to the development of human capital is part of wider state strategies to locate citizens' behaviours in the psyche and the brain, and that seek to modify their actions by targeting them for psychological or neurological activation and enhancement (Pykett 2015; McGimpsey et al. 2016). Of course, we need to be wary of over-determinism – there is nothing inevitable about these attempts to modify the brain. Rather, the ambitions of IBM and Pearson reflect a particular sociotechnical imaginary, linked to business plans and ambitions that project a market for brain-targeting technologies. As Rose (2016) asks, why do some dream that new neurotechnologies will make it possible to 'read' the brain, what practical applications might such technologies lead to, and what mutation in our understandings of the human might result from their development?

The main critical issue here is how the learning brain is represented and modelled by organizations such as Pearson and IBM. The field of neuroeducation has been criticized for representing the brain in reductive computational or algorithmic terms, as a multiply connected, neurally networked device that might be debugged, rewired and optimized (Pykett 2015). The educational writer and founder of Duke University's Center for Cognitive Neuroscience (CCN) Davidson (2011: 14–15), for example, likens the brain to an iPhone, 'with apps for just about everything':

> Those apps can be downloaded or deleted and are always and constantly in need of a software update. … The brain is similar. How we use our brain … changes our brain. … In this way the iPhone also corresponds nicely with recent advances in what we know about neural plasticity, the theory that the brain adapts physically to the sensory stimuli it receives.

The view that the brain can be understood as 'mental software' that is 'being updated all the time' also assumes that an increasingly networked social and technical environment is 'retooling' the brain. Her argument, in fact, is that educational institutions remain wedded to a linear machine-like model of brain development, which is reinforced by standardized curricula and testing regimes developed during the era of scientific industrialization and assembly-line manufacturing, and should be reformed instead to reflect more closely both the networked character of the Internet and the neural networking of the brain.

This reimagining of the brain reflects a longstanding tendency by scientists and technologists to liken the functions of the brain to the operations of a computer (Epstein 2016). Cognitive science has repeatedly utilized metaphors of computing for the functions and processes of the brain, such as that the brain is hardware, a rapid, complex calculating machine, made up of digital switches; that the mind is an information machine, or software, a program or set of programs which manipulates symbolic representation; that thinking is computation; that memory is looking up stored data; and that the function of the mind and brain is information processing (Edwards 1997: 161). Such computing metaphors assume that the complexity of the human brain, processes of thinking and the production of behaviour can therefore be reduced to the relatively simpler processes of computer programming, with behavioural 'bugs' and thought patterns viewed as amenable to being de-bugged, re-programmed or re-wired (Edwards 1997).

The computing metaphor of the brain matters because it assumes that neural functioning – and by default processes of learning – can be computationally modelled to construct technologies that are taken to have 'natural' and 'human' qualities of learning and cognition. But what are taken to be natural human qualities of cognition are themselves the construction of cognitive science, a field which has tended to see the brain in computer-like ways. IBM's imaginary of the brain represents it as a complex networked platform that is multiply connected, adaptive and constantly 'rewiring' itself according to environmental input and experiential stimuli received from a vast ecosystem of both human and non-human cognitive platforms. It is 'based on an altered and expanded knowledge of the body and biological processes ... as an information network rather than a physical substrate or an anatomical machine' that makes 'the reality of life conceivable and calculable in such a way that it can be shaped and transformed' (Lemke 2011: 118–19). IBM's ideal that cognitive systems can 'rewire the ways we learn' inscribes the computing metaphor onto the plasticity of the learning brain. A reimagining of the human subject is instantiated by such claims, as networks of neural patterns connected to a world of information and communication networks (Castells 2009: 139). Yet even the field of neuroscience is deeply divided in its conceptualization of the brain, with different branches of neuroscientific expertise seeking to model the brain differently. For other critics, even the most sophisticated computational modelling and simulation of the vast pattern of the brain's neural network *would mean nothing outside the body of the brain that produced it* and 'be meaningless unless we knew the *entire life history* of that brain's owner – perhaps even about the *social context* in which he or she was raised' (Epstein 2016, original italics).

While the systems that IBM and Pearson are promoting may be brain-based and brain-targeted then, they reproduce a problematic understanding of mental life in terms of computational information processing and networking platforms. Even more specifically, they conflate the neurobiological neural networks of the brain that are the objects of neuroscientific imaging and basic research with the artificial or convolutional neural networks that are being developed in applied R&D in AI and cognitive computing. A rewiring of the biological neural networks of the brain via machine intelligence is being premised on the analysis of the artificial neural networks known to computational neuroscience. They not only treat the neural networks of the learning brain as computable, but may be confusing brain-inspired machine learning and information processing with the complexity of embodied, culturally relevant and socially situated learning. This is not to question the pursuit of expert neuroscientific knowledge through computational methods, but to raise questions about the ways such expertise is being translated and applied by commercial vendors of educational machine intelligences.

Conclusion

Artificial intelligence and cognitive computing are at the cutting edge of big data analytics. They are both the product of huge efforts to map the brain using sophisticated technologies that can translate it into analysable data, and based on computational theories which hold that the brain is itself an advanced big data processor consisting of malleable neural networks. A shared language and imaginary of computation now binds together the kinds of neuroscientific and technical R&D being mobilized by Pearson and IBM, as demonstrated by the announcement of their global partnership to embed Watson in Pearson courseware in 2016, and even further by the uptake of positive visions of AI in education by think tanks, research centres and even political centres such as the White House. Moreover, neurocomputational technologies such as AI and cognitive computing are now seen as the most advanced applications of big data analytics and machine learning, designed with the capacity to analyse huge amounts of unstructured and unpredictable data in ways that do not require hard programming, training data or supervised learning. Instead, modelled on human brain qualities of learning from experience and neuroplasticity, technologies being built and promoted by IBM and Pearson are designed to learn and adapt to environmental stimuli and input, just like humans.

Contentious assumptions about human learning as a computational process, or as a process determined by genetic variance, have come into play, all rationalized via the concept of personalization. While educational genomics advances the case that education can be personalized according to the DNA profile of individuals, developments in neuroeducational AI and cognitive systems also emphasize the development of data-processing technologies that can learn and adapt to the learner in order to provide personalized feedback and content that might stimulate the brain's plasticity.

The application of these developments in the design of adaptive neuroeducation technologies of course raises real implications for educational practices. They are not just biologically rationalized and brain-based, but brain-targeted too, and aimed at actively extending cognition and intelligence through activating neurobiological dynamics. This raises all sorts of questions about how learners and learning processes might be assessed when they are thoroughly hybridized with other forms of machine intelligence. Questions are also raised about the desirability (or not) of artificially extended forms of cognition and thinking. Perhaps not least, serious issues arise when we recognize that both Pearson and IBM are global commercial businesses with products to sell. Artificial tutors and cognitive assistants for learning – whether desirable additions to the classroom or not – could become highly prized acquisitions for wealthy educational institutions, which will be able to integrate them into the pedagogic apparatus of the institution to the benefit of staff and students, at the expense of less wealthy institutions. This could exacerbate and reinforce existing inequalities, giving some institutions with existing economic capital more neurocomputational capital too.

A concept that has emerged with critical biosocial research is that of 'local biologies', the understanding that there is a 'continuous exchange between the social and the biological in the production and reproduction of bodies in situated socio-cultural contexts' (Meloni 2014). From this perspective, local contexts leave biological markers on the 'embedded body' and brain, as biological signatures of socio-environmental exposure. The implication for educational contexts and environments in which machine intelligences and cognitive tutors might enact a cognitive extension of human capacities – through rewiring the plastic brain – is potentially significant. It suggests the possibility of new kinds of local neurobiologies of education – of socio-environmental contexts and spaces where the neurobiological structures of learners' brains bear the signature of their interaction with machine-based forms of intelligence.

Again, caution is required before assuming that neurocomputation will determine neurobiological structure and functioning. But the possibility that local neurobiologies may appear as the result of socially situated interaction with machine intelligences is an emerging issue deserving future scrutiny. Could such technologies lead to new hierarchical striations of education as institutions and individuals are ranked in terms of their hybrid neurocomputational intelligences and cognitively enhanced capacities? The stated ambitions of IBM particularly are to extend human capacities for cognition, based on evidence about how the brain can be moulded and rewired. In this sense, its business plan is to reshape neurobiology by creating new markets for its products. Insofar as its products are likely to be unevenly distributed across education institutions, and that neuroplasticity is now taken seriously by neuroscientists and social scientists alike, then we need to attend to the possible emergence of new locally contingent and hierarchically ranked neurobiologies of learning.

8
MAKING AND CODING CULTURES
Digital citizens, DIY makers and apprentice data analysts

In June 2016, Google Research announced the launch of Project Bloks, a 'tangible programming' platform that would enable children to learn to produce computer code through the physical manipulation of electronic blocks. The Project Bloks platform consists of base boards and electronic 'programmable pucks', the tangible interface components, which are all connected by a 'brain board' to provide power and connectivity. Together, the elements of the platform can be used to code instructions for other linked devices, to instruct sensor devices, to compose music, or myriad other programming activities. The project is intended as an open hardware and software platform that makes it easy to invent novel ways for children to learn how to code. In a position paper accompanying the project launch, the Project Bloks team (consisting of researchers from Google, Stanford University and the design consultancy IDEO) claim that the platform combines educational theories of experiential, hands-on learning with computational thinking and problem solving, particularly citing Seymour Papert's influential work on 'constructionism' as a precursor of the 'coding-for-children' and 'maker movement' that has emerged 40 years later (Blikstein et al. 2016). They also approvingly reference 'constructivist' developmental psychology such as that of Jean Piaget from the mid-twentieth century for its emphasis on how children's 'innate' playfulness allows them to learn from the experience of 'building stuff'.

The idea that young people should learn to code in order to be able to program and make digital products has become a major educational movement in recent years, spearheaded by a range of philanthropic and charitable organizations, businesses, academic researchers, influential media voices and entrepreneurs, and government departments. The Project Bloks researchers are careful in their position paper to distance themselves from the narrow view that children should learn to code and make digital artefacts in order to become employable future programmers and skilled human capital for the digital industries. However, the learning to code and maker movement with which Project Bloks is associated is in fact a highly messy result of a variety of competing perspectives and ways of thinking about training children to program computational devices. It consists of political and economic claims about building industry capacity, concerns from the computer science field about disciplinary development, and theoretical interests in psychological constructivist and constructionist learning, alongside more rampantly commercial attempts to build an educational market in coding and making products and platforms.

At the same time, the rapid growth of the Web, social media and big data has begun to animate significant debates about identity and citizenship in the digital age, and the role of education in shaping 'digital citizens' (Emejula and McGregor 2016). Particularly as social media has repositioned web users as also producers of content, it has been claimed that new ways of expressing one's identity and one's self as a citizen who makes digital artefacts and produces data rather than simply consuming them are becoming available.

This chapter examines the global emergence of the 'maker movement' and 'learning to code' initiatives to explore the emergence of a new imaginary of digital citizenship. The imaginary of digital citizenship is produced through particular ways of thinking about both digital technologies and citizens, and therefore reflects statements about what citizenship is and ought to be that embody norms, values, ideologies and technologies (Isin and Ruppert 2015). The particular form of digital citizenship associated with making and coding, which originated in North American coding and hacking cultures, has been termed 'entrepreneurial citizenship', a way of being a citizen that 'voices a broader enthusiasm for bringing Silicon Valley's practices of hacking, designing, and crowdsourcing to the practice of public life' (Irani 2015: 800). Entrepreneurial citizens are invited to view themselves as 'agents of social progress through software' and as subjects who can make a social difference through digital hacking and making (2015: 800). In other words, the notion of a digital or entrepreneurial form of citizenship registers how technical practices have become models for particular social practices and the expression of one's self in public life.

In recent research literature, making has been associated with a form of 'DIY citizenship' (Ratto and Boler 2014) and a 'participatory politics' that incites citizens to merge the cultural and the political to understand, express and reshape public affairs (Soep 2014). It has been argued that maker activities are also contributing to new identities, or 'making subjectivities' (Lindtner 2015). Coding and making, then, promotes the ideal of the do-it-yourself (DIY) potential of citizens to participate in the production of new public services, create new value-producing products, and contribute to the cultural dynamics of cities and regions. It is embedded in pedagogical strategies intended to re-educate citizens as productive and participatory makers who can contribute culturally, politically and economically in social life. Making is intended not just to make *things*, but to remake society and make digital citizens. Coding and making are not simply neutral technical tasks, but embody deeply political aspirations about the future of a digitized society and the conduct deemed appropriate to being a digital citizen (Williamson 2016d).

The digital citizen who can code and make is the hybrid subject of varied political, economic, commercial, civic and psychological discourses, or a particular subjectivity that young people are being invited to inhabit and project for themselves. So powerful has this movement to produce skilled coders, computational thinkers and digital makers become that, as we shall see in this chapter, massive attempts have been made to integrate programming into school curricula at national levels, opening up vast new opportunities for providers and vendors of technology platforms, materials and resources from across the public, private and charitable sectors. The pedagogies of learning to code and digital making are not just pedagogies of technical craft but rather pedagogies designed to sculpt and model a form of subjectivity that is deemed appropriate to contemporary digital citizenship.

In order to reach that point, the chapter is organized to outline the origins of the learning to code and digital making movement; to examine how coding and making has been linked to the production of technically skilled human capital; to detail how coding and making have begun to integrate into school curricula; to detail some of the commercial markets for products and resources that have accompanied this movement; to consider how it has been linked to 'civic' interests; and then to discuss how the varied coding and making initiatives emerging in education are contributing to the making of a new kind of participatory, DIY form of digital citizenship. The digital citizen-subject projected through these activities and their sponsors is one imagined to possess technical skills of programming, building and analysis, who can work with data as a form of digital labour but also play with data as a productive consumer in the circuits of social media cultures. The ultimate argument is that making and coding is being governmentalized as governments are coming to realize the potential economic and social benefits of producing a new talent pool of skilled producers as well as encouraging citizens to see themselves as 'solutions engineers' who can contribute as DIY participants to the solving of complex public and social problems. In this sense, citizens are being made governable as digital citizens within the logic of emerging objectives of digital governance.

The Making of Making

The origins of the coding and making movement lie in psychological theories of constructivism popularized in the mid-twentieth century – particularly their adoption within constructionist perspectives on children learning through programming, building and otherwise constructing computer-based artefacts–combined with the Silicon Valley culture of hacking, programming and making. For constructivist theorists, learning is said to be a psychological process that occurs as children and young people explore, experiment and play with the linguistic, visual and material resources they encounter through experience. The field of constructionism, chiefly associated with Seymour Papert of MIT from the early 1970s onwards, took the psychological principles of constructivism and applied it to the educational use of construction kits and toys such as LEGO (Papert 1980). Constructionists took a special interest in programmable computing systems and advocated 'cybernetics for children' as an approach to learning. Through programming environments such as LOGO, constructionists aimed to promote transferable problem-solving skills and at the same time to grant young people agency and authorship. The constructionist outlook saw 'users programming the computer rather than the computer programming them' and viewed the act of programming as a way of enabling 'users to embody their agency computationally' (Ito 2009: 146).

The constructionist approach underpins many projects, initiatives and platforms designed more recently to encourage young people to learn to code. Google's Project Bloks makes explicit mention of constructionism and Papert. Papert's legacy at MIT also informs Scratch, a successful MIT platform for visual programming that is designed to be accessible to young children. In the UK, the successful Code Club initiative – an after-school coding class run by volunteer programmers – also invokes the constructionist idea that young people should learn to program the computer rather than be programmed by it. The Code Club curriculum is designed so that children attending a class encounter Scratch as their first experience of programming. More widely, the 'maker movement' is indebted to constructionism, 'the theory of learning that undergirds the maker movement's focus on problem solving and digital and physical fabrication' (Halverson and Sheridan 2014: 497). The maker movement is generally understood to refer to writing computer code, creating apps, 3-D printing and other modes of 'personal manufacturing', often through makerspaces, hackerspaces and hackathons, manufacturing workshops, fabrication labs, learning to code clubs, and other makers programs.

Making has become a global phenomenon, though it is playing out differently in different national and cultural contexts according to different driving forces and factors. While the maker movement is theoretically and practically indebted to constructionism, it has also been forcefully catalysed by technology entrepreneurs. One of the most high-profile advocates of the maker movement is Chris Anderson, former chief editor of *Wired* magazine, who has described making in epochal terms as 'the next industrial revolution'. An entrepreneurial making scene has developed with the emergence of specialist magazines and websites such as *Make:* and the proliferation of new makerspaces and other fabrication labs. The entrepreneurial dimensions of the maker movement have emerged from the Silicon Valley culture of technology utopianism, which tends to view all social problems as solvable through the application of well-designed new technologies (Irani 2015). The influence of the hacker culture of Silicon Valley, with its emphasis on tinkering, playing with programming languages, taking systems apart and rebuilding them, infuses the kind of maker advocacy put forward by people like Anderson and materials such as *Make:* magazine.

A more critically-driven approach to making and coding has been offered by other sources. The US media commentator Rushkoff (2010) for example has adapted Papert's arguments into the slogan 'program or be programmed' to argue that young people need to understand code in order to understand how the dominant technology companies of the age are subtly shaping their lives. In the UK the newspaper columnist Naughton (2012) has vigorously campaigned for children to learn to code in schools according to a similar argument, culminating in his publication of a 'manifesto for teaching computer science' in the *Observer* newspaper:

[I]n a world shaped and dependent on networking technology, an understanding of computing is essential for informed *citizenship*. ... [E]very child should learn some computer science from an early age because they live in a world in which computation is ubiquitous. ... Doing so will yield economic and social benefits – and ensure they will be on the right side of the 'program or be programmed' choice that faces every citizen in a networked world.

The notion that learning to code is key to becoming an informed citizen of a networked world underpins the rationale proffered by Code Club, which Naughton has enthusiastically promoted.

From an explicitly educational perspective, a huge number of online courses, software platforms and hardware has been developed to support young people to learn to code and make, much of it discursively promoted by organizations such as Maker Ed and publications produced through academic initiatives with an emphasis on digital technologies and education. A growing political and education policy emphasis on making has been associated with the science, technology, engineering and maths (STEM) subjects, widely seen as crucial talent pipelines for the digital, creative and technical industries that support advanced economies (Sefton-Green 2013).

As these examples demonstrate, the making of making has been informed by a variety of perspectives and arrangements, involving actors speaking from diverse standpoints. In relation to the learning to code movement specifically, it has been suggested that nine different 'metaphors of code' are in circulation:

- *Machine*: code as a mechanistic, linear sequence of commands.
- *Organism*: code as a combination of objects.
- *Brain*: code is intelligence.
- *Flux and transformation*: code will save the world.
- *Culture*: code-creating communities.
- *Political system*: code structuring the society.
- *Psychic prison*: code restricting human behaviour.
- *Instrument of domination*: knowledge and control of code is power.
- *Carnival*: understanding of code can be created through creative use of code. (Dufva and Dufva 2016)

Indeed, it is helpful to think of making and coding as the subject of multiple translations between these different metaphors of code and coding. By 'translation', what is meant is that diverse perspectives about coding and making have been synthesized, juxtaposed and made seemingly commensurate with one another. Many of the long histories of constructionism and Silicon Valley hacking that underpin this movement are simply taken for granted as making and coding have become seen as seemingly common-sense activities.

Coding Human Capital

Coding and making have become translated into the focus of political interest. In many countries, especially the US and the UK, politicians at the very highest levels of government have publicly advocated the benefits of learning to code and become digital makers. However, this level of political support has been achieved through the work of key intermediary actors who have performed the task of translating coding and making into political discourse, and at the same time begun to open up opportunities for commercial and technical providers. In this respect, learning to code and digital making is a good example of 'fast policy', an accelerated policy process that operates within compressed timescales and also exhibits extended reach across governmental, commercial and intermediary sectors (Peck and Theodore 2015). Think tanks, lobbying alliances, pressure groups, professional and industry associations, and commercial coalitions have been central to how coding and making have become the object of fast policy processes and mainstream political discourse.

A prominent example of the transformation of code into political discourse is the Hour of Code project in the US. The Hour of Code campaign was set up in 2013 by code.org, 'a non-profit dedicated to expanding participation in computer science by making it available in more schools' – its 'vision is that every student in every school should have the opportunity to learn computer programming' (Code.org 2014). Code.org was founded by the entrepreneurs Ali and Hadi Partovi, twins with a long history of 'angel investment' and venture capitalism in Silicon Valley, and supported by Microsoft, Google, Amazon, Dropbox, Facebook and many others, as well as by philanthropic individuals from across commercial computing and the field of venture capital. US President Barack Obama completed an hour of code in late 2014 to much media attention, announcing a year later his ambition for every American school student to receive instruction in computer science. In a weekly address, Obama said:

> 'New technology replaces any job where work can be automated. Workers need more skills to get ahead. These changes aren't new, and they're only going to accelerate. So the question we have to ask ourselves is, "How can we make sure everyone has a fair shot at success in this new economy?"' (Shapiro 2016)

Similarly, in the UK, the Year of Code campaign was established in 2014 to help people 'learn code and create exciting things on computers' (Year of Code 2014). The Year of Code was sponsored by an extensive network of partners from across government, commercial media and civil society. The executive director and advisors of Year of Code were almost all drawn from the fields of entrepreneurship, venture capital and the computing industry. Although the UK's Year of Code was seen as an unsuccessful political intervention, the US Hour of Code has become an international phenomenon, with a dedicated UK Hour of Code initiative established in 2015 with the high-profile backing of Tim Berners-Lee (widely seen as the inventor of the World Wide Web) and Boris Johnson (then Mayor of London).

Organizations from a range of different positions have also been closely involved in promoting coding and making. At about the same time as the Year of Code, the innovation charity Nesta, in partnership with the philanthropic Nominet Trust and the Internet company Mozilla, launched an initiative called Make Things Do Stuff to promote various forms of learning to code, programming and digital making. Described as an 'open movement', Make Things Do Stuff was directly partnered with technology companies, education businesses, third-sector organizations and government agencies. The Chancellor of the Exchequer at that time, George Osborne MP, launched the initiative in May 2013 claiming that 'this campaign is backing the entrepreneurs of the future and helping ensure that Britain is equipped to succeed in the global race' (HM Treasury 2013). Similarly, the Nominet Trust Chief Executive claimed a 'serious and economic imperative' besides the 'fun and learning that digital making offers young people', namely that the 'UK and global jobs market are crying out for digital skills and we need to make sure that the next generation can meet this need' (Nominet Trust 2013). Subsequent high-profile government reports from the Design Commission and the UK Digital Skills Taskforce have similarly recommended political support for coding and making in order to boost digital skills for the economy.

As Year of Code, Hour of Code and Make Things Do Stuff demonstrate, a global political discourse of future economic productivity has been attached to making and learning to code. These initiatives are the product of intermediary organizations such as venture capital investors, charities and trusts, which have performed the task of translating coding and making into an imperative for political intervention. Through the work of such intermediaries, coding and making have been partially detached from their constructionist and hacker culture origins and reframed by discourses of human capital development.

One key rationale for the reframing of coding and making as human capital development is the alleged demand for data analysis talent. The innovation charity Nesta, one of the organizers of Make Things Do Stuff, in particular has advanced arguments about the needs of an 'Analytic Britain'. Its two reports, *Skills of the Datavores: Talent and the data revolution* (Mateos-Garcia et al. 2015) and *Analytic Britain: Securing the right skills for the data-driven economy* (Nesta 2015), explicitly connect learning to code and digital making to the data analytics industry and the UK's digital economy. It regards education in programming and analytical problem solving as the 'talent pipeline' required for the UK to become a competitive, innovative and leading nation in the analysis of big data and in the maximization data-driven insights for economic productivity and prosperity across a range of sectors.

According to the political discourse that has framed it, digital making and learning to code embodies a host of assumptions and working practices based on ideas such as computational thinking, systems thinking, scientific rationality and procedural algorithmic logic that have their origins in the working practices and codes of conduct associated with the 'culture of code' of software development (Hayes 2015). These are very specific kinds of social practices which reflect sometimes quite functionalist and technicist modes of thinking that approach the world in computational terms rather than in relation to cultural, economic or political contexts (Kitchin 2014b). In this sense, learning to code may be interpreted as a material practice of 'algorithmic ideology' (Mager 2012), a kind of introduction into the working codes of conduct, practices, assumptions and values that underpin the production of code. Learning to code initiatives such Hour of Code, Year of Code and Make Things Do Stuff are designed to initiate learners into the systems of thinking and practice associated with the professional regime of programmers. Learning to code and digital making are premised on a fantasy of the material practices associated with coding which simplifies and glamorizes the reality of disciplinary practice in the digital economy.

Computing Curricula

The promotion of making and coding has begun to influence school curricula at the national and state level. In the US, President Barack Obama announced in 2016 $4 billion of federal support for a Computer Science for All initiative, while Canada has similarly supported computing as a future subject for schools. In the UK, a new computing subject was established in the National Curriculum in 2014 (this applies specifically to England, though computing has also become the focus for renewed curricular attention under Scotland's Curriculum for Excellence). The new computing programmes of study were introduced following the disapplication of ICT, which critics claimed over-emphasized basic functional skills for using computers, and in its replacement a new focus on computer science, programming skills and 'computational thinking' (Peyton Jones et al. 2013; Computing at School 2014).

The creation of the computing curriculum in the UK was not the result simply of a political agenda. Instead, it was the end-product of a series of lobbying and campaigning activities involving private sector, public sector and civic sector organizations. Initial support for the idea of learning to code and for enhancing programming and computer science in the curriculum in the UK came from Computing at School (CAS). CAS is a member-led subject association for computing teachers initiated at Microsoft Research in 2008, which is chaired by a senior Microsoft researcher and is funded by Microsoft, Google and the British

Computing Society (BCS), the national association for computing professionals. The CAS (2010) 'white paper' was among the first documents to argue for the replacement of ICT in the National Curriculum with computing. Its authors argued that 'computing is the study of how computers and computer systems work, and how they are constructed and programmed', and it suggested that a new computing curriculum would include the study of 'how computers work', how algorithms, data structures, systems and networks are used to solve computational problems, as well as teaching the knowledge and skills of programming. CAS has also argued strongly for an emphasis on 'computational thinking' in the computing curriculum, as a 'philosophy that underpins computing' or a framework which consists of processes of decomposition, pattern recognition, abstraction, pattern generalization and algorithm design (Computing at School 2014).

However, it was in 2011 after the innovation charity Nesta published a report entitled *Next Gen* (Livingstone and Hope 2011) that the key messages about computing and learning to code took on policy significance. *Next Gen* demanded more 'rigorous teaching of computing in schools' and recommended putting computer science into the national curriculum for schools in England. The report was commissioned as a review of the skills required for the videogames and visual effects industries – rather than of provision in computing education in schools – which have long been seen as economically valuable and innovative sectors of the UK economy. The authors, Ian Livingstone and Alex Hope, were industry leaders in the videogames and visual effects sector and the report was commissioned by Ed Vaizey, then Conservative Party Minister for Culture, Communications and Creative Industries. At the same time, the Royal Society (2012) was compiling a report entitled *Shut Down or Restart?* which was focused on the lack of adequate computer science education in schools. It too added pressure on government to replace ICT with computing in the curriculum. The report was directly commissioned by Microsoft, Google and university computer science departments.

The key messages of CAS, Nesta and the Royal Society began to gather political interest after Google chief executive Eric Schmidt used the platform of the MacTaggart Lecture at the Edinburgh television festival in 2011 to express his dismay that computer science was not taught as standard in UK schools. This was a message repeated by Google executives in a global lecture circuit urging governments to support young people to learn to code in order to produce a skilled workforce for a digital economy (Cave and Rowell 2014). One of the co-authors of Nesta's *Next Gen* has argued explicitly that it was Eric Schmidt's MacTaggart Lecture that mobilized political support for its curriculum recommendations (Livingstone 2012). The subsequent formation of a 'Next Gen Skills coalition' consisting of members from Nesta, BCS, Google, Microsoft, CAS and Raspberry Pi finally convinced the Department for Education to support the disapplication of ICT and its replacement by a new computing curriculum (Livingstone 2012). After that, a working group was established by the Department for Education to draft the new computing curriculum, with membership largely drawn from the BCS, the Royal Academy of Engineering and CAS. Between them, the organizations BCS, the Royal Academy, CAS, Nesta and the webs of affiliates they have drawn together, have made computing and coding in schools into a successful agenda for curriculum policy reform. In so doing, they have stitched together the economic interests of government, the disciplinary aspirations of computer scientists, and the educational goals of computing teachers into a set of shared objectives.

The involvement of Nesta as an intermediary between government and commercial organizations and lobbying groups has also been key to the political acceptance of the language of digital making. Nesta's report *Young Digital Makers* (Quinlan 2015) claims that learning to code is a key part of growing a nation of 'digital makers', individuals with the skills and knowledge to create the digital products of the future, grow the economy, and contribute to societal improvement. It refers to 'digital making' as:

> distinct from simply using digital devices, and as the best way of understanding how technology works. Our work to date has focused on helping young people to 'look under the hood' of technology while they are making. From programming entirely on a computer to designing and 3D printing physical objects, digital making represents a diverse range of activities. (Quinlan 2015: 7)

Many of these activities had previously been promoted through Nesta's own Make Things Do Stuff campaign. But Young Digital Makers signals a mainstreaming of these activities:

> A huge expansion is needed if we are to grow a nation of digital creators who can manipulate and build the technology that both society and industry are increasingly reliant on. This expansion cannot be left exclusively to professionals, however, as we simply don't have enough of them. It will require the mobilisation of enthusiasts and interested amateurs, from parents and non–expert teachers, to those working in the tech industry, working and learning alongside young people to help meet this demand. (Quinlan 2015: 8)

The report also argues that 'Schools must exploit their potential as a hub for digital making opportunities, work with informal learning organisations, raise parents' awareness and recruit volunteers' (Quinlan 2015: 11).

Major public institutions such as the BBC have also been enrolled into the learning to code and digital makers movement. *Young Digital Makers* features a foreword by Tony Hall, Director-General of the BBC, who used his prefatory remarks to announce the BBC's major 2015 campaign Make It Digital. Upon its launch, the BBC described Make It Digital as 'a major UK-wide initiative to inspire a new generation to get creative with coding, programming and digital technology' (BBC 2015). In addition to a range of broadcast programming and online content, the BBC announced its intention to give away a million micro:bit coding devices to every high-school student in the UK. Finally launched in 2016, the device was clearly designed to resonate with the legacy of the BBC Micro. Launched in the 1980s, the BBC Micro was the product of a partnership with the hardware company Acorn and received backing from government departments. It included the Computer Literacy Project, consisting of courses, supporting books and software, a strong liaison network for teachers and learners, as well as the licensed production of its own microcomputer. The legacy of the BBC Micro and the associated Computer Literacy Project was examined in another Nesta report, which stated that 'the BBC Micro was complemented by activities that increased demand for computing generally, by promoting cultural shifts in attitudes towards computing and delivering learning into homes and schools' (Blyth 2012: 7). Following a similar model, the BBC has subsequently established a non-profit foundation to roll out the micro:bit internationally, clearly capitalizing on its global status as an educational computing provider.

As a final key event in this historical narrative about how computing has been embedded in the curriculum for schools in the UK, in 2016 the UK Secretary of State for Education announced plans to open two new free schools that will focus specifically on computer programming skills. The schools are being founded by Ian Livingstone, the videogames entrepreneur who co-authored the Nesta report *NextGen* in 2010 and continued to chair the Next Gen Skills campaign afterwards. The two Livingstone Academies are planned around the 'creative application of digital technologies':

> Our aim is that all our students will be equipped with the skills and qualifications required to play an active and successful role in today's knowledge-based, interdependent, highly competitive, fast-changing digital world. Our new school will have a rich partnership with the digital industry to ensure that students gain the skills and knowledge that are central to a successful life as a digital citizen in modern Europe. We believe that there is a role for a new local school specialising in computing, science and technology that will provide wider opportunities for future careers for a new generation of successful and confident citizens who will contribute to local, national and international economic success. This will be a new school that will combine modern technology with specialist science labs, design studios and an onsite business hub for start-up and tech businesses to ensure that our students will combine excellent academic results with enterprising practical experience tailored to the needs of contemporary society. (Livingstone Aspirations 2016)

The emphasis on preparing young people for work and enterprise in the knowledge economy, for new forms of participatory digital citizenship, combined with its industry partnerships and in-house facilities for startup tech businesses, reiterate many of the key messages that Ian Livingstone himself has been promoting since overseeing NextGen. The Livingstone Academies can therefore be seen as institutional realizations of the NextGen campaign, and demonstrate the significant influence in contemporary education of technology entrepreneurs and lobbyists. In the governmental press release announcing the new schools, Ian Livingstone himself argued:

> It is the combination of computer programming skills and creativity by which today's world-changing companies are built. I encourage other digital entrepreneurs to seize the opportunity offered by the free schools programme in helping to give children an authentic education for the jobs and opportunities of the digital world. (Gov.uk 2016)

The Livingstone Academies embody how the existing priorities of the learning to code movement have been translated directly into the school classroom itself.

As noted earlier, much of the advocacy for learning to code, digital making and related computing projects reflect a modern political preoccupation with sculpting an enterprising mind and body with the technical skills, knowledge and capacity for entrepreneurship and value-creation in the digital economy. In this sense, the Livingstone Academies might be seen as inducting young people into the commercial culture of computing associated with the software development industry, as well as introducing them to the systems of thought associated with the professional regime of programmers that approach the world in computational terms rather than in relation to cultural, economic or political contexts. The Livingstone Academies emphasize and prize the production of economically valuable assets over other culturally valued forms of knowledge. Their business model, ultimately, is concerned with the production of human capital for the digital economy, while simultaneously weaving a narrative of informed digital citizenship around it.

However, the dominant discourse being wrapped around the new computing curriculum – of which the Livingstone Academies are an institutional model – is that computing is a scientific subject, rooted in the expert discipline of computer science. As the history of computing has shown, when computer science emerged as an academic discipline in the late 1960s its key advocates worked hard to distance it from the practical and applied business of programming (Ensmenger 2010). In a contemporary parallel, there is some question about whether the new computing curricula, which emphasize programming and learning to code, genuinely serve the needs and interests of the computer science discipline. Hayes (2015), for example, claims that most coding courses are oriented towards software development rather than the more abstract mathematical analysis of fundamental algorithms that concerns computer scientists.

By prioritizing code, the new computing curricula developed in the UK and North America appear to reinforce and reproduce the historical division between computer science and software development, downplaying the abstract analyses of the former in favour of the applied agenda of the latter to produce human capital with the technical skills to write useful programs. Though this may seem contradictory, it is also strategic. By blurring the lines between the fundamentals of computer science and the practical application of programming, advocates of computing in schools have been able to appeal simultaneously to disciplinary interests in maintaining expertise, and to economic interests in building skilled human capital for the technical industries.

Given the political framing of coding and making by the discourse of human capital development and software skills, it is perhaps not surprising that a large commercial industry, sponsored by many corporate businesses, has emerged to support this educational movement. For example, the global computing company the Oracle Corporation has invested over $200 million in the US Computer Science for All initiative, and in 2016 announced $1.4 billion investment to provide a mix of software, curriculum and professional development for teachers of computing in European Union member states (Cavanagh 2016). Oracle's massive financial support for coding education is ample evidence of how commercial companies are seeking to accelerate government activities in relation to computing in schools in ways that cut across national and governmental boundaries. The juxtaposition of commercial and governmental priorities was most clearly signalled by the Year of Code in the UK. As the *Guardian* newspaper columnist Naughton (2014) argued, 'Year of Code is a takeover bid by a corporate world that has woken up to the realization that the changes in the computing curriculum … will open up massive commercial opportunities'. As if to demonstrate this, the Chief Executive of Codecademy has claimed to have 'struck oil' as the computing curriculum is 'forcing an entire country to learn programming' (Dredge 2014). At about the same time, however, the director of Code Club was forced to quit by its board after criticizing the 'corporate mass surveillance' practices of its commercial sponsor Google (Sandvik 2014).

A significant marketplace for vendors has appeared in the wake of the establishment of the computing curriculum in the UK. With the support of the Department of Education, massive international computing organizations including Google and Microsoft have become significant suppliers of classroom resources and training materials to support the computing curriculum. This is not just about commercial firms influencing education policy and practice. It is indicative of the increasing entanglement of business and government in contemporary policy processes. In their book on political lobbying in the UK, Cave and Rowell (2014) describe the various activities surrounding the learning to code movement and the reform of the computing curriculum as a lobbying tool for technology firms with a clear, vested interest in digitizing learning, as well as enthusing a new generation of coders. Noting the involvement of Nesta and the Education Foundation (an education think tank with strong links to the computing industry), Cave and Rowell (2014: 260–61) argue that this 'campaign of business-backed think tanks and education technology lobbyists' has now 'got what it wanted' in the shape of the computing curriculum and strong political support for the educational technology market.

Civic Coding

Learning to code and digital making is also closely related by key advocates such as Nesta with ideas about 'hackathons', 'mob programming' and 'codefests' for public service design, and 'government hacking' events. 'Hack' events put teams of computer programmers together, using code-sharing tools, to engineer solutions to government and public sector problems. The voluntary producer is the ideal subject for a governmental context where the state is seeking to deconcentrate its responsibilities and enable more 'people-powered public services' and co-produced solutions facilitated by 'people helping people', as Nesta documents describe it (Clarence and Gabriel 2014).

Along these people-powered lines, Nesta manages projects such as 'local government digital making', 'civic tech' and 'coding for civic service' that involve a mixture of coding skills, design skills and user experience to explore 'solutions to challenges' – merging 'what is (technically) possible and what is (politically) feasible' (Bell 2014). These projects apply what Nesta terms a 'code for x model' (Bell 2014) which assume that computer code can be applied as a solution for almost any problem. It rests on the assumption that the problems with the social world can be addressed with solutions written in code – or applying software engineering to the task of human, social and political engineering. In that sense it represents the embedding of computational thinking – the expression of problems in the language that computers can understand – in the main style of contemporary governmental thought. Nesta's work with the UK Government Cabinet Office, for example, has proposed treating 'government as a platform', utilizing new digital services, apps and technical designs to solve its problems. Such a mode of governance requires citizens with particular kinds of skills to enact it, and emphasizes the role of 'civic hackers' and 'civic laboratories' in the creation of citizen-centred urban services, where 'knowing how to code will be an important skill for civic improvement' (Townsend 2013: 243).

Two UK civic coding projects exemplify the emerging juxtaposition of coding and making with questions of citizenship and governance. The Future Makers program, part of Glasgow's Future City initiative in the UK (a £24million government-funded smart cities showcase project) emphasizes the 'literacies' required to 'empower and educate people in using city data' and the 'knowledge and skills to participate, understand or contribute to the Future

City' (Open Glasgow 2014: 4, 9). In order to promote these smart city literacies, the Future Makers program, facilitated by the Nesta-funded CoderDojo programming club, provides an 'innovative coding education programme' to develop programming and coding skills among young people (Open Glasgow 2014: 14). Future Makers consists of coding clubs and workshops all aimed at enabling young people to help shape and sustain the Future City. Related activities in the Glasgow Future City include 'Hacking the Future' events putting citizens, programmers, designers and government staff together in teams to focus on coding citizen-centred solutions to urban problems. Future Makers thus acts in part to ensure young people are equipped with the relevant technical expertise of coding and computational urbanism to help 'hack' or code the future of the smart city.

Similarly, the Milton Keynes' Smart City program, a collaboration between the local government and the Open University known as MK:Smart, includes a major educational initiative, the Urban Data School. The aims of Urban Data School are to teach young people 'data literacy' to access and analyse urban datasets; create tools and resources to 'bring data skill education into the classroom'; and to encourage new forms of 'active citizenship' through using data 'to design and evaluate Urban Innovation Projects' and to devise 'effective solutions on the local, urban and global level' (Urban Data School 2015). The MK:Smart Urban Data School, like Glasgow's Future Makers, seeks to enlist young people into the data practices associated with forms of digital governance that assume public services can be optimized by enrolling citizens into the computational circuits of civic coding. Through learning to code and become digital makers, young people are treated as technical participants in such government platforms, equipped both with the necessary skills to use new kinds of digital government services but also, crucially, the coding and making talents to help build new services. Both projects are concerned with producing apprentice data analysts, civic hackers and computational experts who can act supportively of new digitized environments and governance approaches (Williamson 2015c).

According to internet commentator Morozov (2013a) this kind of 'solutionist' thinking originates in the Silicon Valley hacker culture of technological innovation. Such thinking recasts complex social phenomena like politics, public health and education as neatly defined problems with definite, computable solutions that can be optimized if the right code and algorithms are available. Here we find social phenomena translated into computational models that can be operated upon by algorithmic procedures. These technical models are now being recast as possible solutions to the problems of governments and states. Civic hackers have therefore been described as 'a diverse range of individuals who improve community life by creating and modifying digital infrastructure. Policymakers optimistically describe them as driving new economies using government data. Critical scholars note how they precariously labor for waning institutions' (Hunsinger and Schrock 2016: 537). Through various advocacy coalitions, campaigns, lobbying groups and networks of likeminded organizations, learning to code and digital making have been positioned as equipping young people with the computational skills required to become solutions-engineers and hackers of the future. These apprentice civic hackers are being made responsible for societal improvement and progress through software, and encouraged as participatory citizens to provide free labour for the state. The current political preoccupation with children learning to code is reflected in how governments are also seeking to apply computational thinking and procedural algorithmic solutions to 'hack' public and social problems.

These developments together demonstrate how coding, making and new computing curricula have become the objects of speeded-up policy processes. Understood as the products of fast policy, making and coding have been enrolled into national curriculum policies through highly compressed timescales of policy development and diffusion. The temporal acceleration of policies related to computing in schools has also involved a spatial distribution of influence to diverse actors from government departments, commercial businesses, universities, charities, venture capital firms, think tanks and policy innovation labs, many of them working in joined-up networks and relationships through campaigning alliances, pressure groups and political lobbying coalitions.

Making Up Digital Citizens

Originating in constructionist learning theory and practice, and supported by interests in building human capital, learning to code and digital making have been commercialized and governmentalized. In this final discussion, I want to consider how all of these developments impact on the figure of the citizen, particularly the 'digital citizen' that is increasingly the subject of debate and contestation. Programmes such as Make Things Do Stuff and Code Club justify themselves not just through the prospective economic and commercial value of children learning to code, but through a wider cultural argument about citizens producing and not simply consuming technology. They assume that new kinds of 'DIY citizens' can assume active roles as interventionists, makers, hackers, modders and tinkerers, in pursuit of new forms of engaged and participatory democracy, and can unlock the black box of technological infrastructures to engage and innovate through open and participatory critical making (Ratto and Boler 2014). The apprentice data analysts assumed by civic coding projects take this participatory model of citizenship and apply it to government problems.

One way to understand the preoccupation with coding clubs, programming and related digital making activities, then, is to view it as promoting 'participatory' practices of 'co-production', 'crowdsourcing' and 'prosumption' in new social media practices. The term 'prosumption' registers the alleged blurring of production and consumption as consumers of digital media increasingly also become its producers. The media theorist Manovich (2013), for example, argues that software development is gradually becoming more democratized as social media – Facebook, Twitter, YouTube, Wikipedia and so on – enables users to create and post content, contribute to 'crowdsourced' forms of 'co-production', and perform their own customizations, mash-ups and remixes of existing material.

Critics, however, claim the increasing participation of people in the formation of media content is leading to the 'significant phenomena of the growing amount of "labouring" people are undertaking as they "play" with these new technologies' (Beer and Burrows 2013: 49). 'Free labour' is the perfect business model for contemporary digital forms of capitalism, with networked digital technologies seen as part of the solution to the economic shocks of the global financial crisis (Schiller 2015). As such, prosumption firmly embeds people in the social media 'infrastructures of participation' that are subject to the commercial interests of for-profit social media corporations (Beer and Burrows 2013). Within such infrastructures, the prosumerist individual is encouraged to share personal information and data; maximize sociality through horizontal networks of connected friends and by liking and sharing digital artefacts; and to contribute through everyday participatory forms of digital making, software programming and coding. Learning to code is a direct outgrowth of this concern with co-production, crowdsourcing and prosumption, enabling young people to become able prosumers of social media content and thus providers of the content and data required by the business models of today's major digital companies. Consequently, learning to code is not a neutral, decontextualized or depoliticized practice, but shaped, patterned, ordered and governed by powerfully commercialized coded infrastructures.

New forms of DIY, digital citizenship rest on this image of the productive, participatory digital consumer. Indeed, the DIY prosumer is increasingly of interest to government authorities. Isin and Ruppert (2015: 9) note that the emerging figure of the 'digital citizen' has become 'a problem of government: how to engage, cajole, coerce, incite, invite, or broadly encourage it to inhabit forms of conduct that are already deemed to be appropriate to being a citizen'. In particular, they ask how the lives of digital citizens, as 'political subjects', are 'configured, regulated and organized by dispersed arrangements of numerous people and things such as corporations and states but also software and devices as well as people such as programmers and regulators' (2015: 4). Activities such as learning to code and digital making have become everyday acts that co-produce the political subjectivity of digital citizens: individuals and social groups that can act through the digital to forge styles of participation, but are simultaneously shaped and constrained by the coded software devices, infrastructures and institutional arrangements that make such forms of participation possible. The digital citizen projected by making and coding activities such as civic tech is therefore a hybrid of the Silicon Valley entrepreneur and the democratic progressive:

> Importantly, these digital citizens practice a kind of utopian politics that seeks to accelerate the gains of digital technology ... By attempting to 'democratise knowledge' about coding, ... algorithms and Big Data for the benefit of those groups who are failing to be flexible in a disrupted world, these nomadic digital citizens seek to intervene and repurpose technocapitalism for progressive ends. (Emejula and McGregor 2016: 9)

In this way, coding and making contribute to the production of digital citizens who can participate in the emerging dynamics of 'digital governance':

> the adaptation of the public sector to completely embrace and imbed electronic delivery at the heart of the government business model, wherever possible. For instance ... new forms of automation using 'zero touch' technologies that do not require human intervention; and ... making (able) citizens do more, developing isocratic administration – or 'do-it-yourself' government. (Margetts and Dunleavy 2013: 6)

Strategies of digital governance both depend on data systems that can collect information about citizens, and also on citizens themselves becoming enabled as DIY participants, 'doing more' for themselves. It is this imaginary of a hybrid form of digital, DIY government that infuses the activities of key organizations such as Nesta, which has promoted the learning to code and digital making movement while simultaneously promoting new activities of government hacking, civic coding and people-powered public services. From a digital governance perspective, making and coding will equip citizens with technical capacities and ways of thinking about how to solve contemporary social and public problems. It will allow them to become DIY participants in strategies of digital governance which treat citizens as co-producers of societal solutions, in the same way social media treats its users as prosumers who co-create content and produce data on its platforms.

The philosopher of science Hacking (2007) has influentially written about 'making up people'. By this term he is referring to the various governmental and technical ways in which people and citizens are incited to see, understand and act upon themselves as certain 'kinds of people'. The figure of the digital citizen is a key contemporary governmental imaginary of a kind of person, one that is to be made up in practice by educating and enabling people to become skilled in coding, digital making and diverse forms of working and playing with data. The process of making up digital citizens is the objective of diverse authorities from across the sectoral spectrum, and is being achieved through teaching citizens – and especially young people as digital citizens-in-the-making – how to code, hack and make stuff as the willing subjects of digital governance.

Conclusion

Educational coding and digital making initiatives and products are the hybrid result of a heterogeneous array of activities, agendas and aspirations being enacted at speed by actors and organizations from across the private, public and civic sectors of society. Originating in constructionist theory and practice as well as in the entrepreneurial hacker culture of Silicon Valley programmers, learning to code and digital making have become the focus of concerted attention by governments looking to boost human capital development for the digital economy, commercial vendors seeking to construct talent pipelines for future employees and markets for their products, and charitable organizations aiming to re-educate citizens as DIY participants in data-driven digital governance. The result is highly accelerated and globally networked policy activities that seek to build students' skills in the programming languages of software, the creation of new technologies, and the realization of value through coded products. The digital citizen-in-the-making that is being produced through learning to code and digital making is an able, entrepreneurial and skilled computational operative who can both work with data – as potential data talent required by the data analytics industry – and play with data as the ideal prosumer of social media who voluntarily provides free labour through the consumption and production of content.

9

CONCLUSION

Programmable public pedagogies of software and big data

Ongoing attempts to utilize big data in education have been animated by an imaginary of the digital future of educational policy, knowledge production, the mind, behaviour and brain of the learner, and of digital citizenship. The big data imaginary of education is, however, becoming a material reality as, increasingly, data analytics are inserted into policymaking processes, as data scientific practices become part of the methodological repertoire of educational research and knowledge production, as emotion and behaviour tracking devices are attached to learners' bodies and proliferate across classrooms, as R&D labs focus on developing brain-targeted devices, and as young people are exhorted to become apprentice data analysts and programmers. For sociologists, education has always been seen as a microcosm of the wider society, reflecting various social, economic, political and cultural trends, values and ideologies. The kind of big data-driven education systems, institutions and processes currently being imagined and materialized therefore constitute a microcosm of a much more expansive shift that is catalysing the embedding of big data technologies and practices in many aspects of everyday life.

The focus of this book has been on the processes of digitizing aspects of education as software and then subjecting it to datafication. The examples have been primarily drawn from the schools sector, though it is clear how higher education institutions are being similarly metricized, monitored and managed through data processing software. Furthermore, we can think of digital data software as constituting a kind of 'public pedagogy' that teaches lessons to citizens in all walks of everyday life. 'Public pedagogy' is a term used to refer to the lessons that are taught outside of formal educational institutions by popular culture, informal institutions and public spaces, dominant cultural discourses, and public intellectualism and social activism (Sandlin et al. 2011). A public pedagogy, then, is the manifestation of particular ways of thinking that may be carried out into the wider culture by media, by corporate business, by government policies, by the design of spaces and so forth. In slightly different geographical terms, the idea of 'built pedagogy' denotes how 'spaces teach proper comportment through affordances that privilege certain movements, activities, or states of being over others' and that 'manifests itself everywhere (homes, schools, offices, streets), teaching bodies what should and should not be done in silent, subtle and insistent ways' (Monahan 2005: 34). What the ideas of public and built pedagogies give us is the understanding that educative experiences are confined neither to the formal enclosures of school and university, nor to the relatively less formal spaces of cultural appreciation classes, reading groups or gym classes and so on. Instead, public and built pedagogies surround people in all walks of everyday life, subtly communicating lessons in how to live one's life as a citizen, a consumer, or a political subject, and 're-educating' them all the time (Pykett 2012).

Digital media are perhaps today's most successful public pedagogues, with the 'lines of code' that constitute software providing 'rules of conduct' which 'operate at a distance' to 'constantly direct how citizens act' (Thrift 2005: 172–3). The spaces that individuals – understood variously as consumers, citizens or political subjects – inhabit are increasingly layered with digital technologies and data which transforms how those spaces function and how people apprehend them. The programmability and datafication of social media environments, for example, means that many aspects of everyday life are mediated by the code written by programmers and by the feedback provided to them based on their data (van Dijck and Poell 2013). In this context, contemporary public pedagogies do not just flow into the world through built spaces, but are filtered into it through programmable environments that are designed to act as recursive feedback loops, constantly capturing individuals' data, analysing it, and then modifying and optimizing their experience as a result. The term 'programmable public pedagogies' perhaps captures the dynamic educative processes involved in the feedback loops of contemporary digital media.

Recent public events can help to illuminate the significant social consequences that occur when social media begin to act as programmable public pedagogies. Most of this book was written over the summer and autumn 2016. At the beginning of that summer, the British public voted in a referendum to leave the European Union. Later, as autumn gave way to winter, the US voted Donald Trump to the presidency. In the year that saw 'post-truth' named as word of the year by Oxford Dictionaries, social media fueled by big data was blamed for creating deep political polarization. At the same time, the organization of formal education was itself accused of increasing inequalities and widening a gap in the worldviews between young people who leave education with high-status qualification and those who do not. Both the UK's Brexit referendum and the US election have therefore raised significant questions about education.

The Education Gap

One question was about why, on average, people with fewer educational qualifications had tended to vote for the UK to leave the EU, or for Trump to take the presidency despite his lack of political experience, while those with more qualifications tended to vote the other way. One explanation is that a new 'education gap' has emerged as an apparent determinant of people's political preference, which has begun to raise concerns about divisions in democracy itself:

> The possibility that education has become a fundamental divide in democracy – with the educated on one side and the less educated on another – is an alarming prospect. It points to a deep alienation that cuts both ways. The less educated fear

they are being governed by intellectual snobs who know nothing of their lives and experiences. The educated fear their fate may be decided by know-nothings who are ignorant of how the world really works. (Runciman 2016)

Of course, plenty of wealthy educated people in the UK voted out of the EU, and voted for Trump in the US. But statistics from both votes did indicate significant population differences in terms of educational qualification, in relation to a range of other social factors, in determining voting patterns.

Significantly, the statistics from the EU referendum indicate that the vote for leaving the EU was concentrated in geographical areas already most affected by growing economic, cultural and social inequalities, as well as by mental and physical health and rising mortality rates. The sociologists Savage and Cunningham (2016) have vividly articulated the consequences of growing inequalities for citizens' political participation:

> There is ample evidence that political dynamics are being increasingly driven by the dramatic spiraling of escalating inequalities. To put this another way, growing economic inequalities are spilling over into all aspects of social, cultural, and political life, and that there are powerful feedback loops between these different spheres which are generating highly worrying trends.

Education, of course, is itself highly unequally distributed in terms of how well children achieve in schools, in ways that reproduce all sorts of social, cultural and economic inequalities. The increasing separation of children from more or less affluent backgrounds, and according to geographical locales and social and cultural contexts, is part of the dramatic spiralling of inequalities observed by sociologists. The kind of political polarization that materialized during both Brexit and the US election is the result of the related dynamics of education, geography, economics, and cultural and social networks, and the feedback loops between them.

It would be naive to suggest that those people with fewer qualifications are somehow to blame for not being critically aware of how their perspectives were being sculpted by populist propaganda during these campaigns. Anxiety among highly educated elites about the consequences of a lack of political awareness are far from novel. Moreover, the challenge here is to reconcile the polarizing interests of both those who are highly educated and those who are less educated. As Savage and Cunningham (2016) concluded, 'the way that the wealthy elite are increasingly culturally and socially cocooned, and the extent to which large numbers of disadvantaged groups are outside their purview is deeply worrying'. In the EU referendum and the US presidential election alike, neither side appeared to have any deep awareness of the other or of the deep-seated social issues that led to such distinctive and divided patterns of voting:

> Social media now enhances these patterns. Friendship groups of like-minded individuals reinforce each other's worldviews. Facebook's news feed is designed to

deliver information that users are more inclined to 'like'. Much of the shock that followed the Brexit result in educated circles came from the fact that few people had been exposed to arguments that did not match their preferences. Education does not provide any protection against these social media effects. It reinforces them. ... [T]he gap between the educated and the less educated is going to become more entrenched over time, because it ... represents a gulf in mutual understanding. (Runciman 2016)

This point raises the other question, which was couched much less explicitly in terms of education. This concerned the role of social media in filtering how people learned about the issues on which they were being invited to vote.

Personalized Political Learning

The issue of how social media has participated in filtering people's exposure to diverse political perspectives was one of the defining debates in the wake of Brexit and the US election in 2016 – though the role of social media in 'political turbulence' has been unfolding for several years (Margetts et al. 2016). An article in the tech culture magazine *Wired* on the day of the US election even asked readers, uncharacteristically, to consider the 'dark side of tech':

Even as the internet has made it easier to spread information and knowledge, it's made it just as easy to undermine the truth. On the internet, all ideas appear equal, even when they're lies. ... Social media exacerbates this problem, allowing people to fall easily into echo chambers that circulate their own versions of the truth. ... Both Facebook and Twitter are now grappling with how to stem the spread of disinformation on their platforms, without becoming the sole arbiters of truth on the internet. (Lapowsky 2016)

The involvement of social media in the spread of 'post-truth politics' (Viner 2016) points to how it is leading citizens into informational enclaves designed to feed them news and knowledge that has been filtered to match their interests, based on data analysis of their previous online habits, what they have 'liked' or watched, what news sources they prefer, who they follow and what social networks they belong to. 'Platforms like Twitter and Facebook now provide a structure for our political lives' as social algorithms allow 'large volumes of fake news stories, false factoids, and absurd claims' to be 'passed over social media networks, often by Twitter's highly automated accounts and Facebook's algorithms' (Howard 2016).

Since the US election, it has been revealed that Trump's campaign team worked closely with Facebook data to generate audience lists and targeted social media campaigns (Hercher 2016). It allegedly employed the 'psychographic' data analytics company Cambridge Analytica to data mine the personal details, online behaviours and sentiments of 220 million potential voters, and then sent them personalized, micro-targeted political messages (Cambridge Analytica 2016), exemplifying the use of what has been described as a new 'data-industrial complex' of behaviour tracking and identification technology in contemporary politics (Albright 2016a). Added to this, other more politically-activist social media sites such as Breitbart and Infowars have actively disseminated right-wing political agendas, reaching audiences that count in the tens of millions (Krasodomski-Jones 2016). Some of this content proved to be fake news, actively disseminated by a strong network of 'micro-propaganda sites' that was able to amplify itself through social media sites such as Facebook (Albright 2016b). 'Computational propaganda' involving automated 'political bots' spreading sensationalist political memes across social media networks have further compounded the problematic polarization of news consumption (Woolley 2016). All of this has been possible because social media changes the ways that information is presented for users' engagement and consumption:

> Facebook, Twitter, Snapchat and other platforms are fostering an emerging linguistic economy that places a high premium on ideas that are pithy, clear, memorable and repeatable (that is to say, viral). Complicated, nuanced thoughts that require context don't play very well on most social platforms, but a resonant hashtag can have extraordinary influence. (Weisenthal 2016)

Facebook and Twitter now accelerate the spread of fake news or sensationalized political bias through mechanisms such as trending topics and moments, which are engineered to be personalized to users' preferences.

Clearly there are important implications here for how young people access and evaluate information, and how they might be taught critical thinking and scepticism online to 'allow them to better identify outright lies, scams, hoaxes, selective half-truths, and mistakes' (Bartlett and Miller 2011). But the debate is not just about how to enable young people to deal with online trolling, propagandist bias and fake news. Just as with the debate about the education gap, it's important to note that people from across the political spectrum, whether highly educated or not, are all increasingly 'socially and culturally cocooned' (Savage and Cunningham 2016). Education and social media are both involved in producing these cocooning effects. Big data-driven social media creates not just 'networked publics' who cohere together online around shared tastes and preferences, but 'calculated publics': algorithmically produced snapshots of the public and what most concerns it (Gillespie 2014a). Search engines, recommendation systems, algorithms on social networking sites, and 'trend' identification algorithms not only help us find information, but provide a means to know what there is to know and to participate in social and political discourse.

Algorithmic calculations are now at the very centre of how people are learning to take part in political and democratic life, by filtering, curating and shaping what information and news we consume based on calculations of what most concerns and engages us. The logic of social media personalization now applies to political life as techniques of personalization deliver us political information that is most likely to engage us, and that we might 'like'. In other words, we are now living in a period of *personalized political learning*, whereby existing political preferences are being reinforced by the consumption of news and information via social media and participation in calculated, networked publics, with the consequence that alternative perspectives are being systematically curated out of our feeds and out of our minds. By no means has this situation been caused by social media – it's clear that a well-oiled political machinery of micro-targeted messaging and propagandist news production lies behind it, which is also related to existing social divisions – but social media and the big data that fuels it are certainly exacerbating social and political polarizations.

So seriously is this problem being taken that, in the fallout from the US election, it was reported that a team of 'renegade' Facebook employees established itself to deal with fake news and misinformation, although Mark Zuckerberg at first denied Facebook had anything to do with it (Frenkel 2016). The web entrepreneur O'Reilly (2016) has suggested it would be a mistake for Facebook to reinstate human editors – whose alleged political bias was itself the centre of a major controversy not so long before – but to design more intelligent techniques for separating information from sensationalist misinformation:

> The answer is not for Facebook to put journalists to work weeding out the good from the bad. It is to understand, in the same way that they've so successfully divined the features that lead to higher engagement, how to build algorithms that take into account 'truth' as well as popularity.

Spearheading the quest for truth-divining algorithms, Google in Europe announced within a week of the US election support for a startup company that is developing automated fact-checking software for online news, while the BBC hosted a 'hack-athon' to develop new technologies to detect fake news (Wakeford 2016). The appeal of apparently objective, impartial and unbiased truth-seeking algorithms in post-truth times is obvious, though as recent work in digital sociology and geography has repeatedly shown, algorithms are always dependent on the choices and decisions of their designers and engineers. The power of algorithms such as those of Facebook to intervene in the chaotic pluralism of contemporary political life may not easily be resolved by new algorithms, since 'social media inject turbulence into political life' (Margetts et al. 2016: 19).

Public Pedagogies of Political Mis-Education

The post-truth spread of misinformation twinned with the magnification of political and social polarization via social media platforms and algorithms is at the core of a new public pedagogy of political mis-education. Big data and social media are fast becoming the most successful sources of public pedagogy in the everyday lives of millions around the world. They are educating people by sealing them off into filter bubbles and echo chambers, where access to information, culture, news and intellectual and activist discourse is being curated algorithmically, sometimes via computational propaganda and fake news. The filter bubbles or echo chambers that calculated publics inhabit when they spend time on the Web are consequential because they appear to close off access to alternative perspectives, and potentially lead people to think that everyone thinks like they do, shares their political sentiments, their aspirations, their fears. This is further related to, reproduced and exacerbated by social inequalities in education, economics and cultural access. Doing well in formal education or not now appears to be a determinant of which kinds of social networks and calculated publics you belong to. 'The educational divide that is opening up in our politics is not really between knowledge and ignorance', Runciman (2016) argues, but 'a clash between one worldview and another'.

In an age where highly-educated people and less-educated people are being sharply divided both by social media and by their experience of education alike, serious issues are raised for the future of education as a social institution itself and the part it plays in supporting democratic processes. Existing educational inequalities and the experience of being parts of calculated publics in social media networks are now in a dynamic feedback loop. The public pedagogies of social media are becoming mis-educational in their effects, polarizing public opinion along different axes but most especially between the highly educated and the less educated.

Forms of measurement using data have long been at the core of how governments have known and managed populations. Today, the measurement of people's interests, preferences and sentiments via social media, and the use of that information to feed back content that people will like and that matches their existing preferences, is leading to a form of calculating governance that is exacerbating divisive politics and eroding democratic cohesion. Via social media data, people are being educated and governed according to measurements that indicate their existing worldview, and then provided access to more of the same. As Brexit and the US election indicate, increasingly people in the UK and US are being governed as two separate publics, with many of the less-educated incited to support political campaigns that the more-educated find alien and incomprehensible, and vice versa. Latour (2016) has described them as 'two bubbles of unrealism', one clinging to an imagined future of globalization and the other retreating to the imagined 'old countries of the past', or 'a utopia of the future confronting a utopia of the past':

> For now, the utopia of the past has won out. But there's little reason to think that the situation would be much better and more sustainable had the utopia of the future triumphed instead. … If the horizon of 'globalization' can no longer attract the masses, it is because everyone now understands more or less clearly that there

is no real, material world in the offing corresponding to that vision of a promised
land. ... Nor can we count any longer on returning to the old countries of the past.

Education has long reinforced these utopias of unrealism. Contradictory policy
demands over the last two decades have pointed simultaneously towards an
education for the future of a high-skills, globalized knowledge economy and an
education of the past which emphasizes traditional values, national legacy,
social order and authority (Ball 2008). Social media algorithms and architectures
have further enabled these utopias of unrealism to embed themselves across the
US and Europe. The mis-education of democratic society by the public pedagogies of big data and social media is being enabled by algorithmic techniques that
are designed to optimize and personalize people's everyday experiences in digital
environments. But in the name of personalization and optimization, the same
techniques are leading to post-truth forms of political mis-education and democratic polarization.

The field of education needs to involve itself in this new problem space. It
needs to probe how young people are measured and known through traces of
their data from an early age; how their tastes and preferences are formed through
social media feedback loops; how these relate to entrenched patterns of
educational and other social inequalities; and how their sense of their place and
their futures in democratic societies is formed as they encounter the public
pedagogies of big data and social media in their everyday lives. These issues
point toward important objectives for educational research to make sense of
both the sociotechnical imaginaries and concrete effects of the programmable
public pedagogies of digitization and datafication in everyday life.

New Agendas For Educational Research

Throughout this book, I have sought to demonstrate how educational research
focused on the rise of new forms of digital data in education might need to
engage with newly-emerging approaches such as digital sociologies, critical data
studies and software studies. In a recent chapter developing 'a digital sociology
of school', Selwyn et al. (2017: 148) likewise call for 'something better for
researchers concerned with the critical study of schools and technology'. They
call in particular for studies that take a critical perspective on (1) the political
economy of schools and technology, such as the new forms of digital education
being promoted by commercial interests, ideologies and agendas; (2) the management and governance of schools through accountability and performativity
mechanisms associated with digital data; (3) the digital labour of schools and
schooling, both as sites for the production of future workers and as sites of
increasingly digitized forms of work for teachers, administrators and students

alike; and (4) the digital surveillance of schools and schooling, as surveillance practices increasingly pervade public schools and allow school populations to be monitored, measured and controlled.

In previous chapters, we have seen how digitization and datafication of education is being imagined and enacted by large and powerful organizations that criss-cross the political, commercial and civil society sectors. Educational digitization and datafication is a matter of political economy, as new educational problems are identified by organizations that also possess the digital capacity to solve them. Governance and management of education is being performed through digital policy instruments and database technologies that allow information to flow at speed across the system to influence decision making and active interventions. Teachers are working more than ever with digital technologies, in particular by being required to become data collectors in the classroom and data literate analysts who can make sense of statistical performance information, while students are encouraged to see themselves as apprentice data analysts and programmers who might make a difference to society through software. And we have seen that big data technologies amount to a vast new infrastructure of surveillance that is able to capture the activities of students, staff, schools and whole education systems alike for purposes of measurement and management. At the end of 2016, big-data driven approaches to personalized learning through educational technologies were being promoted with particular enthusiasm and optimism in the US. The earlier introduction of the Every Student Succeeds Act had already opened the door for more involvement of the edtech sector in public education, and the incoming political administration was understood to be supportive of using software tools 'to meet the individual educational needs of each child, providing a digital version of what a one-on-one tutor would do' (Levy 2016). Supported by wealthy entrepreneurs, politicians and the non-profit sector alike, big data in education has been transformed from an imaginary into an emerging material reality for schools.

Educational research is just beginning to make sense of some of these significant transformations and the challenges they introduce. These are going to be complex issues to explore fully. As we have also seen, the rise of data in education is occurring through mixing with other diverse factors. New forms of scientific expertise from psychology, cognitive science and neuroscience are being developed as big data interacts with other fields and practices. Critical studies of the digitization and datafication of education will need to make sense of psychoinformatics, new behavioural techniques of persuasive 'hypernudge' computing, new brain-based technologies inspired by neuroscience, new biosensing techniques based on biomedical classifications and physiological categories of the body, new emotion-sensing technologies and the psychological innovations that inspire them, as well as other emerging explanations of human and social lives. In turn, each of these developments is linked to political agendas, philanthropic interests and commercial aspirations, such as those concerned with public health, emotional well-being, cognitive enhancement, digital governance and the sculpting of new kinds of citizens and political subjects. These developments are affecting education in schools and universities as well as intervening in the public pedagogies that shape how citizens learn in their everyday encounters with digitized and datafied environments. Far from being merely technical, the big data phenomenon in education is the contingent result of complex social, scientific, political and economic factors.

Educational researchers will need to develop conceptual and methodological tools to investigate the social lives of educational data by performing genealogical investigations of their tangled social, technical, political, economic and scientific threads. Though big data may be a hyped concept, and often loose in its technical definition, it is catalysing significant imaginative re-visioning of the future of education, and already animating technical projects, innovations and interventions. The term 'big data' itself may wane in future years, but the practices it describes are likely to proliferate, gain traction, and mutate into new sources of social, technical, economic, scientific and political power and influence. Educational research needs to engage closely and carefully with big data as a technical, social, scientific, economic and political force if it is to play a part in shaping the future of education.

REFERENCES

Adams, J. M. (2014) Measuring a 'growth mindset' in a new school accountability system. *EdSource*, 5 May. Available at http://edsource.org/2014/measuring-a-growth-mindset-in-a-new-school-accountability-system/63557

Alamuddin, R., Brown, J. and Kurzweil, M. (2016) *Student Data in the Digital Era: An overview of current practices*. New York: Ithaka S+R. Available at https://doi.org/10.18665/sr.283890

Alba, D. (2016) Silicon Valley's new-age AltSchool unleashes its secrets. *Wired*, 18 October. Available at www.wired.com/2016/10/altschool-shares-secrets-outside-educators/

Albright, J. (2016a) How Trump's campaign used the new data-industrial complex to win the election. *LSE US Centre blog*, 26 November. Available at http://blogs.lse.ac.uk/usappblog/2016/11/26/how-trumps-campaign-used-the-new-data-industrial-complex-to-win-the-election/

Albright, J. (2016b) Data is the real post-truth. *Medium*, 27 November. Available at https://medium.com/@d1gi/data-is-the-real-post-truth-so-heres-the-truth-about-post-election2016-propaganda-2bff5ae1dd7#.a78ocb123

AltSchool (2015a) AltSchool hires top execs from Google, Uber, Rocket Fuel and Zynga to help reinvent education from the ground up. *AltSchool Press Releases*. Available at www.altschool.com/press-release-3-15

AltSchool (2015b) AltSchool raises $100 million in funding to reimagine education for U.S. students and teachers. *AltSchool Press Releases*. Available at www.altschool.com/press-release-5-4-15

AltSchool (2016) Our Education Approach. *AltSchool*. Available at https://www.altschool.com/lab-schools/approach

Ambrose, M. (2015) Lessons from the avalanche of numbers: big data in historical perspective. *I/S: A Journal of Law and Policy for the Information Society*, 11 (2): 201–77.

Amoore, L. and Poitukh, V. (eds) (2016) *Algorithmic Life: calculative devices in the age of big data*. Abingdon: Routledge.

Anagnostopoulos, D., Rutledge, S. A. and Jacobsen, R. (2013) Mapping the information infrastructure of accountability. In Anagnostopoulos, D., Rutledge, S. A. and Jacobsen, R. (eds), *The Infrastructure of Accountability: data use and the transformation of American education*. Cambridge, MA: Harvard Education Press. pp. 1–20.

Andrejevic, M., Hearn, A. and Kennedy, H. (2015) Cultural studies of data mining: introduction. *European Journal of Cultural Studies*, 18 (4–5): 379–94.

Asdal, K. (2011) The office: the weakness of numbers and the production of non-authority. *Accounting, Organizations and Society*, 36: 1–9.

Axline, K. (2014) The universe is programmable. We need an API for everything. *Wired*, 30 April. Available at www.wired.com/2014/04/the-universe-is-programmable/

Baker and Siemens, G. (2013) Educational data mining and learning analytics. Available at www.columbia.edu/~rsb2162/BakerSiemensHandbook2013.pdf

Ball, S. J. (2008) *The Education Debate*. Bristol: Policy Press.

Ball, S. J. (2012) *Global Education Inc. New policy networks and the neoliberal imaginary*. Abingdon: Routledge.

Ball, S. J. (2016) Following policy: networks, network ethnography and education policy mobilities. *Journal of Education Policy*, 31 (5): 549–66.

Ball, S. J. and Junemann, C. (2012) *Networks, New Governance and Education*. Bristol: Policy Press.

Barber, M. with Ozga, J. (2014) Data work: Michael Barber in conversation with Jenny Ozga. In Fenwick, T., Mangez, E. and Ozga, J. (eds), *Governing Knowledge: comparison, knowledge-based technologies and expertise in the regulation of education*. London: Routledge. pp. 75–85.

Barnes, T. J. and Wilson, M. W. (2014) Big data, social physics, and spatial analysis: the early years. *Big Data and Society*, 1 (1). Available at http://dx.doi.org/10.1177/2053951714535365

Barocas, S., Hood, S. and Ziewitz, M. (2013) Governing algorithms: a provocation paper. *Social Sciences Research Network*. Available at http://dx.doi.org/10.2139/ssrn.2245322

Bartlett, J. and Miller, C. (2011) *Truth, Lies and the Internet*. London: Demos.

Bayne, S. (2015) Teacherbot: interventions in automated teaching. *Teaching in Higher Education*, 20 (4): 455–67.

BBC (2015) Make it Digital. *BBC Media Centre*, 12 March. Available at www.bbc.co.uk/mediacentre/mediapacks/makeitdigital

Beer, D. (2013) *Popular Culture and New Media: the politics of circulation*. London: Palgrave Macmillan.

Beer, D. (2016a) *Metric Power*. London: Palgrave Macmillan.

Beer, D. (2016b) How should we do the history of big data? *Big Data and Society*, 3 (1). Available at http://dx.doi.org/10.1177/2053951716646135

Beer, D. (2017) The social power of algorithms. *Information, Communication and Society*, 20 (1): 1–13.

Beer, D. & Burrows, R. (2013) Popular culture, digital archives and the new social life of data. *Theory, Culture and Society*, 30 (4): 47–71.

Behrens, J. (2013) Harnessing the currents of the digital ocean. Paper presented at the Annual Meeting of the American Educational Research Association, San Francisco, CA, April.

Bell, H. (2014) Coding for civic service: what we are learning? *Nesta blogs*, 11 March. Available at www.nesta.org.uk/blog/coding-civic-service-what-we-are-learning

Beneito-Montagut, R. (2017) Big data and educational research. In Wyse, D., Smith, E., Suter, L. E. and Selwyn, N. (eds), *The BERA/Sage Handbook of Educational Research*. London: Sage. pp. 913–33.

Big Brother Watch (2014) Biometrics in schools: the extent of biometrics in English secondary schools and academies. *Big Brother Watch*. Available at www.bigbrotherwatch.org.uk/files/reports/Biometrics_final.pdf

Big Brother Watch (2016) Classroom management systems: another brick in the wall. *Big Brother Watch*. Available at www.bigbrotherwatch.org.uk/wp-content/uploads/2016/11/Classroom-Management-Software-Another-Brick-in-the-Wall.pdf

Blikstein, P., Sipitakiat, A., Goldstein, J., Wilbert, J., Johnson, M., Vranakis, S., Pedersen, Z. and Carey, W. (2016) Project Blok: designing an development platform for tangible programming for children. *Project Bloks*. Available at https://projectbloks.withgoogle.com/static/Project_Bloks_position_paper_June_2016.pdf

Blyth, T. (2012) *Legacy of the BBC Micro: effecting change in the UK's cultures of computing*. London: Nesta.

Boden, L. (2016) Going with the affective flows of digital school absence text messages. *Learning, Media and Technology*. Available at http://dx.doi.org/10.1080/1743 9884.2017.1247859

Bogost, I. (2014) Welcome to dataland: design fiction at the most magical place on Earth. *Re-Form*, 28 July. Available at https://medium.com/re-form/welcome-to-dataland-d8c06a5f3bc6#.lfwivht3g

Bogost, I. (2015) Programmers: stop calling yourselves engineers. *The Atlantic*, 5 November. Available at www.theatlantic.com/technology/archive/2015/11/programmers-should-not-call-themselves-engineers/414271/

Bone, J. (2016) The nature of structure: a biosocial approach. *Sociological Review Monograph Series: Biosocial Matters: Rethinking Sociology-Biology Relations in the Twenty-First Century*, 64: 238–55.

Bowker, G. C. (2008) *Memory Practices in the Sciences*. London: MIT Press.

Bowker, G. C. (2013) Data flakes: an afterword to 'Raw Data' is an Oxymoron. In Gitelman, L. (ed.), *'Raw Data' is an Oxymoron*. London: MIT Press. pp. 167–72.

Bowker, G. C. and Star, S. L. (1999) *Sorting Things Out: classification and its consequences*. Cambridge, MA: MIT Press.

Boyd, D. and Crawford, K. (2013) Critical questions for big data: provocations for a cultural, technological, and scholarly phenomenon. *Information, Communication and Society*, 15 (5): 662–79.

Bradbury, A., McGimpsey, I. and Santori, D. (2013) Revising rationality: the use of 'nudge' approaches in neoliberal education policy. *Journal of Education Policy*, 28 (2): 247–67.

Bright, J. and Margetts, H. (2016) Big data and public policy: can it succeed where e-participation has failed? *Policy and Internet*, 8 (3): 218–24.

Buckingham Shum, S., Baker, R. S. J., Behrens, J., Hawksey, M., Jeffery, N. and Pea, R. (2013) Educational data scientists: a scarce breed? LAK '13, 8–12 April, Leuven, Belgium. Available at http://simon.buckinghamshum.net/wp-content/uploads/2013/03/LAK13Panel-EducDataScientists.pdf

Bulger, M. (2016) Personalized learning: the conversations we're not having. *Data and Society*, 22 July. Available at www.datasociety.net/pubs/ecl/PersonalizedLearning_primer_2016.pdf

Burger, M. (2015) The perception of the effectiveness of ClassDojo in middle school classrooms: a transcendental phenomenological study. Unpublished doctoral dissertation, Liberty University, Lynchburg, VA.

Burrows, R. (2012) Living with the h-index: metric assemblages in the contemporary academy. *The Sociological Review*, 60 (2): 355–72.

Busso, D. and Pollack, C. (2015) No brain left behind: consequences of neuroscience discourse for education. *Learning, Media, and Technology*, 40 (2): 168–86.

Cambridge Analytica (2016) Election 2016: the data game. *Cambridge Analytica news blog*, 18 November. Available at https://cambridgeanalytica.org/news/blog/election-2016-the-data-game

Carvalho, L. M. (2014) The attraction of mutual surveillance of performances: PISA as a knowledge-policy instrument. In Fenwick, T. Mangez, E. and Ozga, J. (eds), *Governing Knowledge: comparison, knowledge-based technologies and expertise in the regulation of education*. London: Routledge. pp. 58–72.

Castells, M. (1996) *The Rise of the Network Society*. Oxford: Blackwell.

Castells, M. (2009) *Communication Power*. Oxford: Oxford University Press.

Castro, D. and New, J. (2016) *The Promise of Artificial Intelligence*. Washington, DC: Center for Data Innovation.

Cavanagh, S. (2016) Tech giant Oracle makes billion-dollar pledge for coding education in Europe. *EdWeek Market Brief*, 2 December. Available at https://marketbrief. edweek.org/marketplace-k-12/tech-giant-oracle-makes-billion-dollar-pledge-coding-education-europe/

Cave, T. and Rowell, A. (2014) *A Quiet Word: Crony capitalism and broken politics in Britain*. London: Bodley Head.

Cederstrom, C. and Spicer, A. (2015) *The Wellness Syndrome*. Cambridge: Polity.

Ceglowski, M. (2016) The moral economy of tech. SASE conference, Berkeley University, 26 June. Available at http://idlewords.com/talks/sase_panel.htm

Cerruzzi, P.E. (2012) *Computing: a concise history*. London: MIT Press.

Chadwick, A. and Stromer-Galley, J. (2016) Digital media, power, and democracy in parties and election campaigns: party decline or party renewal? *The International Journal of Press/Politics*, 21 (3): 283–93.

Character Lab (2016) About us. *Character Lab*. Available at https://characterlab.org/

Cheney-Lippold, J. (2011) A new algorithmic identity: soft biopolitics and the modulation of control. *Theory, Culture and Society*, 28 (6): 164–81.

Chung, E., Cromby, J., Papadopoulos, D. and Tufarelli, C. (2016) Social epigenetics: a science of social science? *Sociological Review Monograph Series: Biosocial Matters: Rethinking Sociology-Biology Relations in the Twenty-First Century*, 64: 168–85.

Clarence, E. and Gabriel. M. (2014) *People Helping People: the future of public services*. London: Nesta.

ClassDojo (2016a) ClassDojo expands from classrooms to schools. *PR Newswire*. Available at www.prnewswire.com/news-releases/classdojo-expands-from-classrooms-to-schools-300242206.html.

ClassDojo (2016b) Stanford PERTS lab and ClassDojo partner to bring growth mindset to every classroom. *ClassDojo Press Releases*. Available at https://s3.amazonaws. com/static.classdojo.com/docs/Press/press_releases.zip

Clow, D. (2013) An overview of learning analytics. *Teaching in Higher Education*, 18 (6): 683–95.

Code.org (2014) Overview. *Code.org*. Available at https://code.org/files/Code.org Overview.pdf

Compendium of Physical Activities (2011) Home page. *Compendium of Physical Activities*. Available at https://sites.google.com/site/compendiumofphysical activities/home

Computing at School (2010) Computing at School White Paper. *Computing at School*. Available at www.computingatschool.org.uk/data/uploads/Computing_at_ School.pdf

Computing at School (2014) Computing in the national curriculum: a guide for secondary teachers. *Computing at School*. Available at www.computingatschool.org. uk/data/uploads/cas_secondary.pdf

Cope, B. and Kalantzis, M. (2015) Interpreting evidence-of-learning: educational research in the era of big data. *Open Review of Educational Research*, 2 (1): 218–39.

Cope, B. and Kalantzis, M. (2016) Big data comes to school: implications for learning, assessment and research. *AERA Open*, 2 (2): 1–19.

Crawford, K. (2014) The anxieties of big data. *The New Inquiry*, 30 May. Available at http://thenewinquiry.com/essays/the-anxieties-of-big-data/

Dalton, C. and Thatcher, J. (2014) What does a critical data studies look like, and why do we care? Seven points for a critical approach to 'big data'. *Society and Space*: Available at http://societyandspace.com/material/commentaries/craig-dalton-and-jim-thatcher-what-does-a-critical-data-studies-look-like-and-why-do-we-care-seven-points-for-a-critical-approach-to-big-data/

Daniels, J., Gregory, K. and McMillan Cottom, T. (eds) (2016) *Digital Sociologies*. Bristol: Policy Press.

Davidson, C. (2011) *Now You See It: how the brain science of attention will transform the way we live, work and learn*. London: Viking.

Davies, W. (2012) The emerging neocommunitarianism. *The Political Quarterly*, 83 (4): 767–76.

Davies, W. (2015) *The Happiness Industry: how business and government sold us well-being*. London: Verso.

Davies, W. (2016) Happiness and children. *Open Democracy*, 11 May. Available at www.opendemocracy.net/transformation/will-davies/happiness-and-children

de Abaitua, M. (2007) *The Red Men*. Haddenham: Snowbooks.

Decuypere, M. (2016) Diagrams of Europeanization: European education governance in the digital age. *Journal of Education Policy*, 31 (6): 851–72.

Decuypere, M., Ceulemens, C. and Simons, M. (2014) Schools in the making: mapping digital spaces of evidence. *Journal of Education Policy*, 29 (5): 617–39.

Desrosieres, A. (2001) How real are statistics? Four possible attitudes. *Social Research*, 68 (2): 339–55.

DiCerbo, K. E. and Behrens, J. T. (2014) *Impacts of the Digital Ocean*. Austin, TX: Pearson.

Dourish, P. and Bell, G. (2011) *Divining a Digital Future: mess and mythology in ubiquitous computing*. London: MIT Press.

Dredge, S. (2014) Forcing a generation to code is unprecedented, says Codecademy chief. *Guardian*, 5 September. Available at www.theguardian.com/technology/2014/sep/05/codecademy-coding-schools-education-apps

Duckworth, A.L. and Yeager, D.S. (2015) Measurement matters: assessing personal qualities other than cognitive ability for educational purposes. *Educational Researcher*, 44 (4): 237–51.

Dufva, T. and Dufva, M. (2016) Metaphors of code – structuring and broadening the discussion on teaching children to code. *Thinking Skills and Creativity*, 22: 97–110.

Dunleavy, P. and Margetts, H. (2015) Design principles for essentially digital governance. Annual Meeting of the American Political Science Association, San Francisco, 3–6 September.

Dweck, C. S. (2015) The secret to raising smart kids. *Scientific American*, 1 January. Available at www.scientificamerican.com/article/the-secret-to-raising-smart-kids1/

Eassom, S. (2015) IBM Watson for education. *IBM Insights on Business*, 1 April. Available at http://insights-on-business.com/education/ibm-watson-for-education-sector-deakin-university/

Ecclestone, K. and Hayes, D. (2009) *The Dangerous Rise of Therapeutic Education*. Abingdon: Routledge.

EdSurge (2016) The state of edtech: how edtech tools are evolving. *EdSurge Research*. Available at www.edsurge.com/research/special-reports/state-of-edtech-2016

Edtech UK (2015) About us. *Edtech UK*. Available at www.edtechuk.com/about-us/

Education Datalab (2014) About. *Education Datalab*. Available at https://education datalab.org.uk/about/

Education Foundation (2015) EdTech: London capital for learning technology. London: Education Foundation. Available at www.ednfoundation.org/wp-content/uploads/EdtechUK_LP_report.pdf

Edwards, P. N. (1997) *The Closed World: computers and the politics of discourse in cold war America*. London: MIT Press.

Edwards, P. N., Jackson, S. J., Chalmers, M. K., Bowker, G. C., Borgman, C. L., Ribes, D., Burton, M. and Calvert, S. (2013) *Knowledge Infrastructures: Intellectual Frameworks and Research Challenges*. Ann Arbor, MI: Deep Blue.

Edwards, R. (2015) Software and the hidden curriculum of digital education. *Pedagogy, Culture and Society*, 23 (2): 265–79.

Emejula, A. and McGregor, C. (2016) Towards a radical digital citizenship in digital education. *Critical Studies in Education*, September. Available at www.tandfonline.com/doi/full/10.1080/17508487.2016.1234494

Ensmenger, N. (2010) *The Computer Boys Take Over: computers, programmers, and the politics of technical expertise*. London: MIT Press.

Epstein, R. (2016) The empty brain. *Aeon*, 18 May. Available at https://aeon.co/essays/your-brain-does-not-process-information-and-it-is-not-a-computer

Evans, J. and Rich, E. (2011) Body policies and body pedagogies: every child matters in totally pedagogised schools? *Journal of Education Policy*, 26: 361–79.

Facer, K. (2011) *Learning Futures: education, technology and social change*. Abingdon: Routledge.

Fenwick, T. and Edwards, R. (2016) Exploring the impact of digital technologies on professional responsibilities and education. *European Educational Research Journal*, 15 (1): 117–31.

Fenwick, T., Mangez, E. and Ozga, J. (eds) (2014) *Governing Knowledge: comparison, knowledge-based technologies and expertise in the regulation of education*. London: Routledge.

Finn, M. (2016) Atmospheres of progress in a data-based school. *Cultural Geographies*, 23 (1): 29–49.

FitnessGram (2016) What is FitnessGram? *FitnessGram*. Available at www.fitnessgram.net/

Fitzgerald, D. and Callard, F. (2014) Social science and neuroscience beyond interdisciplinarity: experimental entanglements. *Theory, Culture and* Society, 32 (1): 3–32.

Fitzgerald, D., Rose, N. and Singh, I. (2016) Revitalizing sociology: urban life and mental illness between history and the present. *British Journal of Sociology*, 67 (1): 138–60.

Floridi, L. (2016) Should we be afraid of AI? *Aeon*, 9 May. Available at https://aeon.co/essays/true-ai-is-both-logically-possible-and-utterly-implausible

Fogg, B. J. (2002) Persuasive technology: using computers to change what we think and do. *Ubiquity*, December: 89–120.

Fontaine, C. (2016) The myth of accountability: how data (mis)use is reinforcing the problems of public education. *Data and Society*, 8 August. Available at https://datasociety.net/pubs/ecl/Accountability_primer_2016.pdf

Ford, P. (2015) What is code? *Business Week*, 11 June. Available at www.bloomberg.com/graphics/2015-paul-ford-what-is-code

Foresight (2008) *Mental Capital and Wellbeing: making the most of ourselves in the 21st century. Executive Summary*. London: Government Office for Science. Available at https://www.gov.uk/government/uploads/system/uploads/attachment_data/file/292453/mental-capital-wellbeing-summary.pdf

Foucault, M. (1990) *The History of Sexuality, Volume I: The will to knowledge* (trans. R. Hurley). London: Penguin.

Foucault, M. (1991) *Discipline and Punish: the birth of the prison* (trans. A. Sheridan). Harmondsworth: Penguin.

Foucault, M. (2007) *Security, Territory and Population: lectures at the College de France 1977–1978* (trans. G. Burchell). New York: Palgrave Macmillan.

Foucault, M. (2008) *The Birth of Biopolitics: lectures at the College de France, 1978–1979* (trans. G. Burchell). New York: Palgrave Macmillan.

Frenkel, S. (2016) Renegade Facebook employees form task force to battle fake news. *BuzzFeed*, 14 November. Available at www.buzzfeed.com/sheerafrenkel/renegade-facebook-employees-form-task-force-to-battle-fake-n

Friedli, L. and Stearn, R. (2015) Positive affect as coercive strategy: conditionality, activation and the role of psychology in UK government workfare programmes. *Medical Humanities*, 41: 40–47.

Fuller, M. (2003) *Behind the Blip: essays on the culture of software*. Brooklyn, NY: Autonomedia.

Fuller, M. (2008) Introduction. In Fuller, M. (ed.), *Software Studies: a lexicon*. London: MIT Press.

Furedi, F. (2009) *Wasted: why education isn't educating*. London: Continuum.

Gaysina, D. (2016) How genetics could help future learners unlock hidden potential. *Conversation*, 15 November. Available at https://theconversation.com/how-genetics-could-help-future-learners-unlock-hidden-potential-68254

Gehl, R. (2015) Sharing, knowledge management and big data: a partial genealogy of the data scientist. *European Journal of Cultural Studies*, 18 (4–5): 413–28.

Gillespie, T. (2014a) The relevance of algorithms. In Gillespie, T., Boczkowski, P. J. and Foot, K. A. (eds), *Media Technologies: essays on communication, materiality, and society*. London: MIT Press. pp. 167–93.

Gillespie, T. (2014b) Algorithm. *Culture Digitally*, 25 June. Available at http://culturedigitally.org/2014/06/algorithm-draft-digitalkeyword/

Gillespie, T. (2016) Algorithms, clickworkers, and the befuddled fury around Facebook trends. *Social Media Collective*, 18 May. Available at https://socialmediacollective.org/2016/05/18/facebook-trends/

Gitelman, L. and Jackson, V. (2013) Introduction. In Gitelman. L. (ed.), *'Raw Data' is an Oxymoron*. London: MIT Press. pp. 1–14.

Gomes, P. (2015) Your guide to a nation of Edtech accelerators. *EdSurge*, 21 October. Available at www.edsurge.com/news/2015–10–21-your-guide-to-a-nation-of-edtech-accelerators

Gorur, R. (2015) The performative politics of NAPLAN and My School. Working paper, June. Available at www.academia.edu/12817544/The_Performative_Politics_of_NAPLAN_and_My_School

Gov.uk (2016) Games workshop founder and entrepreneur to open 2 free schools. *Gov.uk*. Available at www.gov.uk/government/news/games-workshop-founder-and-entrepreneur-to-open-2-free-schools

Gregory, K., McMillan Cottom, T. and Daniels, J. (2017) Introduction. In Daniels, J., Gregory, K. and McMillan Cottom, T. (eds), *Digital Sociologies*. Bristol: Policy Press. pp. xvii–xxx.

Grek, S. (2009) Governing by numbers: the PISA 'effect' in Europe. *Journal of Education Policy*, 24 (1): 23–37.

Grek, S. (2016) The life and work of the killer chart: on the art of visually assembling education comparisons. European Consortium for Political Research, Prague, September.

Grosvenor, I. and Roberts, S. (2013) Systems and subjects: ordering, differentiating and institutionalising the modern child. In Lawn, M. (ed.), *The Rise of Data in Education Systems: collection, visualization and use.* Oxford: Symposium. pp. 79–96.

Gulson, K., Sellar, S. and Webb, T. (forthcoming) Emerging Biological Rationalities for Policy: (Molecular) Biopolitics and the New Authorities in Education.

Hacking, I. (1990) *The Taming of Chance.* Cambridge: Cambridge University Press.

Hacking, I. (2007) Kinds of people: moving targets. *Proceedings of the British Academy,* 151: 285–318.

Haggerty, K. D. and Ericson, R. V. (2001) The surveillant assemblage. *British Journal of Sociology,* 51 (4): 605–22.

Halford, S., Pope, C. and Weal, M. (2013) Digital futures? Sociological challenges and opportunities in the emergent semantic web. *Sociology,* 47 (1): 173–89.

Halverson, E. R. and Sheridan, K. (2014) The maker movement in education. *Harvard Educational Review,* 84 (4). Available at http://hepg.org/her-home/issues/harvard-educational-review-volume-84-number-4/herarticle/the-maker-movement-in-education

Hardy, I. and Lewis, S. (2016) The 'doublethink' of data: educational performativity and the field of schooling practices. *British Journal of Sociology of Education.* Available at http://dx.doi.org/10.1080/01425692.2016.1150155.

Hartong, S. (2016) Between assessments, digital technologies and big data: the growing influence of 'hidden' data mediators in education. *European Educational Research Journal,* 15 (5): 523–36.

Hayes, B. (2015) Cultures of code. *American Scientist,* 103 (1).

Hayles, N. K. (2013) *How We Think: digital media and contemporary technogenesis.* London: University of Chicago Press.

Hayles, N. K. (2014) Cognition Everywhere: the rise of the cognitive nonconscious and the costs of consciousness. *New Literary History,* 45 (2): 199–220.

Hercher, J. (2016) Trump did have a paid media strategy, and it focused on Facebook. *AdExchanger,* 15 November. Available at https://adexchanger.com/ad-exchange-news/trump-paid-media-strategy-focused-facebook/

Hilbert, M. (2016) Big data for development: a review of promises and challenges. *Development Policy Review,* 34 (1): 135–74.

Hill, P. and Barber, M. (2014) *Preparing for a Renaissance in Assessment.* London: Pearson.

HM Treasury (2013) 100,000 young people to become 'digital makers'. Available at www.gov.uk/government/news/100000-young-people-to-become-digital-makers

Hogan, A., Sellar, S. and Lingard, B. (2015) Network restructuring of global edu-business: the case of Pearson's *Efficacy Framework.* In Au, W. and Ferrare, J. J. (eds), *Mapping Corporate Education Reform: power and policy networks in the neoliberal state.* London: Routledge. pp. 43–64.

Holbein, J. (2016) Left behind? Citizen responsiveness to government performance information. *American Political Science Review,* 110 (2): 353–68.

Housley, W. (2015) The emerging contours of data science. *Discover Society,* 23. Available at http://discoversociety.org/2015/08/03/focus-the-emerging-contours-of-data-science/

Howard, P. (2016) Is social media killing democracy? *Culture Digitally,* 14 November. Available at http://culturedigitally.org/2016/11/is-social-media-killing-democracy/

Howard-Jones, P., Ott, M., van Leeuwen, T. and De Smedt, B. (2015) The potential relevance of cognitive neuroscience for the development and use of technology-enhanced learning. *Learning, Media and Technology,* 40 (2): 131–51.

Hunckler, M. (2015) 'How this hackathon is inspiring students to better education'. *Forbes*, 17 August. Available at: https://www.forbes.com/sites/matthunckler/2015/08/17/how-this-hackathon-is-inspiring-students-to-better-education/

Hunsinger, J. and Schrock, A. (2016) The democratization of hacking and making. *New Media and* Society, 18 (4): 535–8.

Huxley, M. (2007) Geographies of governmentality. In Crampton, J. and Elden, S. (eds), *Space, Knowledge and Power: Foucault and geography*. Aldershot: Ashgate. pp. 185–204.

IBM (2016) IBM Watson Education and Pearson to drive cognitive learning experiences for college students. *IBM Press Release*. Available at www-03.ibm.com/press/us/en/pressrelease/50842.wss

IBM Research (2011) IBM's first cognitive computing chips mimic functions of the brain. *IBM Research News*, 18 August. Available at http://ibmresearchnews.blogspot.co.uk/2011/08/this-cognitive-computing-chip-taught.html

IBM Watson Education (2016a) Education in the cognitive era. *Watson Education POV*. Available at www-01.ibm.com/common/ssi/cgi-bin/ssialias?htmlfid=EDI03007USEN&

IBM Watson Education (2016b) Transform education with Watson. *IBM Watson*. Available at www.ibm.com/watson/education/

Iliadis, A. and Russo, F. (2016) Critical data studies: an introduction. *Big Data and Society*, 3 (2). Available at http://bds.sagepub.com/content/3/2/2053951716674238.full.pdf+html

Imagine K12 (2015) Our program. *Imagine* K12. Available at www.imaginek12.com/our-program.html

Introna, L. (2016) Algorithms, governance, and governmentality: on governing academic writing. *Science, Technology, and Human Values*, 41 (1): 17–49.

Irani, L. (2015) Hackathons and the making of entrepreneurial citizenship. *Science, Technology, and Human Values*, 40 (5): 799–824.

Isin, E. and Ruppert, E. (2015) *Being Digital Citizens*. London: Rowman and Littlefield International.

Ito, M. (2009) *Engineering Play: a cultural history of children's software*. London: MIT Press.

Jasanoff, S. (2015) Future imperfect: science, technology, and the imaginations of modernity. In Jasanoff, S. and Kim, S-H. (eds), *Dreamscapes of Modernity: sociotechnical imaginaries and the fabrication of* power. Chicago, IL: University of Chicago Press. pp. 1–33.

Jones, R., Pykett, J. and Whitehead, M. (2013) *Changing Behaviours: on the rise of the psychological state*. Cheltenham: Edward Elgar.

Jurgenson, N. (2014) View from nowhere: on the cultural ideology of big data. *The New Inquiry*, 9 October. Available at http://thenewinquiry.com/essays/view-from-nowhere/

Keller, E. F. (2016) Thinking about biology and culture: can the natural and human sciences be integrated? *Sociological Review Monograph Series: Biosocial Matters: Rethinking Sociology-Biology Relations in the Twenty-First Century*, 64: 26–41.

Kelly III, J. E. (2015) *Computing, Cognition and the Future of Knowing: how humans and machines are forging a new age of understanding*. Somers, NY: IBM Corporation.

Kelly III, J. E. and Hamm, S. (2014) *Smart Machines: IBM's Watson and the era of cognitive computing*. New York: Columbia University Press.

Kennedy, H. (2016) *Post. Mine. Repeat. Social media data mining becomes ordinary*. London: Palgrave Macmillan.

Kennedy, H. and Moss, G. (2015) Known or knowing publics? Social media data mining and the question of public agency. *Big Data and Society*, 2 (2). Available at http://bds.sagepub.com/content/2/2/2053951715611145

King, M., Cave, R., Foden, M. and Stent, M. (2016) *Personalised Education: from curriculum to career with cognitive systems*. Portsmouth: IBM Corporation.

Kitchin, R. (2014a) *The Data Revolution: big data, open data, data infrastructures and their consequences*. London: Sage.

Kitchin, R. (2014b) Big data, new epistemologies and paradigm shifts. *Big Data and Society*, 1 (1). Available at http://dx.doi.org/10.1177/2053951714528481

Kitchin, R. (2017) Thinking critically about and researching algorithms. *Information, Communication and Society*, 20 (1): 14–29.

Kitchin, R. and Dodge, M. (2011) *Code/Space: software and everyday life*. London: MIT Press.

Kitchin, R. and Lauriault, T. (2014) Towards critical data studies: charting and unpacking data assemblages and their work. *The Programmable City Working Paper 2*. Available at http://ssrn.com/abstract=2474112

Kitchin, R. and McArdle, G. (2015) What makes big data, big data? Exploring the ontological characteristics of 26 datasets. *Big Data and Society*, 3 (1). Available at http://bds.sagepub.com/content/3/1/2053951716631130

Kitchin, R., Lauriault, T. and McArdle, G. (2015) Knowing and governing cities through urban indicators, city benchmarking and real-time dashboards. *Regional Studies, Regional Science*, 2 (1): 6–28.

Knewton (2011) Pearson and Knewton partner to advance next generation of digital education. *Knewton in the News*, 1 November. Available at www.knewton.com/press-releases/pearson-partnership/

Knewton (2013) Knewton Adaptive Learning: building the world's most powerful education recommendation engine. *Knewton*. Available at www.knewton.com/wp-content/uploads/knewton-adaptive-learning-whitepaper.pdf

Knox, J. (2016) *Posthumanism and the Massive Open Online Course: contaminating the subject of global education*. Abingdon: Routledge.

Kolodny, L. (2016) ClassDojo raises $21 million for app to make parent-teacher meetings obsolete. *TechCrunch*, 15 April. Available at http://techcrunch.com/2016/04/15/classdojo-raises-21-million-for-app-to-make-parent-teacher-meetings-obsolete/

Krasodomski-Jones, A. (2016) What does the alt-right do now that 'God Emperor' Trump won? *CNN*, 15 November. Available at http://edition.cnn.com/2016/11/14/opinions/what-next-alt-right-krasodomski-jones-opinion/index.html

Lane, J. E. (2014) *Building a Smarter University: big data, analytics and innovation*. New York: SUNY Press.

Langley, P. and Leyshon, A. (2016) Platform capitalism: the intermediation and capitalisation of digital economic circulation. *Finance and Society*: Available at http://financeandsociety.org/article/early-view-langley-leyshon/

Lapowsky, I. (2015) Inside the school Silicon Valley thinks will save education. *Wired*, 4 May. Available at www.wired.com/2015/05/altschool/

Lapowsky, I. (2016) The 2016 election exposes the very, very dark side of tech. *Wired*, 7 November. Available at www.wired.com/2016/11/2016-election-exposes-dark-side-tech/

Lascoumes, P. and le Gales, P. (2007) Introduction: understanding public policy through its instruments – from the nature of instruments to the sociology of public policy instrumentation. *Governance*, 20 (1): 1–21.

Latour, B. (1986) Visualization and cognition: thinking with eyes and hands. *Knowledge and Society*, 6: 1–40.

Latour, B. (2016) Two bubbles of unrealism: learning from the tragedy of Trump. *Los Angeles Review of Books*, 17 November. Available at https://lareviewofbooks.org/article/two-bubbles-unrealism-learning-tragedy-trump/

Lavecchia, A. M., Liu, H. and Oreopoulos, P. (2014) Behavioral economics of education: progress and possibilities. *National Bureau of Economic Research, Working Paper*. Available at www.nber.org/papers/w20609.pdf

Law, J., Ruppert, E. and Savage, M. (2011) The double social life of methods. *CRESC Working Paper No. 95*. Open University.

Lawn, M. (2013) The rise of data in education. In Lawn, M. (ed.), *The Rise of Data in Education Systems: collection, visualization and use*. Oxford: Symposium. pp. 7–10.

Lawn, M. and Grek, S. (2012) *Europeanizing Education: governing a new policy space*. Oxford: Symposium.

Lemke, T. (2011) *Biopolitics: an advanced introduction*. London: New York University Press.

Lessig, L. (2000) *Code v.2*. New York: Basic Books.

Levy, H. O. (2016) How a Trump administration could back revolutionary education technology. *Fox News Opinion*, 12 December. Available at www.foxnews.com/opinion/2016/12/12/how-trump-administration-could-back-revolutionary-education-technology.html

Lewis, S. and Hardy, I. (2016) Tracking the topological: the effects of standardised data upon teachers' practice. *British Journal of Education Studies*. Available at http://dx.doi.org/10.1080/00071005.2016.1254157

Lewis, S. and Hogan, A. (2016) Reform first and ask questions later? The implications of (fast) schooling policy and 'silver bullet' solutions. *Critical Studies in Education*. Available at http://dx.doi.org/10.1080/17508487.2016.1219961

Lindh, M. and Nolin, J. (2016) Information we collect: surveillance and privacy in the implementation of Google apps for education. *European Educational Research Journal*, 15 (6): 644–63. Available at http://eer.sagepub.com/content/early/2016/06/24/1474904116654917.full.pdf

Lindtner, S. (2015) Hackerspaces and the internet of things in China: how makers are reinventing industrial production, innovation, and the self. *China Information*, 28 (2): 145–67.

Lippert, I. (2015) Environment as datascape: enacting emission realities in corporate carbon accounting. *GeoForum*, 66: 126–35.

Livingstone Aspirations (2016) Home. *Livingstone Aspirations*. Available at www.livingstone-aspirations.org/

Livingstone, I. (2012) The quest to release the ICT curriculum from the jaws of the dragon of dullness. *Wired*, 23 January. Available at www.wired.co.uk/news/archive/2012–01/23/ict-curriculum-ian-livingstone

Livingstone, I. and Hope, A. (2011) *Next Gen*. London: Nesta.

Losh, L. (2014) *The War on Learning: gaining ground in the digital university*. London: MIT Press.

Luckin, R. and Holmes, W. (2016) *Intelligence Unleashed: an argument for AI in education*. London: Pearson.

Lupton, D. (2015a) *Digital Sociology*. London: Routledge.

Lupton, D. (2015b) Lively data, social fitness and biovalue: the intersections of health self-tracking and social media. *Social Sciences Research Network*. Available at http://ssrn.com/abstract=2666324

Lupton, D. (2016) *The Quantified Self: a sociology of self-tracking.* Cambridge: Polity Press.

Lynch, T.L. (2015) *The Hidden Role of Software in Education: policy to practice.* New York: Routledge.

Lyon, D. (2014) Surveillance, Snowden and big data: capacities, consequences, critique. *Big Data and Society*, 1 (1). Available at http://dx.doi.org/10.1177/2053951714541861

Lytics Lab (2016) About Lytics Lab: Available at https://lytics.stanford.edu/about-lytics

MacCormick, J. (2012) *9 Algorithms that Changed the Future: the ingenious ideas that drive today's computers.* Oxford: Princeton University Press.

Mackenzie, A. (2006) *Cutting Code: Software and sociality.* Oxford: Peter Lang.

Mackenzie, A. (2012) More parts than elements: how databases multiply. *Environment and Planning D: Society and Space*, 30: 335–50.

Mackenzie, A. (2013) Programming subjects in the regime of anticipation: software studies and subjectivity. *Subjectivity*, 6 (4): 391–405.

Mackenzie, A. (2015) The production of prediction: what does machine learning want? *European Journal of Cultural Studies*, 18 (4–5): 429–45.

Mackenzie, A. and Vurdubakis, T. (2011) Codes and codings in crisis: performativity, signification and excess. *Theory, Culture and Society*, 28 (6): 3–23.

Mager, A. (2012) Algorithmic ideology: how capitalist society shapes search engines. *Information, Communication and Society*, 15 (5): 769–87.

Mager, A. (2015) Glocal search: search technology at the intersection of global capitalism and local socio-political cultures. *Institute of Technology Assessment (ITA), Austrian Academy of Sciences.* Available at www.astridmager.net/wp-content/uploads/2015/11/Abschlussbericht-OeNB_Mager.pdf

Mager, A. (2016) Search engine imaginary: visions and values in the co-production of search technology and Europe. *Social Studies of Science.* Available at http://sss.sagepub.com/content/early/2016/10/26/0306312716671433

Maltby, P. (2015) A new operating model for government. *Open Policy Making*, 17 March. Available at https://openpolicy.blog.gov.uk/2015/03/17/a-new-operating-model-for-government/

Mandinach, E. B. and Gummer, E. S. (2016) Every teacher should succeed with data literacy. *Phi Delta Kappan*, 97 (8): 43–4.

Manovich, L. (2013) *Software Takes Command: extending the language of new media.* London: Bloomsbury.

Margetts, H. and Dunleavy, P. (2013) The second wave of digital-era governance: a quasi-paradigm for government on the Web. *Philosophical Transactions of the Royal Society A*, 371 (1987).

Margetts, H. and Sutcliffe, D. (2013) Addressing the policy challenges and opportunities of 'big data'. *Policy and Internet*, 5 (2): 139–46.

Margetts, H., John, P., Hale, S. and Yasseri, T. (2016) *Political Turbulence: how social media shape collective action.* Oxford: Princeton University Press.

Markham, A. (2013) The algorithmic self: layered accounts of life and identity in the 21st century. *Internet Research 14.0*, 23–26 October.

Markowetz, A., Błaszkiewicz, K., Montag, C., Switala C. and Schlaepfer, T. E. (2014) Psycho-informatics: big data shaping modern psychometrics. *Medical Hypotheses*, 82 (4): 405–11.

Marres, N. (2012) The redistribution of methods: on intervention in digital social research, broadly conceived. *Sociological Review*, 60 (S1): 139–65.

Martens, K., Niemann, D. and Teltemann, J. (2016) Effects of international assessments in education – a multidisciplinary review. *European Educational Research Journal*, 15 (5): 516–22.

Mateos-Garcia, J. Bakhshi, H. and Windsor, G. (2015) *Skills of the Datavores: talent and the data revolution*. London: Nesta. Available at www.nesta.org.uk/sites/default/files/skills_of_the_datavores.pdf

Mayer-Schönberger, V. and Cukier, K. (2013) *Big Data: a revolution that will change how we live, work and think*. London: John Murray.

Mayer-Schönberger, V. and Cukier, K. (2014) *Learning from Big Data: the future of education*. New York: Houghton Mifflin Harcourt.

McGimpsey, I., Bradbury, A. and Santori, D. (2016) Revisions to rationality: the translation of 'new knowledges' into policy under the coalition government. *British Journal of Sociology of Education*. Available at http://dx.doi.org/10.1080/01425692.2016.1202747

Mead, R. (2016) Learn different: Silicon Valley disrupts education. *The New Yorker*, 7 March. Available at www.newyorker.com/magazine/2016/03/07/altschools-disrupted-education

Mead, S. (2013) Profile of ClassDojo founders Sam Chaudhury and Liam Don. *Education Week*, 11 June. Available at http://blogs.edweek.org/edweek/sarameads_policy_notebook/2013/06/sam_chaudhary_and_liam_don_co-founders_classdojo.html

Meloni, M. (2014) Remaking local biologies in an epigenetic time. *Somatosphere*, 8 August. Available at http://somatosphere.net/2014/08/remaking-local-biologies-in-an-epigenetic-time.html

Meloni, M., Williams, S. and Martin, P. (2016) The biosocial: sociological themes and issues. *Sociological Review Monograph Series: Biosocial Matters: Rethinking Sociology-Biology Relations in the Twenty-First Century*, 64 (1): 7–25.

Merolla, P. A., Arthur, J. V., Alvarez-Icaza, R., Cassidy, A. S., Sawada, J., Akopyan, F., Jackson, B. L., Imam, N., Guo, C., Nakamura, Y., Brezzo, B., Vo, I., Esser, S. K., Appuswamy, R., Taba, B., Amir, A., Flickner, M. D., Risk, W. P., Manohar, R. and Modha, D. S. (2014) A million spiking-neuron integrated circuit with a scalable communication network and interface. *Science*, 345 (6197): 668–73.

Meyers, M. (2015) Connecting the classroom with the internet of things. *EdSurge*, 28 March. Available at www.edsurge.com/news/2015–03–28-connecting-the-classroom-with-the-internet-of-things

Michael, M. and Lupton, D. (2015) Toward a manifesto for the 'public understanding of big data'. *Public Understanding of Science*, 25 (1): 104–16.

Miller, C. (2014) The promise of social media. *Demos Quarterly*, Winter 2013/14. Available at http://quarterly.demos.co.uk/article/issue-1/the-promise-of-social-media/

Miller, P. and Rose, N. (2008) *Governing the Present: administering economic, social and personal life*. Cambridge: Polity.

Mittelstadt, B. D., Allo, P., Taddeo, M. Wachter, S. and Floridi, L. (2016) The ethics of algorithms: mapping the debate. *Big Data and Society*, 3 (2): Available at http://dx.doi.org/10.1177/2053951716679679

Modha, D. (2013) Systems that perceive, think and act. *The Atlantic*, June. Available at www.theatlantic.com/sponsored/ibm-cognitive-computing/archive/2013/06/systems-that-perceive-think-and-act/276708/

Modha, D. (2014) Introducing a brain-inspired computer: TrueNorth's neurons to revolutionize system architecture. *IBM Research*. Available at www.research.ibm.com/articles/brain-chip.shtml

Monahan, T. (2005) *Globalization, Technological Change, and Public Education*. London: Routledge.

Montero, C. S. and Suhonen, J. (2014) Emotion analysis meets learning analytics: online learner profiling beyond numerical data. *Proceedings of the 14th Koli Calling International Conference on Computing Education Research*, 165–9, Koli, Finland: ACM Press.

Morozov, E. (2013a) *To Save Everything, Click Here: technology, solutionism and the urge to fix problems that don't exist*. London: Allen Lane.

Morozov, E. (2013b) The real privacy problem. *MIT Technology Review*, 22 October. Available at www.technologyreview.com/s/520426/the-real-privacy-problem/

Morris, P. (2016) *Education policy, cross-national tests of pupil achievement, and the pursuit of world-class schooling*. London: UCL Institute of Education Press.

Moss, P., Dahlberg, G., Grieshaber, S., Mantovani,, S., May, H., Pence, A., Rayna, S., Blue Swadener, B. and Vandenbroeck, M. (2016) The Organisation for Economic Co-operation and Development's International Early Learning Study: opening for debate and contestation. *Contemporary Issues in Early Childhood*, 17 (3): 343–51.

Mulgan, G. (2016a) A machine intelligence commission for the UK: how to grow informed public trust and maximise the positive impact of smart machines. *Nesta*, 7 February. Available at www.nesta.org.uk/sites/default/files/a_machine_intelligence_commission_for_the_uk_-_geoff_mulgan.pdf

Mulgan, G. (2016b) Government as collective intelligence. *Oxford Government Review*, 1 (August): 44–6.

Nafus, D. (2016) Introduction. In Nafus, D. (ed.), *Quantified: biosensing technologies in everyday life*. London: MIT Press. pp. ix–xxxi.

Nature Neuroscience (2014) Focus on big data. *Nature Neuroscience*, 17 (11): 1429.

Naughton, J. (2012) A manifesto for teaching computer science in the 21st century. *Observer*, 31 March. Available at www.theguardian.com/education/2012/mar/31/manifesto-teaching-ict-education-minister

Naughton, J. (2014) Year of Code already needs a reboot. *The Guardian*, 15 February. Available at https://www.theguardian.com/technology/2014/feb/15/year-of-code-needs-reboot-teachers

Nesta (2015) *Analytic Britain: securing the right skills for the data-driven economy*. London: Nesta. Available at www.nesta.org.uk/sites/default/files/analytic_britain.pdf

New Zealand Ministry of Education (2016) Establishing a regulatory framework for online learning. *Education.govt.nz*, 25 August. Available at www.education.govt.nz/ministry-of-education/legislation/the-education-update-amendment-bill/establishing-a-regulatory-framework-for-online-learning/

New, J. (2016) Building a data-driven education system in the United States. *Center for Data Innovation*. Available at www2.datainnovation.org/2016-data-driven-education.pdf

Neyland, D. (2015) On organizing algorithms. *Theory, Culture and Society*, 32 (1): 119–32.

Nielsen, M. (2015) Who owns big data? Change: 19 Key Essays on How the Internet Is Changing Our Lives. *Open Mind*. Available at www.bbvaopenmind.com/en/book/19-key-essays-on-how-internet-is-changing-our-lives/

Nitta, S. (2014) Cognitive learning content: a vision for how to make learning deeply engaging as well as intuitive. *IBM Insights on Business*, 14 May. Available at http://insights-on-business.com/education/cognitive-learning-content-a-vision-for-how-to-make-learning-deeply-engaging-as-well-as-intuitive/

Nominet Trust (2013) Digital making activities to expand opportunities for UK young people. *Nominet Trust*. Available at www.nominettrust.org.uk/news-events/news/digital-making-activities-to-expand-opportunities-uk-young-people

Novoa, A. and Yariv-Mashal, T. (2014) Comparative research in education: a mode of governance or a historical journey? In Fenwick, T., Mangez, E. and Ozga, J. (eds), *Governing Knowledge: comparison, knowledge-based technologies and expertise in the regulation of education*. London: Routledge. pp. 13–30.

O'Keeffe, C. (2016) Producing data through e-assessment: a trace ethnographic investigation into e-assessment events. *European Educational Research Journal*, 15 (1): 99–116.

O'Reilly, T. (2016) Media in the age of algorithms. *Medium*, 11 November. Available at https://medium.com/the-wtf-economy/media-in-the-age-of-algorithms-63e80b9b0a73

OECD (Organization for Economic Cooperation and Development) (2015) *Skills for Social Progress: the power of social and emotional skills*. OECD Skills Studies. Paris: OECD.

Open Glasgow (2014) Engagement and literacy programme. *Open Glasgow*. Available at http://open.glasgow.gov.uk/content/uploads/LiteracyEngagement.pdf

Orton-Johnson, K. and Prior, N. (eds) (2013) *Digital Sociology: critical perspectives*. Houndmills: Palgrave Macmillan.

Orton-Johnson, K., Prior, N. and Gregory, K. (2015) Sociological imagination: digital sociology and the future of the discipline. *The Sociological Review blog*, 17 December. Available at www.thesociologicalreview.com/blog/sociological-imagination-digital-sociology-and-the-future-of-the-discipline.html

Ozga J. (2009) Governing education through data in England: from regulation to self-evaluation. *Journal of Education Policy*, 24 (2): 149–63.

Ozga, J. (2016) Trust in numbers? Digital education governance and the inspection process. *European Educational Research Journal*, 15 (1): 69–81.

Ozga, J., Dahler-Larsen, P., Segerholm, C. and Simola, H. (eds) (2011) *Fabricating Quality in Education: data and governance in Europe*. London: Routledge.

Pace, L. (2016) How the president-elect can scale personalized learning. *Getting Smart*, 12 December. Available at www.gettingsmart.com/2016/12/how-the-president-elect-can-scale-personalized-learning/

Paglen, T. (2016) Invisible images (your pictures are looking at you). *The New Inquiry*, 8 December. Available at http://thenewinquiry.com/essays/invisible-images-your-pictures-are-looking-at-you/

Papert, S. (1980) *Mindstorms: children, computers and powerful ideas*. New York: Basic Books.

Pariser, E. (2015) Did Facebook's big new study kill my filter bubble thesis? *Backchannel*, 7 May. Available at https://backchannel.com/facebook-published-a-big-new-study-on-the-filter-bubble-here-s-what-it-says-ef31a292da95#.63tcv3oiq

Partnership on AI (2016) About the partnership. *Partnership on AI*. Available at www.partnershiponai.org/

Pasquale, F. (2015) *The Black Box Society: the secret algorithms that control money and information*. Cambridge: Harvard University Press.

Patton, B. (2016) The trouble with taking biometric technology into schools. *Conversation*, 6 January. Available at https://theconversation.com/the-trouble-with-taking-biometric-technology-into-schools-52355

Pea, R. (2014) *A Report on Building the Field of Learning Analytics for Personalized Learning at Scale*. Stanford: Stanford University.

Pearson (2016) IBM Watson Education and Pearson to drive cognitive learning experiences for college students. *Pearson News*. Available at www.pearson.com/news/media/news-announcements/2016/10/ibm-watson-education-and-pearson-to-drive-cognitive-learning-exp.html

Peck, J. and Theodore, N. (2015) *Fast Policy: experimental statecraft at the thresholds of neoliberalism*. Minneapolis, MN: University of Minnesota Press.

Perrotta, C. and Williamson, B. (2016) The social life of learning analytics: cluster analysis and the performance of algorithmic education. *Learning, Media and Technology*. Available at http://dx.doi.org/10.1080/17439884.2016.1182927

Persson, J. (2016) School census changes add concerns to the richest education database in the world. *Parenting for a Digital Future*, 19 July. Available at http://blogs.lse.ac.uk/parenting4digitalfuture/2016/07/19/school-census-changes-add-concerns-to-the-richest-education-database-in-the-world/

Peyton Jones, S., Mitchell, B. and Humphreys, S. (2013) Computing at school in the UK. *Microsoft Research Papers*. Available at http://research.microsoft.com/en-us/um/people/simonpj/papers/cas/computingatschoolcacm.pdf

Piattoeva, N. (2015) Elastic numbers: national examinations data as a technology of government. *Journal of Education Policy*, 30 (3): 316–34.

Picard, R. W. (2016) What happened to the Q sensor? *MIT Media Lab*. Available at http://affect.media.mit.edu/projectpages/iCalm/iCalm-2-Q.html

Pickersgill M. (2013) The social life of the brain: neuroscience in society. *Current Sociology*, 61 (3): 322–40.

Piety, P. J., Behrens, J. and Pea, R. (2013) Educational data sciences and the need for interpretive skills. *American Educational Research Association*, 27 April–1 May.

Piety, P. J., Hickey, D. T. and Bishop, M. J. (2014) Educational data sciences – framing emergent practices for analytics of learning, organizations and systems. *LAK '14*, 24–28 March, Indianapolis.

Pluim, C. and Gard, M. (2016) Physical education's grand convergence: FitnessGram, big-data and the digital commerce of children's bodies. *Critical Studies in Education*. Available at http://dx.doi.org/10.1080/17508487.2016.1194303

Popkewitz, T. S. (2012) Numbers in grids of intelligibility: making sense of how educational truth is told. In Lauder, H., Young, M., Daniels, H., Balarin, M. and Lowe, J. (eds), *Educating for the Knowledge Economy? Critical perspectives*. Abingdon: Routledge. pp. 169–91.

Pykett, J. (2012) The pedagogical state: education, citizenship, governing. In Pykett, J. (ed.), *Governing Through Pedagogy: re-educating citizens*. London: Routledge. pp. 1–20.

Pykett, J. (2013) Neurocapitalism and the new neuros: using neuroeconomics, behavioural economics and picoeconomics for public policy. *Journal of Economic Geography*, 13: 845–69.

Pykett, J. (2015) *Brain Culture: shaping policy through neuroscience*. Bristol: Policy Press.

Pykett, J. and Disney, T. (2015) Brain-targeted teaching and the biopolitical child. *Politics, Citizenship and Rights:* Available at http://dx.doi.org/10.1007/978–981–4585–94–1_22–1

Quinlan, O. (2015) Young digital makers: surveying attitudes and opportunities for digital creativity across the UK. *Nesta*. Available at www.nesta.org.uk/sites/default/files/young-digital-makers-march-2015.pdf

Rabinow, P. and Rose, N. (2006) Biopower today. *BioSocieties*, 1: 195–217.

Raley, R. (2013) Dataveillance and counterveillance. In Gitelman, L. (ed.), *'Raw Data' is an Oxymoron*. London: MIT Press. pp. 121–46.

Ratto, M. and Boler, M. (eds) (2014) *DIY Citizenship: critical making and social media*. London: MIT Press.

Reveley, J. (2015) School-based mindfulness training and the economisation of attention: a Stieglerian view. *Educational Philosophy and Theory*, 47 (8): 804–21.

Reynolds, L. and Birdwell, J. (2015) *Mind Over Matter*. London: Demos.

Rich, E. and Miah, A. (2014) Understanding digital health as public pedagogy: a critical framework. *Societies*, 4: 296–315.

Rieder, G. and Simon, J. (2016) Datatrust: or, the political quest for numerical evidence and the epistemologies of big data. *Big Data and Society*, 3 (1). Available at http://dx.doi.org/10.1177/2053951716649398

Rienties, B. and Rivers, B. A. (2014) *Measuring and Understanding Learner Emotions: evidence and prospects*. Bolton: University of Bolton.

Rizvi, F. and Lingard, B. (2010) *Globalizing Education Policy*. Abingdon: Routledge.

Roberts-Holmes, G. (2015) The 'datafication' of early years pedagogy: 'If the teaching is good, the data should be good and if there's bad teaching, there is bad data'. *Journal of Education Policy*, 30 (3): 302–15.

Roberts-Mahoney, H., Means, A. J. and Garrison, M. J. (2016) Netflixing human capital development: personalized learning technology and the corporatization of K12 education. *Journal of Education Policy*, 31 (4). Available at http://dx.doi.org/10.1080/02680939.2015.1132774

Robertson, H. and Travaglia, J. (2015) Big data problems we face today can be traced to the social ordering practices of the 19th century. *LSE Impact of Social Sciences*, 13 October. Available at http://blogs.lse.ac.uk/impactofsocialsciences/2015/10/13/ideological-inheritances-in-the-data-revolution/

Rogers, R. (2013) *Digital Methods*. London: MIT Press.

Rose, G., Degen, M. and Melhuish, C. (2014) Networks, interfaces and computer-generated images: learning from digital visualizations of urban regeneration projects. *Environment and Planning D: Society and Space*, 32: 386–403.

Rose, N. (1996) *Inventing Our Selves: psychology, power and personhood*. Cambridge: Cambridge University Press.

Rose, N. (1999a) *Powers of Freedom: reframing political thought*. Cambridge: Cambridge University Press.

Rose, N. (1999b) *Governing the Soul: the shaping of the private self* (2nd edn). London: Free Association Books.

Rose, N. (2016) Reading the human brain: how the mind became legible. *Body and Society*, 22 (2). Available at http://dx.doi.org/10.1177/1357034X15623363

Rose, N. and Abi-Rached, J. (2013) *Neuro: the new brain sciences and the management of the mind*. Oxford: Princeton University Press.

Rose, N. and Abi-Rached, J. (2014) Governing through the brain: neuropolitics, neuroscience and subjectivity. *Cambridge Anthropology*, 32 (1): 3–23.

Rose, N., Aicardi, C. and Reinsborough, M. (2016) *Future Computing and Robotics: a Foresight report from the Human Brain Project lab*. London: King's College London.

Rose, S. (2013) Beware 'brain-based learning'. *Times Higher Education*, 12 December. Available at www.timeshighereducation.com/features/beware-brain-based-learning/2009703.article

Rosenberg, D. (2013) Data before the fact. In Gitelman, L. (ed.), *'Raw Data' is an Oxymoron*. London: MIT Press. pp. 15–40.

Royal Society (2011) *Brain Waves II: neuroscience implications for education and lifelong learning*. London: The Royal Society.

Royal Society (2012) *Shut Down or Restart? The way forward for computing in UK schools*. London: The Royal Society.

Runciman, D. (2016) How the education gap is tearing politics apart. *Guardian*, 5 October. Available at www.theguardian.com/politics/2016/oct/05/trump-brexit-education-gap-tearing-politics-apart

Ruppert, E. (2012) The governmental topologies of database devices. *Theory, Culture and Society*, 29 (4–5): 116–36.

Ruppert, E. (2015) Who owns big data? *Discover Society*, 30 July. Available at http://discoversociety.org/2015/07/30/who-owns-big-data/

Ruppert, E., Harvey, P., Lury, C., Mackenzie, A., McNally, R., Baker, S. A., Kallianos, Y. and Lewis, C. (2015) Socialising big data: from concept to practice. *CRESC Working Paper no. 138*. Available at www.cresc.ac.uk/medialibrary/workingpapers/wp138.pdf

Ruppert, E., Law, J. and Savage, M. (2013) Reassembling social science methods: the challenge of digital devices. *Theory, Culture and Society*, 30 (4): 22–46.

Rushkoff, D. (2010) *Program or Be Programmed: ten commends for a digital age*. New York: OR Books.

Sahlberg, P. and Hasak, J. (2016) Data was supposed to fix education. *Washington Post*, 9 May. Available at www.washingtonpost.com/news/answer-sheet/wp/2016/05/09/big-data-was-supposed-to-fix-education-it-didnt-its-time-for-small-data/

Saltman, K. (2016) Corporate schooling meets corporate media: standards, testing, and technophilia. *Review of Education, Pedagogy, and Cultural Studies*, 38 (2): 105–123.

Sandlin, J. A., O'Malley, M. P. and Burdick, J. (2011) Mapping the complexity of public pedagogy scholarship, 1894–2010. *Review of Educational Research*, 81 (3): 338–75.

Sandvik, L. (2014) Resignation. *GitHub*, 26 August. Available at https://gist.github.com/drtortoise/5dc254c614d6b6a19116

Savage, M. (2013) The 'social life of methods': a critical introduction. *Theory, Culture and Society*, 30 (4): 3–21.

Savage, M. and Cunningham, N. (2016) Why inequality matters: the lessons of Brexit. *Items: Insights from the Social Sciences*, 20 September. Available at http://items.ssrc.org/why-inequality-matters-the-lessons-of-brexit/

Schechtman, N., DeBarger, A. H., Dornsife, C., Rosier, S. and Yarnall, L. (2013) *Promoting Grit, Tenacity and Perseverance: critical factors for success in the 21st century*. Washington, DC: US Department of Education, Office of Educational Technology.

Schiller, D. (2015) Digital capitalism: stagnation and contention? *Open Democracy*, 13 October. Available at www.opendemocracy.net/digitaliberties/dan-schiller/digital-capitalism-stagnation-and-contention

Sclater, N., Peasgood, A. and Mullan, J. (2016) *Learning Analytics in Higher Education: a review of UK and international practice*. Bristol: Jisc.

Scottish Government (2016) *Delivering Excellence and Equity in Scottish Education: a delivery plan for Scotland*. Edinburgh: Scottish Government.

Sefton-Green, J. (2013) *Mapping Digital Makers*. Oxford: Nominet Trust.

Sellar, S. (2015a) Data infrastructure: a review of expanding accountability systems and large-scale assessments in education. *Discourse: Studies in the Cultural Politics of Education*, 36 (5): 765–77.

Sellar, S. (2015b) A feel for numbers: affect, data and education policy. *Critical Studies in Education*, 56 (1): 131–46.

Selwyn, N. (2011) *Schools and Schooling in the Digital Age: a critical analysis*. Abingdon: Routledge.

Selwyn, N. (2015) Data entry: towards the critical study of digital data and education. *Learning, Media and Technology*, 40 (1): 64–82.

Selwyn, N. (2016) *Is Technology Good for Education?* Cambridge: Polity Press.

Selwyn, N., Nemorin, S., Bulfin, S. and Johnson, N. F. (2017) Toward a digital sociology of school. In Daniels, J., Gregory, K. and McMillan Cottom, T. (eds), *Digital Sociologies*. Bristol: Policy Press. pp. 147–62.

Shapiro, J. (2016) President Obama wants every kid to learn coding – for all the wrong reasons. *Forbes*, 31 January. Available at www.forbes.com/sites/jordan shapiro/2016/01/31/president-obama-wants-every-kid-to-learn-coding-for-all-the-wrong-reasons/

Sharples, J. and Kelley, P. (2015) Introduction to learning, media and technology: neuro-science and education special edition. *Learning, Media and Technology*, 40 (2): 127–30.

Shepard, M. (2011) Toward the sentient city. In Shepard, M. (ed.), *Sentient City: ubiquitous computing, architecture, and the future of urban space*. Cambridge, MA: MIT Press. pp. 10–35.

Siemens, G. (2013) Learning analytics: the emergence of a discipline. *American Behavioral Scientist*, 57 (10): 1380–400.

Siemens, G. (2016) Reflecting on learning analytics and SoLAR. *Elearnspace*, 28 April. Available at www.elearnspace.org/blog/2016/04/28/reflecting-on-learning-analytics-and-solar/

Simon, S. (2012) Biosensors to monitor US students' attentiveness. *Reuters*, 13 June. Available at www.reuters.com/article/us-usa-education-gates-idUSBRE85C 17Z20120613

Sleeman, C. (2016) The state of interactive data visualisation. *Nesta*, 12 May. Available at www.nesta.org.uk/blog/state-interactive-data-visualisation

Sobe, N. (2013) Educational data at late nineteenth- and early twentieth-century inter-national expositions: 'accomplished results' and 'instruments and apparatuses'. In Lawn, M. (ed.), *The Rise of Data in Education Systems: collection, visualization and use*. Oxford: Symposium. pp. 41–56.

Soep, E. (2014) *Participatory Politics: next-generation tactics to remake public spheres*. London: MIT Press.

Solove, D. J. (2006) A taxonomy of privacy. *University of Pennsylvania Law Review*, 154 (3): 477–564.

Soroko, A. (2016) No child left alone? The ClassDojo app. *Our Schools/Our Selves*, 25 (3): 63–74.

Sqord (2016) About Sqord. Available at http://sqord.com/

Summit Basecamp (2016) Explore base camp. Available at http://summitbasecamp. org/explore-basecamp/

Summit Learning (2016) Bring personalized learning to your students. *Summit Personalized Learning*. Available at www.summitlearning.org/

Suoto-Otero, M. and Beneito-Montagut, R. (2016) From governing through data to governmentality through data: artefacts, strategies and the digital turn. *European Educational Research Journal*, 15 (1): 14–33.

Taylor, E. (2013) *Surveillance Schools: security, disciplines and control in contemporary education*. Basingstoke: Palgrave Macmillan.

TeacherMatch (2015) About TeacherMatch. *TeacherMatch*. Available at www.teacher match.org/about-us/

Thompson, G. (2016) Computer adaptive testing, big data and algorithmic approaches to education. *British Journal of Sociology of Education*. Available at http://dx.doi.org/ 10.1080/01425692.2016.1158640

Thompson, G. and Cook, I. (2016) The logic of data-sense: thinking through learning personalisation. *Discourse: Studies in the Cultural Politics of Education*. Available at http://dx.doi.org/10.1080/01596306.2016.1148833

Thrift, N. (2005) *Knowing Capitalism*. London: Sage.

Thrift, N. (2014) The promise of urban informatics: some speculations. *Environment and Planning A*, 46: 1263–6.

Townsend, A. M. (2013) *Smart Cities: big data, civic hackers and the quest for a new utopia*. London: Norton.

Tufekci, Z. (2014) Engineering the public: big data, surveillance and computational politics. *First Monday*, 19 (7). Available at http://dx.doi.org/10.5210/fm.v19i7.4901

Uber (2015) Uber + HackingEDU: gaining momentum in education. *Uber Newsroom*. Available at https://newsroom.uber.com/2015/09/uber-hackingedu-gaining-momentum-in-education/

UNICEF Kid Power (2016) Home. *UNICEF Kid Power*. Available at http://unicefkidpower.org/

Urban Data School (2015) Aims. *Urban Data School*. Available at http://urbandataschool.org/

van Dijck, J. (2013) *The Culture of Connectivity: a critical history of social media*. Oxford: Oxford University Press.

van Dijck, J. (2014) Datafication, dataism and dataveillance: big data between scientific paradigm and ideology. *Surveillance and Society*, 12 (2): 197–208.

van Dijck, J. and Poell, T. (2013) Understanding social media logic. *Media and Communication*, 1 (1): 2–14.

van Dijk, P. E. E. (2016) ClassDojo and PERTS launch growth mindset toolkit. *Stanford Daily*, 17 February. Available at www.stanforddaily.com/2016/02/17/classdojo-and-perts-launch-growth-mindset-toolkit/

Vander Schee, C. (2009) Fruit, vegetables, fatness, and Foucault: governing students and their families through school health policy. *Journal of Education Policy*, 24 (5): 557–74.

Viner, C. (2016) How technology disrupted the truth. *Guardian*, 12 July. Available at www.theguardian.com/media/2016/jul/12/how-technology-disrupted-the-truth

Wakeford, J. (2016) Fake news detector plug-in developed. *BBC News*, 2 December. Available at www.bbc.co.uk/news/technology-38181158

Watters, A. (2016) Ed-tech patents: prior art and learning theories. *Hack Education*, 12 January. Available at http://hackeducation.com/2016/01/12/patents

WEF (World Economic Forum) (2016) *New Vision for Education: fostering social and emotional learning through technology*. Cologny/Geneva: World Economic Forum.

Weisenthal, J. (2016) Donald Trump, the first President of our post-literate age. *Bloomberg*, 29 November. Available at www.bloomberg.com/view/articles/2016–11–29/donald-trump-the-first-president-of-our-post-literate-age

White House (2016a) The people's code – now on code.gov. *White House blog*, 3 November. Available at www.whitehouse.gov/blog/2016/11/03/peoples-code-now-codegov

White House (2016b) Preparing for the future of artificial intelligence. *Executive Office of the President National Science and Technology Council Committee on Technology*. Available at www.whitehouse.gov/sites/default/files/whitehouse_files/microsites/ostp/NSTC/preparing_for_the_future_of_ai.pdf

Wilkins, A. (2015) Professionalizing school governance: the disciplinary effects of school autonomy and inspection on the changing role of school governors. *Journal of Education Policy*, 30 (2): 182–200.

Williams, S., Katz, S. and Martin, P. (2011) The neuro-complex: some comments and convergences. *Media Tropes*, 3 (1): 135–46.

Williamson, B. (2015a) Governing methods: policy innovation labs, design and data science in the digital governance of education. *Journal of Educational Administration and History*, 47 (3): 251–71.

Williamson, B. (2015b) Algorithmic skin: health tracking technologies, personal analytics and the biopedagogies of digitized health and physical education. *Sport, Education and Society*, 20 (1): 133–51.

Williamson, B. (2015c) Educating the smart city: schooling smart citizens through computational urbanism. *Big Data and Society*, 2 (2). Available at http://dx/doi.org/10.1177/2053951715617783

Williamson, B. (2016a) Digital education governance: data visualization, predictive analytics and 'real-time' policy instruments. *Journal of Education Policy*, 31 (2): 123–41.

Williamson, B. (2016b) Digital methodologies of education governance: Pearson plc and the remediation of methods. *European Educational Research Journal*, 15 (1): 34–53.

Williamson, B. (2016c) Coding the biodigital child: the biopolitics and pedagogic strategies of educational data science. *Pedagogy, Culture and Society*, 24 (3): 401–16.

Williamson, B. (2016d) Political computational thinking: policy networks, digital governance, and 'learning to code'. *Critical Policy Studies*, 10 (1): 39–58.

Williamson, B. (2017) Computing brains: learning algorithms and neurocomputation in the smart city. *Information, Communication and Society*, 20 (1): 81–99.

Williamson, B. (forthcoming) Who owns educational theory? Big data, algorithms and the expert power of education data science. *E-learning and Digital Media*.

Willson, M. (2017) Algorithms (and the) everyday. *Information, Communication and Society*, 20 (1): 137–50.

Wilson, K. and Nichols, Z. (2015) The Knewton platform: a general-purpose adaptive learning infrastructure. *Knewton*. Available at www.knewton.com/wp-content/uploads/knewton-technical-white-paper-201501.pdf

Wolf, M., Taimurty, M., Patel, M. and Meteyer, J. (2016) The Dean's information challenge: from data to dashboard. *EduCause Review*, 28 November. Available at http://er.educause.edu/articles/2016/11/the-deans-information-challenge-from-data-to-dashboard

Woolgar, S. (1991) Configuring the user: the case of usability trials. In Law, J. (ed.), *A Sociology of Monsters: essays on power, technology and domination*. London: Routledge. pp. 57–99.

Woolley, S.J. (2016) Automating power: social bot interference in global politics. *First Monday*, 21 (4). Available at http://firstmonday.org/ojs/index.php/fm/article/view/6161/5300

Year of Code (2014) What is year of code? Available at http://yearofcode.org/

Yeung, K. (2017) Hypernudge: big data as a mode of regulation by design. *Information, Communication and Society*, 20 (1): 118–36.

Youdell, D. (2016a) A biosocial education future? *Research in Education*, 96 (1). Available at http://rie.sagepub.com/content/early/2016/09/16/0034523716664579

Youdell, D. (2016b) New biological sciences, sociology and education. *British Journal of Sociology of Education*, 37 (5): 788–800.

Young, J. R. (2016) What clicks from 70,000 courses reveal about student learning. *Chronicle of Higher Education*, 7 September. Available at www.chronicle.com/article/What-Clicks-From-70000/237704/

Zamzee (2016) Zamzee home page. Available at www.zamzee.com/

Zeide, E. (2016) Student privacy principles for the age of big data: moving beyond FERPA and FIPPS. *Drexel Law* Review, 8: 339.

Zernike, K. (2016) Testing for joy and grit? Schools' nationwide push to measure students' emotional skills. *New York Times*, 29 February. Available at www.nytimes.com/2016/03/01/us/testing-for-joy-and-grit-schools-nationwide-push-to-measure-students-emotional-skills.html

INDEX

Ofsted (Office for Standards in
Education) 82–3
Oracle Corporation 188
Osborne, George 182
ownership
of big data 115, 118
concerns about 118
by profit-making, private organizations
116–17, 118

Papert, Seymour 176, 178, 179
Partnership on AI 151
PBIS (Positive Behavior Interventions and
Supports) 142, 145
Pea, R. 105, 109, 135
Pearson 7, 87
AIEd intelligent learning environments
161–4
Center for Digital Data, Analytics and
Adaptive Learning 104, 110–11, 161
Center for NextGen Learning &
Assessment 104
*Intelligence Unleashed: An argument for AI in
education* 161
Learning Curve Data Bank 87, 88, 89,
161, 163
ownership of educational data 115
partnership with IBM 168–9
partnership with Knewton 110
Peck, J. and Theodore, N. 67–8
performance
measurement 75
nations, comparisons of 87–8
schools, comparisons of 84
see also measurement
performativity 75, 76, 78
Perrotta, C. and Williamson, B. 114
personalized learning 90, 102
DNA profiling 155
learning analytics 108
see also Altschool; Knewton
Persson, J. 81
persuasive computing 127, 128, 130, 144
physical activity monitors/trackers 137–8,
138–9, 140
Piety et al. 103–4, 136
platform capitalism 129
policy instrumentation 74–5
policymaking
changing people's behaviour 126–7
government interest in neuroscience 153
psychological conceptions,
influence of 132
see also education policymaking

political analytics 70–4
politics
analytics turn 26
participatory 177
post-truth 27, 199
populations
governance and control 62
government information on 26, 56, 70, 71
management of 32, 63
statistical knowledge of 30–1
positive psychology (PP) 132
post-truth politics 27, 199
prediction(s)
algorithmic machine learning
techniques 111
algorithms, use of 64
learning analytics 108
predictive analytics software 64, 93
production of 34
students' future performances 10
see also machine learning
Preparing for the Future of Artificial
Intelligence report 151
prescriptive analytics 93
privacy 118–21, 122
privacy harms 119–20
profiling
of countries 88
data analytics 43
data mining 43, 63
predictive 42, 93
programmability 45
Programme for International Student
Assessment (PISA) 77, 78, 86
Programme for the International Assessment
of Adult Competencies (PIAAC) 78
programmers 2, 3, 14, 38, 53
cultures of 52
designing values 61
social consequences of work 56–7
systems of thought 56
technical skills 54
see also software developers; software
engineers
programming 51–2
art of 52, 53
integration into school curricula 177
see also code; learning to code; maker
movement; software development
programming languages 54
Project Bloks 176, 179
Project for Education Research that Scales
(PERTS) 142–3
prosumption 191–2